The Deposition Handbook: Strategies, Tactics and Mechanics

Dennis R. Suplee
Diana S. Donaldson

PROFESSIONAL
EDUCATION SYSTEMS, INC.

8-99

#18452223

"This publication is designed to provide general information prepared by professionals in regard to subject matter covered. It is sold with the understanding that the publisher is not engaged in rendering legal, accounting, or other professional service. Although prepared by professionals, this publication should not be utilized as a substitute for professional service in specific situations. If legal advice or other expert assistance is required, the service of a professional should be sought." From a Declaration of Principles jointly adopted by a Committee of the American Bar Association and a Committee of Publishers.

PESI publications are designed to provide accurate information with regard to the subject matter covered. Attorneys and other professionals using PESI publications in dealing with specific legal matters should also research original sources of authority.

Earlier versions of portions of this book have appeared in The Review of Litigation, The Practical Lawyer, *and course materials published by the Pennsylvania Bar Institute.*

For information on this and other PESI manuals, audiotapes and videotapes, please contact:

Customer Relations
Professional Education Systems, Inc.
P.O. Box 1208
Eau Claire, WI 54702

1-800-826-7155

ISBN 0-941161-46-3

AUTHORS

Dennis R. Suplee, a 1964 graduate of St. Joseph's University and a 1967 graduate of the University of Pennslvania Law School, is a partner in the Philadelphia office of Schnader, Harrison, Segal & Lewis. He has a general litigation practice and has handled a wide range of civil cases, including product liability claims; antitrust, securities and RICO cases; commercial disputes; and insurance coverage litigation. He has accepted court appointments in criminal cases, including murder cases.

Mr. Suplee has written and lectured on various aspects of pretrial and trial practice, including depositions, use of experts, voir dire, opening speeches and closing arguments.

He has served on various boards, including the Secretary of the Navy's Advisory Board on Education and Training and the President's Council of St. Joseph's University.

Diana S. Donaldson is also a partner in the Philadelphia office of Schnader, Harrison, Segal & Lewis. She is a *magna cum laude* graduate of Radcliffe College and a *summa cum laude* graduate of the College of Law of The Ohio State University, where she was articles editor of the *Ohio State Law Journal* and was inducted into the Order of the Coif. She also has a master's degree in education, earned in connection with her term in the federal Teacher Corps program. In 1975-76, she was law clerk to the Honorable Max Rosenn of the U.S. Court of Appeals for the Third Circuit.

Her law practice is a diverse one, including commercial disputes, product liability and personal injury cases. She is a coordinator of the firm's litigation training program and active in its recruiting program.

PREFATORY NOTE

We must thank our partners, associates and legal assistants, and the library, secretarial and word processing staffs at Schnader, Harrison, Segal & Lewis for their interest and participation in the preparation of this book and for their patience with us while we worked on it (and talked to them incessantly about it). The book draws from the deposition experiences of lawyers in our firm and elsewhere. We have borrowed the names of many of our partners for the characters that appear in our hypotheticals because we thought that real names were more interesting.

THE DEPOSITION HANDBOOK: STRATEGIES, TACTICS AND MECHANICS

Table of Contents

INTRODUCTION

Depositions are the most important of the pretrial discovery tools. In evaluating the strength of a case for settlement purposes, litigators accord great weight to the performance during depositions of both their own and their opponents' witnesses. Further, if a case should go to trial, the deposition transcripts will usually be the lawyer's most important resource for cross-examination.

Of all the pretrial discovery tools, depositions require the greatest technical skill. The interrogator must plan and craft questions carefully — yet be prepared to take a completely different tack depending upon the answers given, the personality of the witness, and the scope of the witness's knowledge. The opposing lawyer must prepare the witness carefully (assuming that the witness is his client or is cooperating with him) since he has little control once the deposition starts.

The lawyer who serves the notice of deposition typically will be the principal interrogator and, aside from the witness, the principal actor. Accordingly, this deposition handbook speaks generally, though not exclusively, from the perspective of the interrogator. For the most part, the witness is assumed to be the adverse party or otherwise hostile to the interrogator. Chapters 9 and 10 cover opposing counsel's task of preparing and defending the witness at the deposition. Chapter 11 deals with use of the deposition transcript at trial.

This guide discusses various objectives, strategies, tactics, mechanics and problems in taking depositions. By and large, there are no "right" answers to the questions raised, but the lawyer who considers such matters in advance of the deposition should do a better job of interrogating the witness.

To make this handbook useful to recent law school graduates, as well as to more experienced litigators, we have articulated basic propositions rather than taking them for granted. Generally, we have assumed that the Federal Rules of Civil Procedure and the Federal Rules of Evidence apply.

Organization of this subject presents problems. Each idea tends to be entangled with several others. Separating them out for individual treatment may be tedious and artificial; leaving them jumbled may be confusing. We have attempted to reconcile the conflict by examining each topic individually but showing how it connects (or is at odds) with others.

Throughout, we have used the masculine pronoun to avoid the cumbersome "he or she" and "his or her" but we intend that pronoun to be universal and to include female and male judges, lawyers, witnesses and clients, without distinction.

CHAPTER ONE

PRELIMINARY CONSIDERATIONS: DISADVANTAGES OF AND ALTERNATIVES TO TAKING DEPOSITIONS

The most important preliminary question is whether to take the deposition.[1] This chapter explores the disadvantages of and the alternatives to depositions.

A.   Disadvantages of Depositions

The attorney must carefully consider several significant disadvantages of depositions.

1.   *Expense*
Depositions are expensive. Consider the time spent preparing for the deposition, taking it, reporting on it to the client and summarizing the transcript, not to mention the cost of serving the subpoena, a witness fee, the reporter's charges and possible travel expenses.

2.   *Preserving Harmful Testimony*
The interrogator may preserve testimony harmful to his client which otherwise would be unavailable at trial.[2] Adverse witnesses may die. Harmful nonparty witnesses may move away or just disappear; their memories may fade and their interest wane. While it is understandable that a lawyer may want to know precisely what testimony he must prepare to meet at trial, it is not impossible to cross-examine a witness without a deposition transcript (as criminal

---

1   "Doctors order tests. Lawyers take depositions. It's the same thing. Half the time we don't really know exactly why we take depositions, but there seems to be some primordial need to do so. 'Hmm,' we say to our client, 'this looks serious. Better take some depositions.' " Hart, *Taking Depositions,* 51 THE SHINGLE 44 (Spring 1988) (Journal of the Philadelphia Bar Association).

2   *See* FED. R. CIV. P. 32(a)(3); FED. R. EVID. 804(b)(1).

lawyers demonstrate every day). At the very least, it may be wise to consider postponing the deposition of a witness expected to give harmful testimony.

3. *Waiving Objections to Competence*

By taking a deposition, counsel may waive an objection to the competence of a witness. For example, a party may waive the Dead Man's Act[3] by deposing a witness who would otherwise be precluded by the act from testifying.[4]

4. *Tipping Off Opponent*

The interrogator almost inevitably reveals to some extent through his questions what he believes to be important to his client's claim or defense and what he plans to prove at trial. For example, if the defendant's counsel presses the plaintiff for an unambiguous statement that he was never previously involved in an accident causing personal injuries, the plaintiff's counsel may accurately sense that the interrogator has evidence of a prior accident. Suppose the plaintiff nevertheless testifies at deposition that he was not involved in any other accident, but later admits to his own counsel that he was in fact previously injured in an accident. Plaintiff's counsel may then instruct his client to correct the deposition transcript[5] and thus effectively dilute the impact at trial of the original inaccurate testimony.

5. *Educating Opponent*

The interrogator forces his opponent to learn the case. His opponent will assimilate a good deal just by preparing witnesses and listening to the questioning.

6. *Dress Rehearsal*

The deposition also provides the witness with a dress rehearsal. The witness will do better next time — at trial — because he knows what to expect. A witness who is rattled, evasive and unresponsive at the deposition may perform

---

3   *See generally* II J. WIGMORE, A TREATISE ON THE ANGLO-AMERICAN SYSTEM OF EVIDENCE IN TRIALS AT COMMON LAW § 578 (Chadbourn rev. 1979).

4   *See* E. WEEKS, TREATISE ON THE LAW OF DEPOSITIONS, § 436 (1880); Annotation, *Taking Deposition or Serving Interrogatories in Civil Case as Waiver of Incompetence of Witness,* 23 A.L.R.3D 389 (1969). In federal court, state competency rules such as the Dead Man's Act have no effect except "with respect to an element of a claim or defense as to which State law supplies the rule of decision." FED. R. EVID. 601. It is not settled whether state law governs waiver when a state competency rule applies in federal court. *Compare* 4A J. MOORE & J. LUCAS, MOORE'S FEDERAL PRACTICE ¶ 32.10 n.1 (2d ed. 1981) ("Taking and filing a deposition does not constitute a waiver of the 'dead man's statute'.") *with* 8 C. WRIGHT & A. MILLER, FEDERAL PRACTICE AND PROCEDURE § 2152 (1970 & Supp. 1982) (state law should govern waiver issue).

5   *See* FED. R. CIV. P. 30(e) and Chapter 7, Section Z.

quite well at trial. His discomfort at the deposition will rarely appear from the dry transcript. The jury will see only the interrogator's chagrin.

7. *Identifying Witness Helpful to Opponent*
The interrogator may alert his opponent to the existence and importance of a witness. For example, in an antitrust case, if counsel for the defendant decides to take the deposition of a relatively low-level employee of the plaintiff on the outside chance that he may know something useful (or from an automatic reflex to leave no stone unturned), the interrogator may find that the witness knows much more about the nitty-gritty of competition between the parties than the interrogator wanted to hear. But for the deposition, plaintiff's counsel might never have considered that employee as a possible trial witness.

8. *Retaliation*
The lawyer serving the notice must recognize that his opponent is likely to respond in kind. If a notice is served for the deposition of the opposing party's secretary, a counterpart notice is likely to be served the next day by the other side.

B.   Alternatives to Depositions

Having considered the disadvantages, the lawyer should examine the alternatives to depositions:

1. *Written Discovery*
Answers to interrogatories and production of documents may suffice, particularly if the amount at issue is small. For example, in a simple breach-of-contract suit for less than $10,000, counsel may be satisfied with written discovery. If the case does not settle, the parties can tell their stories at trial and let the fact finder decide.

2. *Telephone Interview*
A telephone interview may produce remarkably good results. Although a witness is likely to be skittish about a telephone interview with an attorney, he may find that prospect less odious than appearing in person for a deposition. Although a face-to-face interview is usually preferable, a telephone interview will, at the least, give the lawyer a good reading on whether the witness's information is helpful to his client's case. If the lawyer's client maintains good relations with the witness, the client should pave the way by contacting the witness first and explaining that the lawyer will be calling him and that the interview is merely to collect information.

5

The interviewing lawyer should remember that this interview (and the client's conversation with the witness) will not be protected by any privilege and may become the subject of discovery. Although the lawyer's notes of the interview are protected attorney work product, there is no protection against inquiries at the witness's deposition into the substance of his discussion with the lawyer. (Also, lest he be tempted, the interviewer should remember that it is illegal in many states to tape record a telephone conversation without the consent of both participants.)

Certain witnesses are off limits to informal contacts. A lawyer may not communicate directly with any other party represented by counsel without the consent of the lawyer representing the party.[6] In addition, a lawyer should not communicate with an adverse party's expert or investigator.[7]

The extent to which direct contacts with a party's employees are forbidden is a matter of debate. It seems clear that an officer, director or managing agent cannot be contacted, since the Federal Rules of Civil Procedure expressly recognize these individuals as corporate representatives for purposes of testifying.[8] Although some lawyers argue that lower-level employees of the opposing party may be contacted with impunity, most refrain from doing so to avoid arguments about its propriety.[9] After all, communications between a corporation's lawyers and lower-level corporate employees in certain circumstances are protected by the corporation's attorney-client privilege.[10] Moreover, a statement by a party's "agent or servant" about a matter within the scope of his agency or employment during the existence of the relationship is treated as an admission of the party itself at trial.[11] It thus might be argued that counsel would be wise to steer clear of all of the employees of an adverse party. The opposing lawyer should at least give the matter some thought before picking up the telephone.

---

6   *See* MODEL CODE OF PROFESSIONAL RESPONSIBILITY EC 7-18, DR 7-104 (1979); MODEL RULES OF PROFESSIONAL CONDUCT Rule 4.2 (1986).

7   *See* FED. R. CIV. P. 26(b)(3) (trial preparation materials prepared by or for the other party's "representative," including the party's consultant, insurer or agent, are protected).

8   FED. R. CIV. P. 30(b)(6) and 32(a)(2).

9   *See* ABA/BNA LAWYER'S MANUAL ON PROFESSIONAL CONDUCT 71:313-315 (1984) for a discussion of varying approaches to the question.

10   Upjohn Co. v. United States, 449 U.S. 383 (1981).

11   FED. R. EVID. 801(d)(2)(D); MODEL RULES OF PROFESSIONAL CONDUCT Rule 4.2, Comment (1986) (prohibiting contacts with persons whose act or omission in the matter "may be imputed to the organization for purposes of criminal or civil liability or whose statement may constitute an admission on the part of the organization").

3. Face-to-Face Interview

An in-person interview is another alternative to a deposition. Where feasible, it is usually more useful than a telephone interview. It will enable the lawyer to get a better feel for the witness and his potential to be a helpful or harmful trial witness. An in-person interview may also align the witness more closely with the lawyer and his client than a telephone interview can and may make the witness more resistant to similar approaches from the other side (or at least more willing to advise the lawyer when such approaches are made). The lawyer should consider volunteering to travel to the witness's location or to another location convenient to the witness to conduct the interview.

Also, the lawyer may consider asking a favorable witness to speak in the presence of a court reporter so that a stenographic record of the interview is made. It is probably not a good idea to tape record or videotape the interview because these methods of recording the interview will expose (and preserve) any hesitations and pauses as the witness tells his story or, in the case of videotape, any unconvincing or unappealing aspects of his demeanor. If a stenographic record is not an option, the lawyer may want to have another lawyer or a legal assistant present to make extensive notes during the interview.

As with a telephone interview, the face-to-face interview will not be protected by the attorney-client privilege. Although a lawyer's notes of the interview are protected work product, any transcription or videotape may be discoverable, if good cause is shown.[12] If the information that has emerged in the interview is helpful to the interviewer, he may not care that it is discoverable. But if it is harmful, he may prefer just to memorialize it in his notes and not in any discoverable form. Why create a record that can be harmful?

4. Signed Statement

The lawyer may want to follow up either a telephone or a personal interview by sending the witness the transcript or a memorandum or letter summarizing what he said, perhaps with a request that the witness advise the attorney of any inaccuracies and sign and return the document. Generally, the signed statement is not discoverable unless good cause is shown.[13]

5. Deposition on Written Questions

An alternative to oral depositions is the procedure under Rule 31 of the Federal Rules of Civil Procedure for taking testimony of parties and nonparties before an officer on written questions.[14] The scope of discovery is the same as for oral depositions, and a subpoena may be used to compel attendance. Notice of taking a deposition upon written questions may be given at any time after

---

12   *See* FED. R. CIV. P. 26(b)(3).

13   *Id.*

14   FED. R. CIV. P. 31.

commencement of the action. As with an oral deposition, the notice must state the name and address of the deponent, if known, or a general description sufficient to identify him or the class or group to which he belongs, and the name or the descriptive title of the officer before whom the deposition is to be taken.[15]

Rule 31(a) provides that the questions are to be served on all parties along with the notice of the deposition, and within 30 days, a party so served may serve cross questions on all of the other parties to the action. Redirect questions may be served within 10 days after service of the cross questions, and recross questions may be served 10 days after service of the redirect questions.

The party initiating the deposition is obliged to deliver a copy of the notice and copies of all questions served to the officer designated in the notice. The officer then must proceed promptly to record the testimony of the witness in response to each question.[16] After the deposition is filed, the party initiating its taking is required to give prompt notice of the filing to all other parties.[17]

---

15   FED. R. CIV. P. 31(a).

16   FED. R. CIV. P. 31(b).

17   FED. R. CIV. P. 31(c).

CHAPTER TWO

THE ROLE OF DEPOSITIONS IN THE DISCOVERY PLAN

Another important preliminary consideration is where to fit depositions into the overall discovery plan.[1] This chapter will discuss timing, the order in which to take depositions, and the importance of involving the client in the discovery plan, including depositions.

A.   Limitations on Discovery

In an effort to curb discovery abuse, Rule 26 of the Federal Rules of Civil Procedure was amended to require judges to limit "the frequency or extent of use of the discovery methods" authorized by the Rules, including depositions, if:

> (i) the discovery sought is unreasonably cumulative or duplicative, or is obtainable from some other source that is more convenient, less burdensome or less expensive; (ii) the party seeking discovery has had ample opportunity by discovery to obtain the information sought; or (iii) the discovery is unduly burdensome or expensive, taking into account the needs of the case, the amount in controversy, limitations on the parties' resources, and the importance of the issues at stake in the litigation.[2]

Federal courts also have broad discretion to determine the scope of discovery.[3] And courts are increasingly receptive to motions for protective orders

---

1   *See* FED. R. CIV. P. 26(d); *Proposed Amendments to the Federal Rules of Civil Procedure Relating to Discovery*, 48 F.R.D. 487, 506-07 (1970) ; A. MORRILL, TRIAL DIPLOMACY §12.12 (2d ed. 1972) (suggesting that detailed background data such as names and dates be discovered through interrogatories first in order to save time at deposition).

2   FED. R. CIV. P. 26(b)(1).

3   FED. R. CIV. P. 26(c); Herbert v. Lando, 441 U.S. 153, 177 (1979).

prohibiting unnecessary or disproportionately expensive or burdensome depositions, especially where less burdensome alternatives are available.[4] Accordingly, counsel should try to devise a discovery plan, even if sketchy, at the beginning of the case and to keep in mind that his opportunities to take depositions may well be limited by the court and thus should be carefully timed and targeted.

B.   The Timing of Depositions

1.   Waiting for Depositions

Many lawyers prefer to initiate depositions only after their opponent answers comprehensive interrogatories and produces many documents. (Indeed, the lawyer serving answers to interrogatories should carefully select the affiant thereto because opposing counsel may serve a notice for that person's deposition.) By proceeding in this way, the interrogator will be better prepared — but so will the witnesses. The lawyer for the witnesses can prepare them by reviewing (a) the interrogatories as a kind of checklist of subjects likely to be covered at the deposition, (b) the positions that were taken in answering them, and (c) the documents (at least the most important ones) that were produced. The witnesses will have the opportunity to refresh their recollection of the underlying facts and to work on their story.

Moreover, the time for starting depositions will probably be delayed while the information necessary to answer interrogatories is collected and the documents are assembled. Opposing counsel will probably object to some of the interrogatories and requests for documents, which may signal the start of motion practice. Depositions are likely to be further delayed until the motions are decided. This delay may work to the advantage of the witnesses, who have more time to assess possible weak points in their testimony and to plan how to deal with them.

Thus, the interrogator should consider other options. He might serve a short set of interrogatories and a request for certain key documents, along with a notice to start depositions soon after the response date for the interrogatories and document request. Or he may serve only a short document request. As to more comprehensive sets of interrogatories and requests for documents, the interrogator can either (a) serve them at the same time as the shorter ones, but agree that they can be responded to later without delaying the start of depositions, or (b) serve them later in the discovery period.

---

4   See, e.g., Stone City Music v. Thunderbird, Inc., 8 Fed. R. Serv. 3d (Callaghan) 431 (N.D. Miss. 1987). Some courts by local rule limit the number of depositions that may be taken. E.g., E.D. VA. R. CIV. P. 11.1(B) (unless court permits, no party shall take more than five non-party depositions).

By proceeding in the way suggested, the interrogator will know less about the opponent's claim than if he waited for answers to more searching interrogatories and for production of additional documents. In deciding how to proceed, counsel must balance the advantages of having more knowledge in advance of the deposition against those of getting the opponent's witnesses into the witness chair at the earliest possible moment.

For example, the defense counsel in a personal injury suit will often file interrogatories to elicit background information about the plaintiff and detailed information about his damages, but usually will not ask him to give his account of how the accident happened. He saves this question for the deposition. In effect, defense counsel has made the decision that a certain lack of preliminary knowledge on his part is preferable to forcing the plaintiff (with the assistance of his counsel) to think through and write down his account of the accident, which may cause him to confront weaknesses in his story and to develop a strategy to deal with them.

2. Immediate Depositions

The lawyer may also consider scheduling a deposition immediately [5] without waiting for answers to interrogatories and without obtaining documents.[6] The interrogator should first ascertain what he is likely to learn from answers to interrogatories and documents that may be useful in the deposition. If he is likely to learn very little, the interrogator may decide to start discovery with the deposition.

Consider, for example, a case in which the claim is that the seller made oral misrepresentations about his product. The buyer's attorney may conclude that since the seller is not likely to make admissions when given ample time to ponder the questions, interrogatories will elicit little helpful information and may provide the opposition with a list of topics that almost certainly will be covered at the deposition. The buyer's attorney may also decide that the seller has probably not generated documents tending to show the misrepresentations; thus, a document request will not produce much. In this situation, it may be best to take the seller's deposition at the earliest possible time, rather than wait for the completion of less promising discovery.

3. Alternating Discovery

Some cases may call for alternating forms of discovery. For example, in a complicated case in which the deposition is likely to take several days, it

---

5   This is, of course, subject to the time limit imposed on a plaintiff by Fed. R. Civ. P. 30(a).

6   *See* FED. R. CIV. P. 26(d); *Proposed Amendments to the Federal Rules of Civil Procedure Relating to Discovery,* 48 F.R.D. 487, 506-07 (1970). Interrogatories and a document request may be served with the deposition notice, but with a later response date, or served after the deposition is completed.

11

may be worthwhile to schedule only one day for the deposition and then recess until other discovery has been completed. In some cases, the interrogator may schedule a deposition early in the discovery process to learn about the opposing party's documents and thus prepare a reasonably specific document request.

Another option is to attach a document request to the deposition notice and arrange with opposing counsel to receive the documents a week or so before the deposition. Often opposing counsel will agree to this arrangement in order to save time at the deposition. Otherwise there may be a long recess at the deposition while the interrogator reviews the documents. However, opposing counsel who has refused to make the documents available ahead of time cannot convincingly complain of the delay at the deposition. When the volume of documents to be produced is extensive, the interrogator may want to retain the services of an expedited copying service, and should review the documents sufficiently ahead of the deposition date to reasonably determine which documents should be inquired into at the deposition.

4. Depositions Before Action or Pending Appeal

Rule 27 permits the taking of depositions in an ancillary proceeding before the filing of an action, or pending appeal, to perpetuate testimony.[7] An ancillary proceeding is begun by a verified petition, rather than by complaint, in a district where any expected party resides. The contents of the petition are specified by Rule 27(a)(1). A notice stating that the petitioner will apply to the court for the order described in the petition, together with a copy of the petition, must be served upon each person named as an expected adverse party at least 20 days before the date of the hearing in the manner provided in Rule 4 for the service of a summons.[8]

Rule 27(a)(3) provides that the court shall make the order if it is satisfied that the perpetuation of the testimony may prevent a failure or delay of justice. The order must designate the persons to be deposed, the subject matter of the examination, and whether the deposition shall be by oral examination or written interrogatories. A Rule 27(a) deposition may be used "in any action involving the same subject matter subsequently brought in a United States District Court."[9]

Rule 27(b) provides a procedure for perpetuating testimony by deposition while a case is on appeal. Any party may make a motion in the district

---

7   FED. R. CIV. P. 27.

8   FED. R. CIV. P. 27(a)(2).

9   FED. R. CIV. P. 27(a)(4).

court, and, if the court finds that perpetuation of the testimony is proper to avoid a failure or delay of justice, it may issue an order allowing the depositions.[10]

C.   Order of Deponents

Another preliminary decision is the order in which to depose witnesses. In most instances, the lawyer will first depose the more important witnesses and then move to those of secondary importance.[11] In cases with complicated facts, however, it may be best to start with a less important witness who possesses a good, basic knowledge of the operative facts.

For example, in an antitrust case, the plaintiff's counsel may decide to educate himself about the industry and the defendant's method of doing business by deposing a middle-level employee of the defendant. The deposition of the president of the corporate defendant, perhaps the single most important discovery event in the case, may be taken much later. If the corporate president is deposed too early and claims to be uninformed except in the most general way on certain subjects, the interrogator's knowledge of the facts may be too primitive to allow him to press the deponent effectively. If, after other discovery, the plaintiff's attorney wants to resume the deposition of the corporate president, defense counsel may seek a protective order to prevent reopening the deposition.[12] Counsel for the plaintiff may have a difficult time persuading the court that he should have a second stab at the president.

D.   Consulting the Client

The client can be an invaluable resource in developing the discovery plan. He should be consulted about many of these preliminary considerations. He should participate in deciding whether depositions should be taken, what other discovery should be conducted first, and in which order the deponents should be listed. The client often will know who on the opposing side should be knowledgeable about a given subject and may be able to supply useful insights about the personal characteristics of the deponents.

Moreover, the client should know and approve the anicipated cost of the proposed deposition program. A client who understands what the lawyer is

---

10   FED. R. CIV. P. 27(b).

11   "During a trial it is traditional to put your client on after your witnesses have testified. You want him to hear what they say before he testifies . . . Turning this defensive ploy around, generally depose the adverse party before you depose his supporting cast of ruffians and ne'er-do-wells." K. HEGLAND, TRIAL AND PRACTICE SKILLS IN A NUTSHELL 258 (1978).

12   *See* FED. R. CIV. P. 26(b)(1) and (c)(1).

doing and why is more likely to be satisfied, especially if he has had a chance to participate in the underlying strategic decisions.

Where possible, the interrogator should review with the client a list of the opponent's witnesses before their depositions begin to get the client's ideas on the information and admissions that the interrogator should elicit from each witness. If the interrogator can prepare his deposition outlines sufficiently ahead of time, the client may review them and suggest additional or different questions.

The client frequently has a more thorough grasp of the overall facts of the case than does his lawyer at the outset of a case, especially if it involves complex technical details of the client's business. If the case concerns an area unfamiliar to the interrogator (for example, computer software research and development), the client can give the interrogator the proper vocabulary with which to pose the crucial questions to the other side's witness. This help lessens the risk that the witness will be able to retreat behind a smokescreen of jargon.

Indeed, the interrogator may decide to have his client present at the most important depositions. The client may supply good follow-up questions, will know better what to expect at his own deposition, and will better understand the strengths and weaknesses of his claim or defense. But there are disadvantages. Some plaintiffs' personal injury lawyers are pleased to see in-house counsel or some other representative of the defendant attending the depositions because they interpret this to mean that the defendant considers the case to be an important one — which suggests that ultimately a substantial settlement offer will be forthcoming. Once in a while, an opponent may object to the client's presence. (See Chapter 7, Section C, for a discussion of the presence of others at a deposition.)

If the client will be present at depositions, his lawyer should instruct him carefully about demeanor and deposition etiquette so that the client will not inadvertently reveal information or theories pertinent to the case. The client should be told to keep a poker face, not to comment about the testimony no matter how offensive to him, not to whisper to his lawyer during the testimony (notes may be passed within reason), not to let down his guard during the small talk at the breaks, and to make notes discreetly so that opposing counsel will not be alerted to the fact that something important to the client's view of the case has been said.

E.   Consulting the Expert

If the case involves experts, the interrogator should consult his own expert in advance of the deposition of the opposing party's expert. Indeed, he may decide to have his own expert present at the deposition of the opposing expert or at selected other depositions to suggest lines of inquiry based on the answers given. For example, if a securities fraud action involves allegations of improper accounting practices by the defendant corporation, the plaintiff's counsel may want to have his expert accountant present when he takes the deposition of the corporate controller.

Even if an expert is an experienced deponent, he may not have attended others' depositions before. Accordingly, the interrogator should lay down the same rules to the expert as those given to the client about behavior at depositions. The rule about note taking is particularly crucial, as opposing counsel will doubtless be watching for signals as to what interests the expert.

CHAPTER THREE

SCHEDULING AND PREPARING FOR THE DEPOSITION

A.   The Deposition Notice

The lawyer schedules a deposition by serving on all parties a notice stating his intention to depose a certain witness.[1] See Form A in the Appendix. The notice must include the name and address of the deponent, if known, and the date, time and place of the deposition.[2] If the deponent is a party, service of the notice on his counsel is sufficient to require his appearance at the deposition, and a subpoena is unnecessary.[3] No subpoena is required to depose an officer, director, or managing agent of a party; failure of such a person to appear at deposition after counsel has been served with proper notice is treated as the failure of the party.[4]

The notice may include a request that documents and tangible items be produced at the deposition under Rule 30(b)(5), in which event the procedure of Rule 34 applies. It is not clear, however, whether the 30-day response period of Rule 34 applies to a request for production under Rule 30(b)(5).[5] (Chapter 2, Section B.3, discusses the use of this procedure.)

B.   The Deposition Subpoena

If the deponent is not a party, he should be served with a deposition subpoena to which the notice of deposition is attached.[6] See Form B in the

---

1   FED. R. CIV. P. 30(b)(1).

2   *Id.* Rule 29 permits the parties to vary the form of notice by written stipulation. FED. R. CIV. P. 29(1).

3   *See* FED. R. CIV. P. 37(d); *Proposed Amendments to the Federal Rules of Civil Procedure Relating to Discovery*, 48 F.R.D. 487, 542 [hereinafter *1970 Advisory Committee Notes*].

4   *See id.* For a discussion of who is considered a "managing agent" of a party, see 4A J. MOORE & J. LUCAS, MOORE'S FEDERAL PRACTICE ¶ 30.55[1] (2d ed. 1981).

5   *See* 8 C. WRIGHT & A. MILLER, FEDERAL PRACTICE AND PROCEDURE § 2108 (1970 & Supp. 1982).

6   FED. R. CIV. P. 30(a) and 45.

Appendix. In some jurisdictions, the district court will issue deposition subpoenas in blank. In others, to obtain a deposition subpoena, counsel must first serve the notice upon the parties and then file with the court a copy of the notice and a certified statement of the date, manner of service and persons served.[7]

A check to cover the witness fee and travel costs must be tendered when the subpoena is served. If a nonparty witness fails to appear because he was not subpoenaed properly or was not paid a witness and mileage fee, the court may impose costs of other counsel upon the party giving notice of the deposition.[8] If a subpoena duces tecum is to be served on the deponent, the notice served upon counsel should include, or have attached to it, a designation of the materials to be produced.[9]

If the nonparty witness is located outside of the district in which the case is pending and does not agree to appear for deposition, the lawyer seeking the deposition must file a copy of the notice and certification of service in the district court of the district in which the deponent is located. That district court will then assign a miscellaneous docket number to the case for purposes of the subpoena and will issue a deposition subpoena.

C.   Rule 30(b)(6) Notice

The deposition notice or subpoena may name as the deponent a corporation, partnership, association or governmental agency and should describe with reasonable particularity the matters on which examination is sought.[10] See Form C in the Appendix. The organization named must then designate one or more officers, directors, managing agents or other persons who consent to testify for the organization to appear at the deposition. The federal deposition subpoena form requires a nonparty organization to file a designation specifying those persons who will testify on its behalf and setting forth the matters on which each will testify. See Form B in the Appendix.

It may be easier to use the Rule 30(b)(6) procedure and thereby compel the organization to identify a witness than to select a name based on limited

---

7   FED. R. CIV. P. 45(d)(1).

8   FED. R. CIV. P. 30(g)(2). *See* CF & I Steel Corp. v. Mitsui & Co., 713 F.2d 494 (9th Cir. 1983) (failure to tender witness fee and estimated mileage charge invalidates subpoena); Harrison v. Pratcher, 404 F.2d 267 (5th Cir. 1968) (subpoena served on witness's counsel rather than witness himself is invalid).

9   FED. R. CIV. P. 30(b)(1). The rationale of this requirement is to enable each party "to prepare for the deposition more effectively." *1970 Advisory Committee Notes, supra* note 3, at 514.

10   FED. R. CIV. P. 30(b)(6).

information and hope that the witness is sufficiently knowledgeable. Indeed, one purpose of the rule is to dispense with the need to depose many witnesses in the search for those with relevant knowledge.[11]

Of course, if the organization is an adverse party, it may be tempted not to identify the most knowledgeable or helpful witness to appear at the deposition. At least one court has compelled a corporation to redesignate witnesses who were prepared to testify for the entire corporation on a specified issue where the corporation had first designated witnesses who had knowledge only about the activities of one particular unit within the corporation.[12] Moreover, there is a possibility that the corporation, having designated a deponent on a particular issue, is then bound by that witness's testimony. It has in effect represented that the witness is authorized to speak for the corporation on the issue, unlike a lower level employee who is directly subpoenaed for his deposition.[13] Moreover, the deposition of a person designated under Rule 30(b)(6) can be used "for any purpose" at trial whether or not the person is available to testify, pursuant to Rule 32(a)(2). Thus, a corporation would be well-advised to choose its deponent with care and not try to hide the ball when faced with a Rule 30(b)(6) notice.

D.   Location

1.   Parties
Nothing in the Federal Rules of Civil Procedure limits the geographic reach of the deposition notice directed to a party. Thus, regardless of the opposing party's location, the interrogator may properly serve notice of that party's deposition to take place at the interrogator's office. (Counsel should be aware that some state courts, by local rule, require that all depositions be taken at the local courthouse, rather than at attorneys' offices.) If the party is a corporation or other entity, its officers, directors and managing agents are also subject to deposition at the interrogator's office.[14]

---

11   *See 1970 Advisory Committee Notes, supra* note 3, at 515.

12   Federal Deposit Ins. Corp. v. Butcher, 116 F.R.D. 196 (E.D. Tenn. 1986).

13   Lapenna v. Upjohn Co., 110 F.R.D. 15, 20 (E.D. Pa. 1986) (ruling that corporate employee designated under Rule 30(b)(6) may be compelled to testify about corporation's subjective opinions and beliefs, whereas employee not so designated was not compelled to testify on such subjects).

14   Fed. R. Civ. P. 37(d)(1). In Nippondenso Co. v. Denso Distributors, Civil Action No. 86-3982 (E.D. Pa. September 21, 1987) (available on Westlaw), the court directed that the deposition of the retired senior managing director of the plaintiff corporation, resident in Japan, who was identified by another deponent as most knowledgeable about significant material facts, take place in the forum district or, alternatively, that the plaintiff pay a defense lawyer's expenses to travel to Japan to take the deposition.

Other counsel may request that the deposition be taken at a location other than that designated in the notice.[15] For example, counsel for a corporate defendant will often successfully argue that the depositions of his client's employees should be taken at the corporate headquarters, particularly when the headquarters are not located within the jurisdiction of the pending case.[16] But counsel should use caution in suggesting that the deposition be held at the head-quarters, since opposing counsel may benefit from overhearing conversations in halls or on elevators or from seeing photographs, slogans or graphs on the wall.

Another drawback to inviting the interrogator to a party's place of business is that the deponents may confirm that the company has certain documents, and the interrogator may request that they be produced immediately at the deposition. Although the deponents are not technically obliged to produce such documents, a refusal to do so (if the records are readily available) may appear arbitrary to the court, and the court may allow the interrogator to reopen the deposition after the documents are produced.

To avoid such dangers, counsel for a corporate party may choose the intermediate course of requesting that the depositions be held near, but not at, corporate headquarters. Local counsel's office may be a logical alternative or a motel near the airport may be convenient for all concerned.

Alternatively, other counsel may accept the designation of place by the party serving the notice but argue that the serving party should pay the witness's and counsel's travel expenses in connection with the deposition.[17] A party serving notice for the deposition of a witness, party or nonparty, outside the jurisdiction of the court where the case is pending should recognize the substantial danger that he will receive a request from some other party for reimbursement of its travel and related expenses.[18]

2. Nonparties

The location of a nonparty's deposition is governed by Rule 45(d) pertaining to deposition subpoenas. Rule 45(d)(2) protects nonparties by requiring them to attend a deposition only at a location within 100 miles from the place

---

15   FED. R. CIV. P. 26(c)(2); *see* 4 J. MOORE & J. LUCAS, *supra* note 4, ¶ 26.70 [1.-2 to -3]. Rule 26(c) may be invoked by a nonparty witness as well as by a party. *See id.*, ¶ 26.70[1.-1].

16   Zuckert v. Berkliff Corp., 96 F.R.D. 161, 162 (N.D. Ill. 1982); Mitchell v. American Tobacco Co., 33 F.R.D. 262, 263 (M.D. Pa. 1963).

17   *See* 4 J. MOORE & J. LUCAS, *supra* note 4, ¶ 26.77, at 26-550 to 26-552.

18   *See id.* at 26-546 to -548; FED R. CIV. P. 26(c)(2). For an example of a local rule on this subject, see E.D.N.Y. CIV. R. 5(a).

where they reside, are employed, transact business in person, or were served, although the court may also fix a convenient place.

3.   Experts
A party seeking to depose the opponent's expert must usually pay a reasonable fee for the time the expert spends responding to discovery, under Rule 26(b)(4)(C)(i). Such payment may be required not only for the time during which the expert is being deposed, but also for preparation and travel time. (See Chapter 8, Section A.2).

4.   Document Production
Production of documents in response to a subpoena duces tecum or a document request included in a deposition notice ordinarily takes place at the location of the deposition. However, if the documents are voluminous and are located at a distance from the deposition, a court may decide not to require that the documents be transported except upon payment of some or all of the costs by the party seeking the documents.[19] The interrogator may find it less expensive to travel to the site of the documents than to pay for moving them to his location.

5.   Witnesses in Foreign Countries
A witness located in a foreign country presents a special problem. There are ways of obtaining testimony from witnesses outside the United States, among them letters rogatory and procedures under the Hague Convention on the taking of evidence abroad in civil and commercial matters, which include the taking of evidence by diplomatic or consular officers of the United States located in the country where the witness is found.

Where a United States court has jurisdiction of a deponent who is abroad, the party seeking discovery has the option of proceeding under either the Federal Rules of Civil Procedure or the Hague Convention.[20] A court may, however, order a party to use Hague Convention procedures as a first resort in a

---

19   *See* Petruska v. Johns-Manville, 83 F.R.D. 32 (E.D. Pa. 1979) (voluminous documents requested from defendant should be examined in place where kept but defendant required to bear half of plaintiff's travel and associated expenses to distant location); Mid-America Facilities, Inc. v. Argonaut Insurance Co., 78 F.R.D. 497, 498 (E.D. Wis. 1978) (corporate defendant not required to bring documents from California to Wisconsin for production).

20   *See* Societe Nationale Industrielle Aerospatiale v. United States District Court, ___ U.S. ___, 107 S. Ct. 2542, 2557 (1987) (concerning interrogatories, production of documents, and requests for admissions in which the Supreme Court cautioned courts to supervise foreign discovery "particularly closely" to prevent discovery abuse).

particular case.[21]   A full discussion of discovery from witnesses in foreign countries is outside the scope of this book.[22]

E.   Recording the Deposition

The deposition will ordinarily be stenographically recorded but the parties "may stipulate in writing or the court may upon motion order that the testimony at a deposition be recorded by other than stenographic means."[23] Although lawyers tend automatically to order a stenographer, the use of a reliable tape recorder may suffice when the witness's testimony is not expected to be controversial or lengthy. Playing back prior questions may become burdensome, however, unless there is someone in charge of running the machine.

F.   Telephone Depositions

Normally the witness will appear in person to testify but the parties may stipulate in writing, or the court may order, that the deposition be taken by telephone.[24]

Although it is understandable that an attorney will wish to depose important witnesses in person, in some cases the savings in cost and travel time will outweigh the advantage of having the interrogator and the deponent physically present in the same room, particularly if the deposition is not expected to be lengthy.

Typically, the lawyers will be in a conference room with a speaker phone in one city and the deponent and court reporter will be in a conference

---

21   *E.g.,* Hudson v. Herman Pfauter Gmbh & Co., 117 F.R.D. 33 (N.D.N.Y. 1987).

22   For helpful discussions of the issue, see Bishop, *Service of Process and Discovery in International Tort Litigation,* 23 Tort & Ins. L. J. 70, 128-34 (Fall 1987); Stein, *Oral Depositions in Federal Civil Practice* in H. Hecht, Deposition Techniques in Commercial Litigation at 56-58 (Practising Law Institute 1987); Comment, *Extraterritorial Discovery Under the Hague Convention,* 31 Vill. L. Rev. 253 (1986).

23   On the issue of what discretion lies in a district court to deny a motion for an order allowing nonstenographic recording, *compare* In re Sessions, 672 F.2d 564 (5th Cir. 1982); Reiter v. United States Dist. Ct., 27 Fed. R. Serv. 2d (Callaghan) 801 (6th Cir. 1979) (per curiam); and International Union v. Nat'l Caucus of Labor Comms., 525 F.2d 323 (2d Cir. 1975), *with* Colonial Times, Inc. v. Gasch, 509 F.2d 517 (D.C. Cir. 1975). *See generally* Annotation, *Recording of Testimony at Deposition by Other Than Stenographic Means Under Rule 30(b)(4) of Federal Rules of Civil Procedure,* 16 A.L.R. Fed. 969 (1973).

24   "The parties may stipulate in writing or the court may upon motion order that a deposition be taken by telephone. For purposes of [Rule 30] and Rules 28(a), 37(a)(1), 37(b)(1) and 45(d), a deposition taken by telephone is taken in the district and at the place where the deponent is to answer questions propounded to him." Fed. R. Civ. P. 30(b)(7).

room with a speaker phone in another city. There is no requirement that the lawyers gather at one place (rather than having a multi-party conference call) but it is logistically easier if they are all at one place. Many lawyers prefer to have the court reporter in the room with them, rather than with the deponent, so that they can see if the court reporter is encountering difficulty in taking the testimony and so the reporter can easily identify which lawyer is making an objection. That, too, can be accomplished by agreement or court order.

The lawyers most vigorously opposed to telephone depositions are those who have never participated in one. The difficulties they predict are usually surmountable.

First, how can the interrogator be sure that no one is prompting the deponent? As a technical matter, the interrogator might seek an order excluding others from the room in which the deponent will be testifying. A more practical approach is simply to ask the deponent in advance not to have others present. If he is agreeable, that arrangement can be confirmed on the record with the deponent after he has been sworn and, if the reporter is with the deponent, he might be asked to note on the transcript the comings and goings of others. If the interrogator is genuinely concerned that the deponent may perjure himself about the presence of others, then the deponent is not a good candidate for a telephone deposition. But few deponents are so suspect.

If the deponent will be represented by opposing counsel who intends to be at the deponent's side during the deposition, the interrogator may want to reconsider whether he wants a telephone deposition. The interrogator will not see nods, looks or gestures between the two. And it is not realistic to ask the reporter to act as a police officer and record the interactions between the deponent and his counsel.

Second, how do counsel use documents during a telephone deposition? The interrogator and other counsel must plan their questioning early enough so that, in advance of the deposition, they can provide the deponent or the court reporter with copies of all documents about which they may want to inquire. Ideally, such documents should be premarked as exhibits.

Major complicated business transactions are negotiated on the telephone every day. There is no reason that a deposition cannot be handled the same way.

G.   Common Sense Considerations

Most judges and clients think that lawyers take too many depositions, all of which are too long. Most litigators believe that this criticism is valid — but place the blame on their adversaries.

The lawyer planning to serve a deposition notice should give thought to the two principal questions his client may ask — "Why is it necessary to take this deposition?" and "What will it cost?" — as well as their numerous alternative formulations:

- What are the disadvantages of not taking the deposition?

- Does the witness have unique information? What is it?

- Does the lawyer need this information to prove his case? Or only to help cross-examine the witness at trial? Can the lawyer cross-examine the witness at trial without a deposition transcript? Why not?

- Can the information be obtained in a cheaper way? Through a telephone interview or a meeting?

- How long will the deposition take? If the witness has crucial information on subject A, does the interrogator plan to limit his questioning to that subject? Why not?

- Why must the deposition be taken now rather than three months from now (by which time the case may have settled)?

- If the deposition will be taken out of town, can it be taken by telephone? Why not? Or can it be taken by counsel in that city? Why not?

- Who will take the deposition? If it is a critical deposition, will it be taken by the senior lawyer on the case? Why not? If it is a rather routine deposition, will it be taken by the junior lawyer on the case? Why not?

If the lawyer satisfies himself and his client that the deposition ought to be taken, he should then give thought to how to expedite his examination. He might consider imposing a time limit on himself. For example, if the case is a complicated one in which the deposition might reasonably be expected to last, say, three days, the interrogating lawyer might decide to try to complete it in one day. This self-imposed discipline will force the interrogator to decide which issues are the important ones and to sharpen his questions to get to the point more quickly. More often than not, the interrogator will meet his own deadline. Even if he does not, his questioning will be more focused and the deposition shorter than would otherwise be the case.

24

A more junior lawyer may be concerned about overlooking a crucial line of questioning or about being second-guessed for not taking an exhaustive deposition. Even he should take the time to think through ways of shortening and focusing the deposition rather than assuming that if the deposition is long enough, he is bound to have asked every question worth asking. A thought-through, focused deposition is much more likely to include the essential questions than a meandering, leisurely one.

H.   Preparing To Take the Deposition

To prepare for the deposition, the interrogator should review the pleadings, answers to interrogatories, documents (his own client's and those produced by the opponent or other witnesses), prior deposition transcripts or summaries of them, and memoranda on the underlying facts. He should consult his client to discover additional areas of inquiry. (See Chapter 2, Section D.) Ideally, the interrogator should take a "hands on" approach and, together with his client, visit the intersection, inspect the punch press, or walk through the site where the toxic fumes are said to have accumulated. The deponent and his counsel should consider doing the same. The attorney who makes this additional effort is almost always better prepared as a result.

The interrogator should also familiarize himself with the important applicable case law, particularly the most recent decisions. After this preparation, the attorney should set aside the file and just think about the case.

If the deponent is not hostile and no ethical barrier prohibits it,[25] the interrogator may elect to talk to him in advance of the deposition to explain the procedure, explore the witness's knowledge of the matters in dispute, arrange a convenient time for the deposition, arrange an unembarrassing time for service of the subpoena, and reach an agreement on the witness's compensation. Technically, the deponent is entitled only to the statutory fee,[26] but the interrogator may agree to compensate him for expenses and lost wages.[27]

Finally, the interrogator should prepare a written list of the questions he intends to ask. This list will ensure that the interrogator raises all pertinent issues and, when the wording of a particular question is critical, that he asks the

---

25   See MODEL CODE OF PROFESSIONAL RESPONSIBILITY EC 7-18, DR 7-104 (1979); AMERICAN BAR FOUNDATION, ANNOTATED CODE OF PROFESSIONAL RESPONSIBILITY 331-42 (1979); MODEL RULES OF PROFESSIONAL CONDUCT Rules 4.2-4.4 (1986). The subject of contacting employees of an opposing party is discussed at Chapter 1, Section B.2, *supra*.

26   See 28 U.S.C. 1821 (Supp. III 1979).

27   See MODEL CODE OF PROFESSIONAL RESPONSIBILITY EC 7-28, DR 7-109(C)(1)-(2) (1979). *Compare* MODEL RULES OF PROFESSIONAL CONDUCT Rule 3.4(b) (1986).

question perfectly. Although the form the deposition outline takes is a matter of personal preference, it is probably advisable not to write out each question in full. Such a detailed script may make it harder for the interrogator to keep the big picture in mind and may hamper his ability to establish rapport with the witness and to respond flexibly to answers he elicits during the deposition.

I.   Last-Minute Details

In preparing for the substance of the deposition, a lawyer may well overlook more basic items, such as making arrangements for a conference room or having a copy of the caption of the case with him at the deposition to provide to the reporter, or even arranging for a court reporter.

When making arrangements for the court reporter for the deposition, the lawyer should alert the reporting service to the following items:

(a)   that the deposition may run into the evening if that is a danger (so that the reporting service does not assign a reporter who cannot continue beyond the normal end of the business day);

(b)   that he will want the transcript on an expedited basis (the next day or within a week or whatever);

(c)   that the deponent will be a medical doctor who will be testifying about his treatment of the plaintiff (since the reporting service may be able to assign a reporter who has facility with medical terminology); and

(d)   that other depositions have been taken in the case (the reporting service may then send the reporter who took the other depositions and is already familiar with names and terms).

The reporter will appreciate receiving in advance of the deposition a list of proper names of people likely to be mentioned during the deposition and a lexicon of unusual words and phrases which may be used. That courtesy will not only simplify the reporter's task, but will speed along the deposition (by eliminating breaks to give spellings).

In some places, reporters ask to be sent a copy of notice so that they can verify the date, time and location and can have a caption ready when they arrive.

26

A checklist of routine items needed for most depositions appears in the Appendix under "Practical Tips."

CHAPTER FOUR

OBJECTIVES

A.   Discovery or Admissions?

The two principal, and often conflicting, objectives of depositions are obtaining discovery and obtaining admissions. Although grappling with these conflicting objectives is always difficult, it becomes more so when the underlying facts are complicated and the legal issues complex. The purposes of discovery are, first, to squeeze the witness dry of all relevant information, and second, to bind the witness by his own testimony to a particular version of the facts. To achieve these discovery purposes, the interrogator must continually invite the deponent to talk. For example, the interrogator may ask, "Are there other facts upon which you base your claim [or defense] that . . .?" until the answer is, "No."

To acquire admissions, on the other hand, the interrogator typically will frame questions narrowly and, should he obtain the admission, switch to another subject to avoid retraction or dilution of the admission by the witness. Of course, by switching subjects, the interrogator necessarily risks sacrificing important discovery.

Obtaining discovery is thus essentially *defensive* since the interrogator wants to learn and pin down the information he must prepare to meet at trial. Obtaining admissions is primarily *offensive* in that the interrogator seeks to obtain ammunition for his own use at trial. This distinction will blur in many places.

It is fair to ask why seeking discovery and seeking admissions are inconsistent with each other. Why cannot the interrogator ask the questions that tend to establish a helpful admission and then ask additional questions on the same subject even though they are likely to elicit answers tending to support the deponent's position? More concretely, if the interrogator might ask 10 questions on a particular subject, seven of which are likely to elicit answers favorable to his client's position and three of which are likely to elicit answers favorable to the deponent's position, why not ask all 10?   Certainly, this approach has the benefit of allowing the interrogator to learn before trial the deponent's explanation of seemingly harmful facts.

To answer these questions, one must recall the various uses of depositions at trial.[1] First, depositions are often used to impeach a witness's trial testimony. A

---

1   *See* FED. R. CIV. P. 32(a). *See generally* Kolczynski, *Depositions as Evidence,* LITIGATION, Winter 1983, at 25.

witness who testifies at trial may be cross-examined concerning statements made at the deposition. Rather than giving the witness an opportunity to reconcile inconsistent portions of his deposition and trial testimony, the cross-examining attorney may read those portions of the deposition transcript at the trial and ask the witness to confirm only that he so testified at the deposition. Opposing counsel must then ask questions on redirect examination to mitigate the harmful aspects of such deposition testimony. If, however, the witness gave an exculpatory explanation at the deposition, he may reply that the cross-examining attorney is reading only a portion of the deposition or, on objection by opposing counsel, the court may require the cross-examiner to read the additional deposition testimony on the same subject.[2] Even if the attorney is not compelled to read the supplementary testimony, the jurors will learn that, in the witness's view, they have heard only a portion of the facts and will retain their objectivity until redirect examination.

If the trial witness is a party, opposing counsel may use the transcript in a second way. Instead of cross-examining a party concerning deposition testimony, opposing counsel, as part of his own case, may read portions of the deposition to the jury.[3] The deponent-party cannot offer any exculpatory explanation for such deposition testimony until opposing counsel has concluded his case, perhaps hours or days later. When the deponent finally takes the witness stand, the delayed explanation may be unconvincing to the jury simply because it was so long in coming. If the explanation appears in the deposition transcript itself, however, counsel for the witness can compel the lawyer introducing the harmful portion of the deposition to read the explanatory portion to the jury as well.[4]

We return to the example of the interrogator with 10 possible questions on a particular subject, seven of which are likely to elicit admissions helpful to the interrogator and three of which are likely to elicit answers supportive of the deponent's position. By stopping after seven questions, the interrogator seeking admissions can create a portion of the deposition that may be used either to cross-examine the witness at trial or to read directly to the jury without an exculpatory explanation by the witness.

But suppose the interrogator has asked all 10 possible questions at deposition. If at trial he reads only the first seven questions and answers, he may appear dishonest to the jury when the witness or opposing counsel brings to light the further explanatory deposition testimony on the same subject. Additionally, the witness's explanation may sound more credible to the jury if he has made it previously. Even if the interrogator does not use the deposition

---

2   FED. R. CIV. P. 32(a)(2). See Chapter 11, Section B.5, *infra*.

3   *Id.*

4   FED. R. CIV. P. 32(a)(4); *see also* FED. R. EVID. 106.

transcript, there is the danger that the witness may answer a question with the preface, "As I explained to you at my deposition. . . ." The explanation given at deposition may then take on the aura of a prior consistent statement, tending to add plausibility to the witness's trial testimony. Conversely, the witness's explanation at trial of a harmful fact which was not previously given at the deposition, even though not given because not asked for, may appear to be a recent fabrication.

After obtaining the admission and proceeding to other areas of inquiry, the interrogator may occasionally chance returning to the original subject to ask remaining questions in order to know what the witness's explanation will be at trial. Then, at trial, the interrogator may read the original admission into the record, or cross-examine the witness about it, and hope that neither the witness nor opposing counsel will cite the later answers. Such an approach is risky.

Unfortunately, in actual practice there is no clear dividing line on questions which are likely to evoke admissions. In reality, lawyers preparing for and taking depositions squirm intellectually as they attempt to determine where to draw the line. If the interrogator asks too few questions and the witness is left with several escape hatches, the "admission" may not be of much value. If, on the other hand, the deposing attorney presses too far, the admission may become diluted as the witness begins to explain away its harmful impact.

The interrogator should decide what information is needed from the witness before the deposition begins. For example, when deposing the plaintiff's damage expert in an antitrust case, counsel for the defendant may seek almost pure discovery, rather than admissions. Thus, he will ask the expert to explain everything he has done, to explain each calculation (where he obtained the numbers, which figures he multiplied or divided and why), and to state what further work, if any, he plans to complete on the case. But the interrogator will not seek a direct admission that the expert did not consider inflation, a general decline in the industry at issue or variable costs. The risks of seeking such admissions at the deposition are that the expert will have prepared good answers by the time of trial or that he may revise his approach to eliminate apparent flaws. Also, if counsel for the defendant causes too much damage at the deposition, counsel for the plaintiff may change experts.

On the other hand, if the interrogator has the facts, he may primarily seek admissions from the witness. In a products liability case, for example, counsel for the plaintiff may seek to compel the corporate defendant's president to admit that he knew of certain literature or studies casting doubt on the safety of his product, that he knew of ways to modify the product to eliminate the hazard, that the cost of such modification was negligible (when balanced against human injury or death), and that such modification was considered but rejected for some unworthy reason. If counsel for the plaintiff obtains one of these admissions, he has moved one step closer to winning the case. If not, he has not

31

sacrificed much since opposing counsel surely knew that such points would arise at some time, and the interrogator now knows what he must prepare to prove at trial.

Typically, however, the interrogator seeks both discovery and admissions on most subjects. In light of the inevitable tension between these objectives, the interrogator should plan what he will settle for on each subject to be covered.[5] As a housekeeping matter, he may want to bracket in his outline those questions of which he is unsure and wait until the deposition to decide whether to ask them.

In deciding how far to go in examining a particular deponent, the interrogator should consider whether he wants to settle the case or try it. If he wants to settle, the attorney may drive his points home during deposition questioning to signal to his opponent the significant risks involved in proceeding to trial. On the other hand, if the interrogator expects the case to be tried, he will question witnesses without being as overt about the potential significance of their testimony.

B.   Other Objectives

1.   *Preserving Favorable or Essential Testimony*

A deposition, of course, serves purposes other than obtaining discovery or admissions. One is to preserve favorable testimony.[6] A lawyer will often decide not to schedule the deposition of a witness favorable to his case, waiting instead to call that witness at trial. The attorney may prefer not to expose the witness to cross-examination by opposing counsel before trial. On the other hand, if a favorable witness is elderly, infirm, nomadic, or beyond the jurisdiction of the trial court, the lawyer should seriously consider scheduling the witness's deposition, particularly if the case will not be reached for trial for, say, two years or more. When deposing such a witness, each attorney should take into account that the witness may not be available for the trial and that the deposition may therefore serve as trial testimony.[7]

---

5   For a discussion of structuring the examination to accomplish its objectives, *see* Gildin, *A Practical Guide to Taking and Defending Depositions*, 88 DICK. L. REV. 247, 251-55 (Winter 1984).

6   *See* FED. R. CIV. P. 32(a)(3).

7   *See id.*

To some extent this risk is always present because any deponent may die before trial or become otherwise unavailable.[8] When the deposition is likely to be used as the witness's trial testimony, each lawyer may hesitate to ask questions tending to elicit testimony harmful to his case. By asking such questions, the attorney can better prepare to meet his opponent at trial. But if the lawyer elects not to ask such questions, potentially harmful testimony may not surface at trial (the witness may die, disappear, or, if he is beyond the subpoena power of the trial court, refuse to appear) and the lawyer may never have to confront that testimony.

The lawyer should also seriously consider deposing the witness who is not only favorable, but crucial to his case — regardless of age, health or residence. He should consider what explanation he will give to his client if he fails to do so and the witness has a heart attack and dies before trial.

2. Exposing Inconsistencies

The interrogator's objective may be to create conflicts between and among the other side's witnesses. Thus, in a suit against the members of a board of directors for breach of their fiduciary duty, counsel for the plaintiff may elect to depose each of the directors in detail about the conversations which led to the challenged transaction. He may figure that no two of them will be able to give completely consistent accounts of those conversations and that as he takes additional depositions, conflicts in the testimony will proliferate, thereby creating doubts about the alleged motive for the transaction.

Similarly, in a suit against an insurance company which has denied coverage on the basis of some exclusion, counsel for the plaintiff may elect to depose everyone at the insurance company who is knowledgeable about the meaning of the exclusion or who participated in the decision to deny coverage. To the extent that he is successful in developing conflicts in their testimony as to the meaning of the exclusion, he marshals support for an argument that it is ambiguous, which is a large step toward winning the case.

3. Weakening the Deponent as a Trial Witness

Depositions may also be used to destroy a deponent's effectiveness as a trial witness. The interrogator may achieve this objective either by demonstrating

---

8   *See* Wright Root Beer v. Dr. Pepper Co., 414 F.2d 887, 889-91 (5th Cir. 1969) (rejecting counsel's argument that deposition could not be used since "he did not extend himself on cross-examination because it was a discovery deposition"); *In re* Asbestos Related Cases, 543 F. Supp. 1142, 1148 (N.D. Cal. 1982) (rejecting defendant's argument that deposition of witness could not be used because defendant had not vigorously cross-examined in light of small number of pending asbestos cases at the time of deposition); United States v. International Business Machines Corp., 90 F.R.D. 377, 381 (S.D.N.Y. 1981) (rejecting plaintiff's argument that depositions of its witnesses could not be used because it chose not to cross-examine those witnesses).

through the deposition examination that the witness's testimony is not credible, or by successfully inviting the witness to commit to a series of propositions which can convincingly be shown at trial to be false.

4.   *Eliminating the Deponent as a Trial Witness*

Another objective of the interrogator may be to eliminate entirely the deponent as a possible trial witness by asking him to confirm that he has no knowledge about the key facts in dispute.

5.   *Supporting a Motion*

Finally, a deposition can provide the interrogator with testimonial support for a motion for summary judgment or for other motions.[9] (See Chapter 11, Section C.) If this is an objective, the interrogator should think about scheduling the key depositions early in the case so that he does not miss the opportunity to obtain helpful admissions before discovery has developed to the point where the witnesses are wary.

---

9   *See* FED. R. CIV. P. 56(c), 43(e).

CHAPTER FIVE

THE LAWYER'S MANNER

A.   Who's in Charge?

A deposition is a kind of meeting, and even at a meeting among equals, one person, for whatever intangible reason, will usually take control. Depositions are no exception, nor should they be. The lawyer who controls the deposition has an edge. Consequently, a certain amount of jockeying for position often occurs at a deposition, particularly at its start, to determine who will seize control. If a lawyer cannot dominate the deposition, he should at least prevent his opponent from doing so.

Learning to take control of a meeting is probably a better subject for a psychology book than a legal one, but it is nonetheless appropriate to observe that a lawyer generally avoids losing control by choosing his ground carefully and not retreating. For example, the interrogator should not demand that one of two witnesses to be deposed that morning be sequestered if he intends to abandon that demand should his opponent refuse. Similarly, the deponent's lawyer should not instruct the deponent not to answer if he plans to withdraw the instruction, either directly or indirectly (by waffling), when the interrogator recesses the deposition to apply for a court ruling. That is not to say, however, that the lawyer should never budge from a position he has taken for fear of forfeiting control. The deponent senses who is in charge from the lawyer's tone and manner, not from his rigid adherence to unreasonable positions, and will react accordingly.

B.   Losing Through Intimidation

An attorney need not be obnoxious to assume control of a deposition.[1] Although lawyers are sometimes successful in bullying their opponents, an experienced attorney can readily deflate a pugnacious opponent, causing the opponent to lose rather than gain control. For example, in one case after the lawyer for the deponent ended a long diatribe questioning the interrogator's motives in taking the deposition and his reasons for delving into certain topics, the interrogator matter-of-factly inquired, "Dick, did you have a flat tire on the way into town this morning?"

---

1   *See* Facher, *Taking Depositions*, in LITIGATION MANUAL, 3, 7 (1983).

The interrogator should consider not only how his manner will affect the deposition testimony elicited but how it will affect the long-term course of the litigation. For example, some personal injury defense lawyers are unremittingly nasty to the plaintiff and openly skeptical of his testimony. The idea seems to be that if the plaintiff expects more of the same in the formal setting of the courtroom, he will be more willing to accept a low settlement offer. Perhaps that approach works in some cases. But, at the least, the interrogator should consider a less hostile approach.

In one death case in which liability was reasonably clear, at the conclusion of the deposition of the decedent's father (the named plaintiff), counsel for the defendant shook hands with the deponent and said, "I'm sorry for your loss, sir." Counsel for the plaintiff later commented that that simple gesture changed his client's attitude about the case so that, for the first time, he was willing to think and talk about settlement.

Similarly, some plaintiffs' attorneys take a very aggressive tone in deposing the chief executive officer of the corporate defendant. Again, the idea seems to be that such an approach will make the deponent more willing to pay a higher sum to settle the case to avoid another session of tough questioning in the courtroom. Undoubtedly that approach succeeds in some cases. But are there not dangers in treating a strong-willed chief executive officer discourteously? If his lawyers tell him that he has an even chance to win the case, might he not direct that it be tried rather than settled? Of course, if counsel for the plaintiff has no interest in settlement, such a reaction will not trouble him. But that is a rare case.

An experienced litigator will sometimes attempt to intimidate a younger opponent. For example, if the experienced attorney is counsel for the deponent, he may disrupt the younger interrogator's questioning by snorting derisively at his questions, arguing about their relevance, interrupting the deposition to make telephone calls, or threatening to walk out with the deponent if the deposition is not concluded in 30 minutes. The younger lawyer should not yield to such antics but should stand his ground and proceed with questioning as planned. If he hurries and abbreviates his questioning, the quality of the deposition will suffer. It is highly improbable that counsel for the witness will follow through on his threat to leave the deposition; if he should, the court will almost certainly order him to return.

C.   Refusing To Rise to the Bait

Some lawyers defending depositions are so offensive to the interrogator that it is hard to refrain from taking the bait and answering them in kind. This is rarely good strategy. If the interrogator diverts his attention from the witness in order to trade barbs with the opposing lawyer, that lawyer will have achieved his objective of disrupting the deposition by successfully interjecting himself between his client and the interrogator.

As difficult as it is, the interrogator should try to ignore provocative comments and firmly and persistently press on with the deposition. If opposing counsel's comments cannot be completely ignored, it is usually best to make the response a matter-of-fact "We disagree," or "Let's move on," or "Let's get the work done and save the chatter for later." If even such a refusal to rise to the bait does not stem the disruptions (and if the record will adequately reflect the intrusive comments or actions), the interrogator may want to state on the record his intention to adjourn the deposition and seek a court order unless opposing counsel stops his attempts to disrupt the deposition.[2] He must be prepared to follow through if the behavior continues.

If the deponent is obviously nervous at the start of the deposition, the interrogator's natural tendency may be to attempt to put him at ease. This may not be wise. If the deponent is the opposing party or is otherwise hostile, the interrogator may obtain more truthful and more helpful answers if the deponent remains nervous. As the deposition progresses, however, the deponent will almost certainly grow more relaxed. Some lawyers succeed in keeping the deponent off balance by alternating their conduct, seeming, at some times, cordial and accommodating and, at others, brusque and unpleasant. It is difficult for the deponent to remain at ease if he perceives the interrogator as unpredictable. There is no steadfast rule. In a given case, the interrogator may decide that a friendly manner and conversational questioning are more likely to disarm the deponent and elicit helpful testimony than a more contentious approach.

Neither the interrogator nor the defending attorney should allow himself to become angry during the deposition, any more than he would allow that to happen during a trial. The lawyer who is genuinely angry is out of control and likely to say and do things which he will regret. Of course, there may be times when the lawyer decides that there is some advantage in appearing to be angry. There is nothing wrong with that — so long as it is strictly an appearance and not a fact.

Inevitably, the deponent will learn something of the interrogator's manner through his questioning. Accordingly, the lawyer in charge of the case may prefer that a younger associate take the deposition. In this way, the senior lawyer, as trial counsel, will arrive as an unknown entity to the witness at trial.

---

2   *See* Unique Concepts, Inc. v. Brown, 115 F.R.D. 292 (S.D.N.Y. 1987) (imposing fine on attorney for "contentious, abusive, obstructive, scurrilous, and insulting conduct" in deposition).

CHAPTER SIX

STRATEGY AND TACTICS

A. Business and Personal Injury Litigation — The Differences

Strategy and tactics may depend on the type of litigation involved. Two broad categories are personal injury litigation and business litigation. In general, there are three principal differences between these categories that affect the techniques which lawyers use in taking depositions:

1. *Time*
In a personal injury case, the key events (a collision at a corner, a slip on a sidewalk, the amputation of a finger by a saw) may have happened in the blink of an eye. By contrast, in a business case, the key events may have unfolded over a protracted period of time, perhaps months or even years.

2. *Plaintiff's Knowledge*
In the typical personal injury case, the plaintiff's knowledge is limited. He will probably be knowledgeable and can testify about how the accident happened. But he will not know much about the basis of the liability contentions which his lawyer is advancing and, in any event, his lawyer will probably instruct him not to answer deposition questions directed to such contentions. For example, the plaintiff may testify at the deposition that there was no guard on the saw and describe how the accident happened. But his lawyer will probably instruct him not to answer questions probing the contention that the saw should have been equipped with a guard, claiming that such questions call for opinion testimony and should be directed to the plaintiff's expert. If such an instruction is tested, it is likely that the court will uphold it.

By contrast, in business litigation, the plaintiff's employees will often be knowledgeable about how the defendant's company operates and about the industry in general. Thus, they may be able to give detailed testimony to support the plaintiff's legal contentions. For example, if the plaintiff alleges that the defendant has attempted to monopolize a certain market, the plaintiff's employees may know a great deal about what actions the defendant has taken to achieve that objective, how those actions have made it difficult or impossible for the plaintiff to compete, and how those actions differ from vigorous but fair competition. The interrogator may subject such witnesses to very probing examination, usually with little objection from counsel for the plaintiff.

3.   Documents

Even in a very serious personal injury case, there may be few documents of importance — perhaps none except medical records; the entire liability case may turn on eyewitness testimony. On the other hand, it is very unusual to encounter a business case without a large volume of documents generated by both sides.

These are differences of degree. In personal injury litigation, counsel may have to deal with events that occurred over many years and with many documents. For example, in a product liability case, the significant steps in the development of the product may have occurred over many years and be reflected in many documents. But, broadly speaking, the three distinctions described here are valid.

These differences in the nature of business litigation will affect counsel's strategic and tactical decisions in deposing the other side's witnesses, as the following discussion of approaches and techniques illustrates.

B.   The Traditional Approach — And Alternatives

When preparing for the deposition, the interrogator should give careful thought to the order in which he will approach various subjects. He must determine whether to begin with the important issues or to postpone those questions until the deponent starts to tire and is further away in time from the cautions his lawyer gave him in their preparation session. The question is often difficult and there is no single right answer.

1.   Getting the Deponent's Background First — or Later

The great majority of depositions begin with questions about the deponent's education and employment history, including his current duties and responsibilities. The interrogator will then ask a question to determine the deponent's first involvement in the subject matter of the dispute ("When and how did you first become involved in the Hotel California construction project?"), and will then trace his activities chronologically to the end.

There is nothing wrong with such an approach. It is an orderly and sensible way to elicit the facts.

But the interrogator should consider other approaches. It can take 15 minutes to an hour or more to learn the deponent's education and employment history. The witness will usually feel relatively comfortable in relating this personal history and will become more so as he establishes eye contact with the interrogator and grows accustomed to the cadence of his voice and his mannerisms. The same witness, even if an experienced deponent, may be surprised and flustered if defense counsel asks in rapid succession whether he attended the key meeting at which the defendant's representatives allegedly made certain false statements, what was said at the meeting, what statements he claims were false, and in what way they were false. The deponent may be somewhat unnerved by the simple fact that the examiner is not playing by "the rules" as the deponent knows them from his own prior experience or has learned them from his own lawyer. The witness's education and employment pedigree can be explored at the end of the deposition or anywhere else that suits the interrogator.

As another example, when deposing a defendant-driver involved in a motor vehicle accident case, counsel for the plaintiff will normally question the defendant about his background, then set the scene (how wide were the streets, which vehicle was in what lane, did anything obstruct the view, etc.), and will finally reach the details of the accident. The defendant will tend to relax since his own lawyer probably told him that the questioning would proceed this way. Occasionally, the plaintiff's counsel may want to take a different apprroach. He may start by asking, for instance, the defendant's name and whether he was involved in an accident on December 14, 1987. Then, without further preamble, he may ask how the accident happened. This approach may differ from what the defendant's lawyer told him to expect. The result may be an answer harmful to the defendant's case, particularly if he tries to include all the detailed information that he recently reviewed with his lawyer about speeds, distances and times.

On the other hand, the interrogator may decide to postpone the significant questions for as long as possible. For example, assume in a personal injury suit that the liability issue is close but the damages are clear and serious. Since, understandably, the plaintiff may be more interested in his own injuries than in the precise dynamics of the accident, counsel for the defendant may decide to question first about those injuries and then, hours later, proceed to liability. By that time, the plaintiff may have only a dim recollection of his own lawyer's warnings about the liability pitfalls.

There are no hard-and-fast rules. As Section C of this Chapter will explain, sometimes it can be a mistake to move too abruptly to the central event.

To be sure, at some point in the deposition, the interrogator should elicit certain background information. For example, the deponent's education and employment experience may be highly relevant both to the claims asserted and to the weight to be given to his testimony. It is also wise to ask a nonparty deponent to give his home and business addresses and telephone numbers and to inquire whether he has plans to move. As the case approaches trial, this information can be very valuable in locating a witness to serve him with a subpoena. Sometimes a witness will refuse to state an unlisted telephone number for the record. If his counsel agrees to provide the information necessary for service of a subpoena upon request, the interrogator need not press for the information on the record.

If the deponent is a party or a director, officer or managing agent of a party, it is usually not necessary to obtain an address and telephone number; a

41

request to opposing counsel that such a person appear at the trial should normally be sufficient to assure his presence. However, a director, officer or managing agent may terminate employment with the corporation before trial, so it may be advisable to obtain this information in all cases.

2.   *Development of the Facts — Chronological or Otherwise*

If the case involves a sharp factual dispute about who said what to whom over an extended course of dealing, the easiest approach for the interrogator is to develop the facts by inquiring about them in chronological order. However, the interrogator should consider using something other than a straight chronological approach. The chronological method may be easiest for the interrogator, but it is also easiest for the deponent.

Consequently, even if the interrogator's approach is generally chrono-logical, hopscotching around from time to time may help to develop inconsistencies in the testimony of an untruthful deponent.   For instance, after questioning the witness about his first four meetings with the interrogator's client, the interrogator may want to return to the second meeting to ask whether a particular subject was discussed there. Of course, in doing so, he runs some risk of an objection and instruction not to answer by opposing counsel on the ground that the questioning is repetitious. Even though such an instruction is not technically proper, the interrogator is then faced with the hard choice whether to abandon the question or seek a ruling from the court.

Once the interrogator has given thought to how he will develop the facts, he should not become so mesmerized by his own outline of questions that intriguing answers fail to register with him. Having settled on the best order in which to cover his subjects, he must repeatedly decide during the deposition whether to adhere to his script or to set it aside and immediately follow up an interesting answer that may, for example, pertain to the final subject on his agenda. The interrogator must quickly and intuitively decide whether the bene-fit of pursuing such an answer outweighs the advantages of his original organi-zation of topics. If the interrogator hesitates too long before asking the follow-up questions, the deponent may interpret the pause as a signal that his answer in some way injured his case, and modify or withdraw his statement.

Suppose that a plaintiff has purchased component parts, which the plaintiff claims are defective, from the defendant supplier. The deponent, a quality control manager employed by the supplier, is describing a series of inspections he made of those parts at the supplier's plant. The interrogator represents the plaintiff. The interrogation goes like this:

Q.   When did the first inspection take place?

A.   Well, I remember that the first one took place on my
       birthday, June 3, because the plant superintendent

> offered me $500 and suggested that I take the day
> off. He said he could sign the inspection forms with
> my initials and no one would be the wiser.

Surely the next question should not be: "And when did the next inspection take place?"

If the interrogator will be deposing several similarly situated witnesses, he should vary his approach. Otherwise the deponent (who may have attended the other depositions or read the transcripts) will anticipate the approach and feel comfortable from the start. At the least, the interrogator's first substantive question to a later witness should differ from his lead questions to previous witnesses.

After determining the order in which to address the various subjects, the interrogator must decide on the order in which to pose specific questions and how to word them. It makes a difference. The following discussion of approaches, while not exhaustive, may illustrate the point.

C. Getting the Deponent Committed to Certain Propositions — Especially on Policy and Practice

The interrogator may want the deponent to commit himself to certain propositions on seemingly noncontroversial matters before turning to the central issues. If the deponent perceives such questions to be unimportant, he may readily make significant concessions.

Two areas in which it may be particularly helpful to establish the deponent's policy and practice, correspondence and note taking, are treated separately below. Other important areas include the deponent's policy and practice with respect to reviewing certain types of documents routinely sent to him (for example, sales reports, personnel evaluations, customer complaints), consulting with or reporting to others about significant events and decisions, making written reports about significant events and decisions, retaining documents, and monitoring activities in particular areas.

1. Correspondence

Suppose that the underlying facts are that there was correspondence between the parties, that at some point the defendant sent a letter to the plaintiff stating that certain facts favorable to the defendant's case were true, and that the plaintiff made no written response to that letter. How does the interrogator representing the defendant obtain the maximum benefit from these helpful facts?

If the interrogator studies the correspondence, he may find that his client sent 11 letters prior to the crucial letter and that the plaintiff's president responded only to the fifth and the eighth to correct some inaccuracy. In deposing the plaintiff's president, the interrogator may take the letters in turn and ask the witness to confirm that he received each letter, that he read it, that the letter contained an accurate statement of the facts, that he did not respond to it, and that he did not respond because the letter was accurate. The interrogator will further ask the deponent to confirm that he responded to the fifth and eighth letters and that he did so to correct their inaccuracies. After discussing perhaps the eighth or ninth letter, the interrogator may ask the deponent to confirm that his general policy or practice was to respond in writing only to letters which were inaccurate in some way.

The deposing attorney should not wait too long to pose this question since the closer he comes to the date of the key document, the greater the risk that the deponent will have his guard up. The interrogator has a greater chance to obtain the admission on policy or practice if he proceeds in this painstaking way than if he asks without preamble whether the deponent's policy or practice was to respond in writing only to inaccurate letters.

The described scenario raises the problem of the conflicting objectives of discovery and admissions. Suppose the deponent concedes that his policy or practice was as the interrogator suggested. The interrogator must decide whether to stop that line of questioning since he has secured a favorable admission or to continue and ask the deponent to confirm that, consistent with his policy or practice, he failed to respond in writing to the key letter because it was fully accurate. If the interrogator halts the questioning, he will have no inkling of how the deponent will answer the critical question at trial.

If the interrogator continues and poses the key question, the deponent may feel compelled to make the desired admission by the force of the series of answers he has just given, thus aiding the interrogator in winning his case. But, just as likely, the deponent may refuse to make the desired admission, and instead give a self-serving but credible explanation of his failure to respond to the key letter. If that happens, the interrogator will learn what he must face at trial; but the witness's explanation at trial may assume an extra patina of credibility since it was also given at deposition.

As an alternative to these approaches, the interrogator could follow a middle course and ask the deponent only whether he received the key letter, whether he responded to it, and nothing more. Even with this approach, however, the interrogator risks losing the admission since the deponent may not cooperate by giving one-word answers without adding an explanatory gloss.

2. Notes of Meetings

The technique of obtaining admissions of preliminary propositions may also be used with respect to notes made at meetings. Assume the defendant claims that the plaintiff made a statement harmful to the plaintiff's case at a meeting between the two parties. Assume further that the notes taken by the defendant at the meeting include no mention of the alleged statement. How can counsel for the plaintiff best utilize that helpful fact in deposing the note taker? One approach is to consider first the notes of other meetings and to confirm that the deponent's general policy or practice at those other meetings was to make notes of what was important and to omit what was unimportant. This proposition is so seemingly obvious and noncontroversial that the deponent may readily agree that he took notes on that basis. Contrast the situation in which counsel for the plaintiff begins his questioning by asking the deponent whether his approach in taking notes during the key meeting between the parties was to transcribe important statements and to exclude those that were unimportant. The deponent might quickly perceive the implications of an affirmative answer and hedge. The deponent might claim, for example, that he made notes randomly without regard to the significance of a particular statement. Although this explanation may be somewhat implausible, the interrogator will have gained nothing from the deposition. In fact, he will have lost ground by permitting the deponent to give a pretrial explanation of his conduct which, if it should surface at trial, may lend credibility to the deponent's trial testimony.

D.   Establishing a Premise That May Tend To Shape the Next Answer

Deponents are generally aware of what they have already said in the deposition and want their testimony to be consistent and believable. Consequently, there may be some advantage to asking a particular question before another. For example, in a personal injury case in which the plaintiff last saw a doctor six months before the deposition, does it make any difference in which order counsel for the defendant asks the plaintiff the following questions?

(a)   Do you still have pain from the injuries you claim to have sustained in this accident?

(b)   When were you last treated by a doctor for the injuries you claim to have sustained in this accident?

Some accident defense lawyers argue that the second question should be asked first. If the plaintiff first answers that he was last treated by a doctor six months ago, he may think that it will sound odd to say he still suffers from intense pain, and so may tend to give a more temperate account of his injury when asked about it later in the deposition. On the other hand, if the plaintiff is first asked to describe his pain and characterizes it as excruciating, he may then rationalize his failure to seek further treatment by claiming that the doctor advised him (or that he concluded himself) that medical treatment would be of no further help and that he would have to live with the pain.

Obviously, asking the questions in one order rather than the other does not assure that the answers will be more favorable to the interrogator. Nevertheless, it should enhance the odds slightly and a successful litigator will constantly watch for small advantages.

E.   Wording the Question Aggressively

Although some lawyers contend that the interrogator may not ask leading questions or cross-examine the deponent, as a practical matter, the interrogator may generally phrase questions as he wants.[1] By wording the questions aggressively, the interrogator can improve the chances of obtaining favorable testimony.

For example, suppose the plaintiff-distributor alleges that he was wrongfully terminated by the defendant-manufacturer without adequate notice. The interrogator could pose his question in either of the following ways:

(a)   As of May 1987, did you expect to be terminated by the defendant?

(b)   In light of the history of your dealings with the defendant in 1986 and 1987, including the unpleasant meetings in October 1986, and February 1987, which you have told us about, did it come as a [big] surprise to you when you received the letter of termination in May 1987?

The interrogator using the second approach should attempt to phrase the question so that it tends to persuade the deponent to assent to the proposition at issue. Sometimes the interrogator may coax the witness to accept a proposition by starting his question with, "Would it be fair to say that . . . ?" or "Would you agree that . . . ?" Since most people want to be fair and agreeable, it may be difficult for the deponent to answer negatively to such a question. Another variation is, "Would I be wrong if I said . . . ?" The witness may hesitate to give the rather abrupt answer, "Yes, you would be wrong . . . ," even if that is the case.

---

1   Rule 30(c) permits examination of a deponent "as permitted at the trial under the . . . Federal Rules of Evidence." FED. R. CIV. P. 30(c). These rules permit examination by leading questions of "a hostile witness, an adverse party, or a witness identified with an adverse party." FED. R. EVID. 611(c).

46

F.   Stating the Deponent's Position Baldly

Sometimes the witness will recoil from and reject one of his own contentions if it is put to him starkly, particularly if an allegation of intentional wrongdoing is at issue. For example, if the plaintiff alleges fraud and breach of contract because of the defendant's alleged misrepresentations, the defendant's attorney may directly confront the plaintiff by asking:

> Do you claim that Mr. Suplee lied to you when he
> described the qualifications of the project manger?

Some lawyers will object to use of the word "lied" on the questionable ground that it calls for a conclusion.[2] If so, the interrogator may often eliminate the objection by rewording the question as follows:

> Do you claim that Mr. Suplee lied to you when he
> described the project manager's qualifications in that he
> knew that such statement was false when he made it?

The plaintiff may stop short of answering that the defendant lied to him even though he is willing to make the substantially identical, though semantically more amorphous, charge that the defendant misrepresented the situation. Even if the plaintiff insists that the defendant lied to him, the interrogator has not lost ground since the plaintiff essentially had charged such deception before the questioning began.

Similarly, if the complaint alleges that the defendant acted for the purpose of inflicting harm upon the plaintiff, defense counsel may ask directly whether the plaintiff contends not only that the defendant's actions hurt him, but also that the defendant took those actions deliberately to harm the plaintiff. The plaintiff may hesitate to answer such a question affirmatively.

G.   Posing the Who-Cares-What-The-Answer-Is Question

Some questions afford the interrogator a line of attack regardless of the witness's answer. The question will often begin with the phrase, "Did it occur to you at that point that . . . ?" This approach can be used effectively in cases ranging from complex fraud to automobile collision to products liability.

Suppose the plaintiff in a complex fraud case alleges that the defendant took nine separate steps, the last of which caused the plaintiff to lose money. After ascertaining the facts of each step, counsel for the defendant may ask the plaintiff:

---

2   Most such objections lack merit. *See* Fed. R. Evid. 701, 704.

> Did it occur to you at that point that Ms. Donaldson
> might be attempting to defraud you?

If the plaintiff answers no, the interrogator may ask him to confirm that the defendant's actions up to that point fell within the range of normal business conduct. Should the plaintiff concede this, the facts allegedly constituting the fraud are narrowed. On the other hand, if the plaintiff responds that it did occur to him that the defendant might have been perpetrating a fraud, he will have a more difficult time demonstrating that thereafter he acted reasonably in continuing to deal with the defendant despite his suspicions.

The same approach may be used in connection with a right-angle collision. Either driver may be asked:

> Did it occur to you at that point that an accident was
> about to happen?

If the driver replies no, the answer may damage his case because the fact finder may conclude that, in view of the circumstances at that point, the driver should have recognized the risk of an accident and acted accordingly. If the driver answers affirmatively, however, then the fact finder will judge his subsequent actions in light of the concededly recognized risk of an accident. Either way, the opponent has gained the edge.

Finally, the same technique may also be used in a products liability case. In questioning the defendant's safety engineer, the plaintiff's attorney may ask:

> In light of the information available to you at that point,
> did you give consideration to a modification in the
> design of the punch press?

If the deponent answers no, he will risk being attacked at trial because "that thought never even crossed your mind, did it?" If the engineer says yes, then he will be forced to explain why, after specific consideration, he made no change.

H.   Establishing the Obvious

The interrogator may ask some questions primarily to obtain a good crisp colloquy with which to cross-examine the witness at trial or to read to the jury. The interrogator may also gain greater control of the witness at trial by covering certain subjects at the deposition. One might say that the interrogator is seeking admissions of what is obvious.

For example, counsel for the plaintiff in a products liability case may ask the defendant's engineer:

In designing the universal joint of the steering wheel did you take safety considerations into account?

Is that because you recognized that a defectively designed universal joint might cause serious personal injuries or death?

Did you take into consideration that a pedestrian such as plaintiff might be seriously injured or killed if this universal joint were defectively designed and malfunctioned?

Particularly if the case is to be tried before a jury, counsel will want to spend time on those obvious points beneficial to his case.

I.   Putting Yourself in the Deponent's Shoes

In preparing for the deposition of an adverse party, the interrogator should assume the role of the deponent and think through the deponent's position in the case. He should then consider two questions.

First, *what possible actions by the deponent would be consistent or inconsistent with his present claim?* The interrogator should think about what steps the opposing party would have taken if events occurred as he claims they did. For example, if the plaintiff claims that he entered into an oral contract with the defendant, which the defendant denies, the interrogator should ask whether the plaintiff arranged to obtain the materials needed for performance. Failure to initiate such arrangements would be inconsistent with the plaintiff's claim that a contract existed.

Similarly, the interrogator should explore what the deponent might have done if the facts were not as claimed. In a dispute between a landlord and tenant as to whether the tenant gave timely notice of his intention not to renew the lease,[3] suppose the tenant contends that he gave timely oral notice and that the landlord assured him that written notice was unnecessary. The interrogator should identify what steps the landlord might have taken if, in fact, the tenant did give notice of nonrenewal. Possible actions by the landlord that would be inconsistent with his claim that he received no such notice include listing the premises with a real estate broker, printing brochures to describe them or showing the premises to a prospective tenant. The interrogator should investigate such possibilities at the deposition.

---

3   *See, e.g.*, Kachigian v. Minn, 23 Ill. App.3d 722, 320 N.E.2d 173 (1974).

Second, *what circumstances may the deponent have faced in which it would have been in his interest to take a position inconsistent with his litigation position?* For example, if the plaintiff avers that the defendant sold him defective goods, the interrogator should inquire whether the plaintiff attempted to resell the goods. If so, did he describe them as defective? The interrogator should at least determine the identities of all prospective buyers with whom the plaintiff dealt. He may further inquire about the details of the plaintiff's conversations with these buyers. On the other hand, he may decide to avoid highlighting the point and, instead, interview the prospective buyers privately at a later time.

J.   Exhausting the Knowledge of the Deponent

The interrogator who seeks full discovery of facts should be careful to exhaust the knowledge of the deponent. If asked who attended a meeting, for instance, the deponent may say that he, Mr. Baccini, and Mr. Leddy did. The interrogator should persist in asking whether anyone else attended the meeting until the witness says no.

In dealing with broader subjects, the interrogator must carefully avoid becoming lost in the details of the deponent's answers. For example, the interrogator may begin by asking the witness which meetings he attended on a particular topic. After the deponent gives the approximate date of one such meeting, the interrogator may question him at length about what occurred. However, when the interrogator completes such particularized questioning, he should return to the general subject and ask whether other meetings on that topic were held. This pattern should be repeated until the deponent confirms that no other meetings were held. The interrogator must concentrate to be sure that he has exhausted all knowledge of the witness about each meeting: who attended, what was discussed, what options were considered, what action was decided upon, and whether there are any documents reflecting the discussions at the meeting.

K.   Delving into the Deponent's Preparation for Deposition

In addition to questioning the deponent on substantive topics, the interrogator should find out how the deponent prepared for the deposition. Of course, the attorney-client privilege protects the substance of preparation sessions with the deponent's lawyer, and the work product shield, in certain circumstances, protects the lawyer's selection of documents for the witness's review.[4] Without trespassing into privileged areas, however, the interrogator may ask questions such as the following:

> How many preparation sessions did the deponent have with his lawyer? How long did each last? Who else attended the sessions or any part of them?

> Did he review documents? On his own? That his lawyer selected? How many? Where did they come from? (Confirm with the deponent's lawyer that they have been produced.)

> What documents did he review? (But see footnote 4 above and the discussion of Federal Rule of Evidence 612 at Chapter 9, Section E.3.).

> Did the deponent talk to anyone besides his lawyer in preparing for his deposition? Who? What was said?

> Did he review transcripts of other depositions in the case? Which ones?

> Did he see any testimony with which he disagrees or that he thinks is inaccurate? (This question may raise an objection that the witness cannot possibly respond with respect to hundreds of pages of transcript, but it sometimes elicits helpful information.)

Interrogation about preparation for the deposition may surface information about documents and witnesses that have not previously been identified. The extent of preparation may also affect the credibility of the deposition testimony when used at trial.

---

4   *See* Sporck v. Peil, 759 F.2d 312 (3d Cir.), *cert. denied*, 474 U.S. 903 (1985), holding that a lawyer's selection and compilation of documents to prepare a witness for deposition is work product, and that Fed. R. Evid. 612 will override the work product protection only if opposing counsel establishes at the deposition that the witness used the documents to refresh his memory and to answer specific, relevant deposition questions (and then only those documents relied on are subject to production). The case is discussed in Solovy & Byman, *Rule 612 and Work-Product Usage in the Preparation of Testimony,* NAT'L L. J., June 10, 1985, 28-29.

CHAPTER SEVEN

MECHANICS AND PROBLEMS (AND MORE TACTICS)

The expectation under the Federal Rules of Civil Procedure is that depositions ordinarily will proceed without court involvement. The interrogator may seek information reasonably calculated to lead to the discovery of admissible evidence.[1] The objections made by other counsel at the deposition will be ruled upon by the court at, or immediately in advance of, trial.[2] Usually, the witness will answer even those questions to which objections have been made, unless counsel instructs the witness not to answer, which is very much the exception.

Depositions are usually conducted in an adversarial but cooperative atmosphere, and thus it is rarely necessary to involve the court. Most litigators take seriously their duty of good faith in participating in the discovery process. The lawyer tempted to disrupt may be deterred by the prospects of reciprocal treatment from opposing counsel and sanctions from the court.[3] Still, problems will inevitably occur from time to time.

This chapter catalogs in a chronological fashion much of what can and does happen during depositions. It begins with who sits where, ends with reading and correcting the transcript, and discusses in between many of the problems which may arise in questioning the deponent.

In general, both the interrogator and the lawyer defending the deponent should be conversant with the rules governing deposition practice: the applicable Federal Rules of Civil Procedure, local rules, and the Federal Rules of Evidence, as well as standing orders and instructions of the individual judge to whom the case is assigned.

A. Who Sits Where

The interrogator and the deponent will usually sit directly across from each other toward one end of the table. The reporter will sit at the same end in

---

1   FED. R. CIV. P. 26(b)(1).

2   *See* FED. R. CIV. P. 32(b), 32(d)(3).

3   *See* FED. R. CIV. P. 37(a).

order to hear their voices clearly. The lawyer for the deponent will normally sit next to the deponent on the side most distant from the reporter.

The interrogator generally holds the deposition in his own conference room and can make the initial decision where to seat the participants. A lawyer may prefer to sit between the deponent and the door, leading the deponent to feel trapped and under the interrogator's control. Conversely, the lawyer who wants to put the deponent at ease may seat the deponent closest to the door. This arrangement also decreases the chance that the witness will walk by the interrogator's side of the table and observe the notes or documents the interrogator plans to use. The interrogator may seat the deponent to face the glare from the window, which can become annoying over the course of the day. (Counsel for the witness should be alert to this tactic and should protect the witness by requiring that something be done about the glare.)

The interrogator may stand momentarily to stretch while continuing with questioning or may stand beside the witness when asking about a photograph or document. However, counsel for the deponent should request that the interrogator be seated once the occasion for standing has ended so that the interrogator is not hovering over the witness. Although the importance of such minor details should not be exaggerated, neither should it be ignored.

B.   The Oath

The interrogator ordinarily will begin the deposition by requesting that the reporter administer the oath to (or swear) the witness.[4] Occasionally, the attorney will encounter a new reporter who is not yet authorized to do this; one solution is to locate a notary public to administer the oath. Although the procedure is not strictly in accordance with Rule 30(c), unless an objection is made at that point, the validity of the transcript as a deposition will not be open to question.[5] Even if such an objection were made and the transcript ruled not to be a valid deposition, the transcript would still be useful for cross-examination as a statement by the witness.[6] And if the deponent were an adverse party, the transcript (whether or not a valid deposition) would be admissible against him.[7]

Some deponents refuse to take the oath for religious or other reasons. The reporter should ask such persons to affirm that they will tell the truth.[8]

---

4   *See* Fed. R. Civ. P. 30(c).

5   *See* Fed. R. Civ. P. 32(d)(2) and 32(d)(3)(B).

6   *See* Fed. R. Evid. 608(b).

7   *See* Fed. R. Evid. 801(d)(2).

8   *See* Fed. R. Civ. P. 43(d); *see also* Fed. R. Evid. 603.

Occasionally, the interrogator may question the witness on what the oath means to him and what he thinks will happen to him should he fail to tell the truth. While one might plausibly argue the relevance of such questioning, it is generally provocative, unproductive, and if it probes into the deponent's religious beliefs or opinions, improper.[9]

C.   The Presence of Others

Who may attend a deposition? May witnesses who will be testifying later at deposition attend? May a party attend all depositions? May the press attend? These questions have not been widely addressed by courts, and answers vary.

The starting point for denying public access may be that depositions are typically conducted in private, that they were not open to the public at common law, and that not all deposition transcripts are filed with the court under local rules promulgated by district courts.[10] On the other hand, deposition transcripts are open to public inspection when they are filed with the clerk of court, and it can thus be argued that the deposition session itself should be open in most cases.[11]

Typically, lawyers do not face the question whether the public may attend the deposition. Rather, they usually want to preclude attendance by private individuals with some connection to the lawsuit, such as other witnesses or parties.

The interrogator may request that persons other than the deponent be sequestered, usually because the interrogator plans to depose them later and does not want them to have the advantage of hearing his questions and growing accustomed to his style. The interrogator who feels sequestration is important should raise the issue with opposing counsel before the day of the deposition. If the attorneys cannot reach an agreement, the interrogator will then have time to obtain a ruling from the court.[12] If he waits until the morning of the deposition, he may be unable to reach the court for a ruling.

---

9   *See* FED. R. EVID. 610.

10   *See* Seattle Times Co. v. Rhinehart, 467 U.S. 20, 33 (1984) (affirming protective order prohibiting dissemination of certain information obtained in pretrial discovery).

11   *See* Avirgan v. Hull, Civil Action No. 87-252 (D.D.C. 1987) (rejecting request for protective order from former CIA officer whose deposition was scheduled in a public conference room in the office of the American Civil Liberties Union); E.D.N.Y. STANDING ORDERS ON EFFECTIVE DISCOVERY IN CIVIL CASES ¶ 9 ("A person who is a party, witness or potential witness in the action may attend the deposition of a party or witness.").

12   FED. R. CIV. P. 26(c)(5) authorizes a court to order that "discovery be conducted with no one present except persons designated by the court."

Although authority is scant, many lawyers adhere to the principle that a party (as distinguished from a witness) has the right to be present at every stage of the proceedings, including depositions.[13] Nevertheless, there is good authority for sequestering even a party in an appropriate case.[14]

The interrogator should instruct the reporter to note the presence of others at the start of the deposition, as well as when they subsequently leave and return. Such information may prove valuable. For example, if a deponent claims at trial to have been nervous and rattled at the deposition and to have thus given inaccurate testimony, the interrogator can show that the deposition environment was comfortable by noting that the deponent's spouse or business associate was present to lend support. Or, if the defendant's attorney brings the defendant to the plaintiff's deposition, counsel for the plaintiff may later depose the defendant, remind him that he was present when the plaintiff was deposed and made certain charges against the defendant, and inquire what actions the defendant has taken to determine the validity of those charges.

Suppose the interrogator's client or expert is present (see Chapter 2, Sections D and E above) and passes the interrogator a note containing a suggested question. The attorney should look at the note but continue with the planned questioning, and then, after several minutes have passed, ask the suggested question without referring to the note. There are two reasons for proceeding in this way. First, the deponent will have noticed the action and is likely to be on guard for the question which immediately follows the interrogator's reading of the note. Waiting a while to ask the suggested question will increase the chances of obtaining a candid answer. Second, opposing counsel will also have noticed the note and will be paying close attention to the next question in the hope of gaining some insight into the thinking of the interrogator's client or expert. If he is thrown off the track by the interrogator's

---

13   *See* 8 C. WRIGHT & A. MILLER, FEDERAL PRACTICE AND PROCEDURE, § 2041 (1970 & Supp. 1982). Fed. R. Evid. 615 authorizes exclusion of witnesses from trial, but excepts parties, including the designated representative of a corporate party, and anyone "whose presence is shown by a party to be essential to the presentation of the party's cause" (such as an expert). Some courts apply Rule 615 to depositions. *See* Lumpkin v. Bi-Lo, Inc., 9 Fed. R. Serv.3d (Callaghan) 395 (N.D. Ga. 1987); Naismith v. Professional Golfers Assoc., 85 F.R.D. 552, 567 (N.D. Ga. 1979) (ordering that lawyers for the parties insure that deponents not discuss their depositions with other witnesses).

14   Galella v. Onassis, 487 F.2d 986, 997 & n.17 (2d Cir. 1973) (sequestration order "appropriate to protect the deponent from embarrassment or ridicule intended by the calling party"); Metal Foil Products Manufacturing Co. v. Reynolds Metals Co., 55 F.R.D. 491, 493 (E.D. Va. 1970) (sequestration to prevent dissemination of trade secrets; *but cf.* Kerschbaumer v. Bell, 112 F.R.D. 426 (D.D.C. 1986) (denying motion to exclude parties who had not yet been deposed from depositions of other parties). *See Roemer Deposition Closed by Judge, but 75 Attorneys Attempt Entry*, ASBESTOS LITIGATION REP., Oct. 22, 1982, at 5708. For a general discussion of who may be present during a deposition, see R. HAYDOCK & D. HERR, DISCOVERY PRACTICE § 3.2.2 (1982).

"burying" the suggested question in the succeeding colloquy, opposing counsel will have no such advantage.

D.   "The Usual Stipulations"

At the start of the deposition the reporter will almost invariably inquire whether the attorneys agree to "the usual stipulations."[15] Even if inclined to accept these stipulations, counsel should state them specifically or ask the reporter to state them, since the formulation may vary from one reporter to another. The lawyer who does not agree to one or more of the stipulations should be sure to check the first page of the transcript upon receiving it. Some stenographers are so accustomed to the usual stipulations that they include them at the start of the transcript even when an attorney specifically directs otherwise.

A fairly common formulation of the usual stipulations is as follows:

> Signing, certification, sealing and filing are waived; all objections except as to the form of the question are reserved until the time of trial.

The attorney should carefully consider whether to enter into these stipulations.[16]

1.   *Signing*

The deponent has the right to examine and to read the transcript of his testimony, and to make changes of form or substance, with a statement of reasons for making them. Ordinarily the deponent will make corrections and then sign the transcript.[17]

To waive the requirement of signing and the corresponding right to examine, read and correct the transcript, all counsel must agree and the deponent also must consent since the rights involved are his.[18] The interrogator may

---

15   "Like a religious service, the deposition starts with prayers and incantations. Like the congregation at a religious service, most of us do not really care what these prayers and incantations mean. Besides it would be embarrassing to admit that we also do not know what they mean. Take, for example, the 'usual stipulations.' The court reporter mumbles something about the usual stipulations and we mumble assent. . . . Maybe the 'usual stipulations' really means questions must be asked from a reclining position. . . ." Hart, *Taking Depositions*, 51 THE SHINGLE 44 (Spring 1988) (Journal of the Philadelphia Bar Association).

16   Other possible stipulations include waiver of notice, waiver of oath, effect of witness's failure to sign, and effect of refusal to answer. *See* D. DANNER, PATTERN DISCOVERY: ANTITRUST 620-23 (1981). For a discussion of the stipulations and their effect, see Facher, *Taking Depositions*, in LITIGATION MANUAL, at 4-5, 8 (1983).

17   FED. R. CIV. P. 30(e).

18   *Id.*

decide to require that the deposition be submitted to the deponent for signature, particularly if the deponent seems devious. Otherwise, the deponent may claim at trial that the reporter erred in transcribing the testimony and that the testimony was slightly, but materially different, and the deponent would have made appropriate corrections had the transcript been submitted.

Counsel for the witness may also prefer to require signing. The witness, even if bright and articulate, may make a mistake, or the reporter may make an error. In that event, however, despite having waived the requirement of signing, the witness nevertheless may choose to follow the formal procedure of reading the transcript, making changes and then signing. Waiver of the right to read and sign does not constitute a prohibition against reading and signing; but by not waiving the right to read and sign, the deponent assures that the transcript will be submitted to him, rather than just to the lawyer. Finally, rather than waive the requirement of signing at the start of the deposition, counsel and the witness may prefer to wait to decide whether they will go to the trouble of making corrections until after they have seen the transcript.

In some jurisdictions, it is customary to have the witness sign the transcript in the presence of a notary although the federal rules do not require it. Another stipulation may be made in such jurisdictions that the witness may sign in the presence of any notary.

2. Certification and Sealing

It is generally unnecessary to insist upon certification by the reporter that the witness was duly sworn and that the deposition is a true record of the testimony given.[19] Similarly, the requirement of sealing (that is, placing the deposition in an envelope to be sealed and appropriately labeled)[20] will usually be waived unless counsel seeks to limit circulation of the information in the deposition. A confidentiality agreement or a protective order may, in fact, require sealing of particular deposition transcripts.

3. Filing

Although lawyers commonly waive filing of the transcript with the clerk of the court,[21] the language of the rules seems to require that depositions

---

19   See FED. R. CIV. P. 30(f)(1).

20   See id.

21   See Lindeman v. Textron, 136 F. Supp. 157, 158 (1955).

be filed unless the court orders otherwise.[22] However, many federal district courts by local rule or standing order have now prohibited the filing of deposition transcripts and other discovery material in an effort to reduce the volume of the record in the clerk's office.[23] In any event, counsel should ensure that a set of transcripts is available for the court when the case reaches trial. Unless the court orders that transcripts shall not be filed, or a local rule prohibits it, any party should be able to file the transcript even if the filing requirement has been waived. Waiver of the requirement of filing does not prohibit filing. Indeed, counsel may elect to file a transcript favorable to his case if there is any possibility that the judge or law clerk may read the deposition for a preliminary view of the case.

4. Reserving Objections Except as to Form

As a general matter, the interrogator should consider refusing to enter into this "usual" stipulation; doing so may be dangerous. Generally, counsel must object at deposition if the ground for the objection is one that might be remedied at that time.[24] Thus, both the federal rules and the usual stipulation would require counsel to interpose an objection to the form of the question to allow the interrogator to reword it.

Rule 32(d)(3)(A), however, goes further than the usual stipulation and requires counsel also to object at the deposition to a question which lacks foundation, in order to permit the interrogator to supply the foundation.[25] The usual stipulation does not require such an objection because it is not an objection to form, and, therefore, leaves the interrogator open to a surprise objection at trial upon attempting to read this portion of the deposition into the record.

The interrogator can avoid this embarrassing scenario by refusing to make the usual stipulation and stating that he will abide by Rule 32(d)(3)(A). The problem with such a refusal is that opposing counsel may be so accustomed to

---

22   *See Amendments to the Federal Rules of Civil Procedure*, 85 F.R.D. 521, 525 (1980) ("By the terms of Rule 5(d) and Rule 30(f)(1) discovery materials must be promptly filed. . ."). The 1980 amendments to the rules allow parties to move for "an order of the court that discovery materials not be filed unless filing is requested by the court or is effected by parties who wish to use the materials in the proceeding." *Id. See* FED. R. CIV. P. 5(d), 30(f)(1).

23   *See, e.g.,* E.D. PA. R. 24(a) ("depositions. . . shall not be filed with the court"); M.D.N.C.R. 19(f) ("Depositions. . . are not to be filed unless on order of the Court or for use in the proceeding."); S.D. ILL. R. 16(a) ("depositions. . . shall be served upon other counsel or parties, but shall not be filed with the Court"); STANDING ORDER FOR ASBESTOS CASES, at 8 (E.D. Tex. July 7, 1982) ("No depositions. . . shall be filed in the District Clerk's office except by order of the Court.").

24   *See* FED. R. CIV. P. 32(d)(3)(A)–(B).

25   *Id.*

the usual stipulation and so unfamiliar with the rule that he does not know which objections to make in the absence of the usual stipulation. Such uncertainty may lead to unnecessary objections and disruptions in the tempo of the questioning.

E.   The Interrogator's Preliminary Instructions to the Deponent

At the outset of the deposition, the interrogator will usually instruct the deponent as follows:

(a)   I am going to ask you some questions to find out what you know about the facts giving rise to this lawsuit.

(b)   If you do not hear a question, say so and I will repeat it.

(c)   If you do not understand a question, say so and I will rephrase it.

(d)   If you realize that an earlier answer you gave was inaccurate or incomplete, say that you want to correct or supplement your earlier answer, and you will be allowed to do so.

(e)   If you want to stop to use the restroom, or to stretch your legs, or to get a cup of coffee or water, or to collect your thoughts, say so, and you will be permitted to do so.

(f)   If you find that you are tired or confused and want to take a short break or even recess for the day, please say so.

(g)   If you do not know or do not remember the information necessary to answer a question, say so.

(h)   If you answer the question, I will assume that you have heard it, and understood it and have given me your best recollection.

(i)   Do you understand the instructions that I have just given you?

Some lawyers also instruct the witness that he may indicate that he wants to consult with his attorney and will be permitted to do so. This can lead to trouble. If the deponent then repeatedly requests to confer with his lawyer, the interrogator is hardly in a position to complain.

Counsel for the witness may respond to instruction (h) above by noting that the witness may think he understands a question when in fact he does not and, thus, the mere fact that the witness answers a question should not be taken as a guarantee that he understood it. If a controversy arises at trial about whether the witness answered a particular question the way he did because he was confused by the question, the interrogator may read these preliminary instructions to the witness and jury to establish that the witness was told what to do in the event he did not understand the question. The witness's failure to state any problem with the question in compliance with the instructions should lead the jury to conclude that he understood the question perfectly well at the time of the deposition. If, however, the witness's counsel has made the comment suggested above, it may lend credibility to the witness who claims that, in retrospect, he must not have understood the question at the deposition.

The interrogator should consider omitting some or all of these instructions.[26] Counsel for the witness probably told him to expect such instructions at the start of the deposition. Fulfilling that prophecy may help put the witness at ease — which may not be desirable. Even if such instructions are not given, the deponent, particularly if he is obviously intelligent and sophisticated, will have difficulty wriggling out of what he said under oath at his deposition.

F.   The Need To Visualize the Transcript

Gestures, inflections and grunts are important to human communication, but they do not appear on a deposition transcript. The lawyers, therefore, must learn to "see" the transcript as the testimony is given. This exercise is similar to visualizing a letter as it is being dictated.

The interrogator should finish each question before the witness starts to answer. Similarly, the witness should complete each answer before the interrogator asks the next question.

The interrogator should not be satisfied with a nod or shake of the head, but should insist that the witness answer with a yes or no. It should not be the reporter's responsibility to determine whether a movement of the head indicates assent or disagreement. Further, the deposition will not read as crisply to

---

26   It has even been suggested that lawyers not begin every deposition by habitually saying to the witness, "State your full name for the record": "Isn't this really very silly? In the first place, we already know the witness' name. How else do we think he got there? Even the court reporter knows the witness' name. Besides, how many times has a witness ever claimed at trial that someone posed as him during the deposition?" Hart, *Taking Depositions*, note 15 *supra*.

the jury if the transcript records such nods and shakes of the head rather than actual yes or no answers. Similarly, the interrogator should not accept "Uh-huh," "Uh-uh," or any comparable response. It is too easy for the witness to claim later that the reporter got it wrong.

Sometimes answers that are clear when given in person will lose their meaning on paper. Suppose the interrogator asks the deponent whether he took certain action and the witness answers, "What do you think?" or "What was I supposed to do?" The witness may intend the answer as a strong affirmative, and the interrogator may take it that way, but the transcript will appear equivocal.

Another danger is that the witness may repeat part of a question which will appear on the transcript as an answer. For example, the defendant's attorney might ask the plaintiff, "Didn't you tell Mr. Kendall, your superior, that the accident was all your fault?" The witness may react with surprise and reply, "I told Kendall that?" The reporter, however, may omit the critical question mark from the transcript. In this situation, counsel for the witness should interrupt to note for the record that the witness has answered with a rising inflection indicating only that he is repeating the gist of the question and reacting with surprise.

Often, using a negative in the question can lead to an unclear transcript. For example, the transcript may read:

> Q. You did not complain to Mr. Barnes about that; is that correct?
>
> A. No.

Although the witness probably meant that he did not complain, the literal meaning of his response is just the opposite. There are countless ways that the question and answer may not match up on paper, as these few examples illustrate.

Additionally, the interrogator should be alert to describe for the record things which will not otherwise be reflected on the transcript. The reporter might not always note for the record the presence of individuals other than the witness and counsel, such as the client or an expert. The interrogator should be careful to have their presence noted. Also, if the witness consults a document or someone else in the room, the interrogator may note such consultation for the record by stating, "Let the record show that . . ." or by asking the witness, "Would you please identify the document to which you referred in answering my last question?"

On the other hand, the interrogator may not want to draw immediate attention to the witness's reference to a document. He may purposely wait until the witness has used the same document several times and then, for example, inquire: "Mr. Tate, you have referred to a pocket calendar three times in the last 15 minutes. Could you tell us what information is recorded there and for what purpose you use it?" The more times a witness refers to a document, the more relevant it appears and the better the interrogator's chances of obtaining it through discovery. If the interrogator makes a comment for the record about the document after the first reference to it, the deponent may claim that it contains no useful information and may never again refer to it. In that event, the interrogator's chances of getting a look at the document are reduced.

G.   Private Conversations Between the Deponent and His Counsel

The witness is free to speak with his lawyer during lunch and other recesses at the deposition. But is he free to consult privately with his lawyer after the interrogator has asked a question and before answering it?

Although there appears to be no reported decision on this issue, several courts have issued general pretrial or standing orders prohibiting consultation with counsel while a question is pending or prohibiting counsel from initiating such consultation at any time during the taking of the deposition, except about a possible assertion of privilege.[27] Such consultation destroys the spontaneity of the deponent's testimony and detracts from the effectiveness of the deposition as a truth-finding device. Consequently, even if unwilling to issue an outright prohibition, the court can usually be persuaded to rule that (1) such consultation should be permitted only on the initiative of the witness, not the lawyer, and (2) it should not be permitted solely because the witness does not understand the question.

If the witness does not understand the question, he should say so and permit the interrogator to rephrase it. If the witness ultimately understands the question but still claims to need the advice of his counsel, the interrogator may decide to permit him a private consultation rather than bother the court with the dispute. However, the interrogator should note for the record that such consultation has occurred. Additionally, the interrogator may consider asking the witness whether, by reason of what his lawyer said, his answer was different from what it otherwise would have been, whether what the lawyer said helped him answer, or whether his attorney pointed out any hazards in the original question. Such follow-up questions will often be met with an instruction not to answer based on the attorney-client privilege. Although the answers to such questions,

---

27   E.D.N.Y. STANDING ORDERS, *supra* note 11, ¶ 13 (attorney for deponent "shall not initiate a private conference with the deponent during the actual taking of a deposition, except for the purposes of determining whether a privilege should be asserted"); *In re* Rhode Island Asbestos Cases, R.I.M.L. No. 1, at 7 (D.R.I. Mar. 15, 1982) (pretrial order No. 2) ("During the questioning of witnesses, while a question is pending, no counsel shall confer with said witness."); *In re* Asbestos-Related Litigation, No. MDCP-82-1, at 7 (M.D.N.C. Feb. 2, 1982) (order coordinating proceedings) (similar order); *In re* Asbestos-Related Litigation, No. CP-81-1, at 6 (E.D.N.C. Sept. 15, 1981) (first pretrial order) (similar order).

even if given, are not likely to be helpful, simply asking them may cause sufficient discomfort to the witness and his counsel that they will discontinue, or reduce the frequency of, their conferences.

H.   Renewing Instructions to the Deponent and Inviting Corrections

If the deposition will last several hours or days, the interrogator may remind the deponent periodically of the instructions given, if any, at the start of the deposition. At the beginning of each new session, the interrogator should also remind the deponent that he is still under oath.

Throughout the deposition, the interrogator should be sensitive to comments by the witness which, although not so intended at the time, may later be used as evidence that the witness was overly tired at the deposition and so gave erroneous harmful testimony. As he prepares to answer a question, the witness will sometimes gratuitously remark, "Gee, this is hard work," or "I didn't realize that this would be so tiring," or "I'm really confused now." The interrogator should not let such comments pass. Instead, he should caution the witness that if he is too tired to proceed, he should say so; that if he needs a break, he should ask for it; and that the interrogator does not want him to give testimony which he will later disclaim on the ground that he was too tired or confused. The attorney should then inquire whether the witness feels fit to continue and, if the answer is affirmative, instruct the witness that he should inform the interrogator if at any point he wants to take a short break or to recess for the day.

Some interrogators will ask the deponent every few hours whether he wants to correct or supplement any of his earlier answers. This practice may later be useful in convincing the jury that the deposition procedure was fair and that the witness should not be permitted to renege on his deposition answers. The danger of inviting such corrections is that the witness, having been alerted at a lunch break to harmful testimony given that morning, will accept the invitation and modify earlier testimony to take the sting out of it. Or the witness may be prompted to give a general disclaimer to the effect that he cannot guarantee that every answer is, in fact, accurate and that he answered to the best of his knowledge at the time. The interrogator will have gained nothing by bringing up the subject of corrections.

I.   Recapitulating Contradictory and Disjointed Testimony

To be most useful at trial, the deposition testimony must be reasonably encapsulated. The judge and jury may have difficulty following and become impatient with counsel reading long passages extending over many pages. Consequently, the interrogator should recapitulate or summarize the deponent's testimony, particularly if the witness has given contradictory testimony over several pages (*e.g.*, first denying that he attended a meeting and then recalling that he did, first claiming to be unsure whether a certain topic was discussed and then saying that it was, and so on). The interrogator may want to ask:

> So that we have it straight in one place, is it correct that you did attend the meeting of November 19, 1987, in Mr. Wellington's office; that the meeting lasted about 45 minutes; that Mr. Wellington was present during the entire meeting; that Mr. Simon joined the meeting 15 minutes after it started and was then present until the end; and that the subjects discussed while all three of you were present at the meeting included the termination of Mr. Hart and whether he would be entitled to severance pay?

Opposing counsel will sometimes object to the interrogator's efforts to summarize prior testimony on the ground that the question is repetitive, leading or not a fair summary. But if the recapitulation is in fact a fair summary of the deposition testimony, the opposing attorney usually will allow the witness to answer. To head off an objection, the interrogator should avoid express references to the prior testimony and should not phrase his question in terms such as, "Would it be a fair summary of your testimony that . . ." or "Now you have testified that . . . ."

J. The Deponent Who Knows — or Claims To Know — Too Little

The interrogator may discover that the witness is not knowledgeable about many of the subjects of planned questions. In this situation, the interrogator should obtain a clear statement of the limited scope of the witness's knowledge without disclosing his entire script of questions (which could be used by his opponent to prepare more informed witnesses for depositions). Thus, the interrogator may ask only that the witness describe in general terms his knowledge of the underlying facts; or he may press further and ask the witness to confirm that he knows about subject A, but not about subjects B through K. Requesting such confirmation nails things down, but also provides opposing counsel with a useful checklist of topics in which the interrogator has an interest.

Further, even if the knowledge of the witness is very limited, he may be able to identify other possible witnesses. The interrogator should ask the witness to identify those persons who possess the knowledge to answer questions the witness could not.

In outlining his questioning, the interrogator should consider the possibility that a generally knowledgeable witness will claim not to recall the information necessary to answer a question. The interrogator should decide whether such an answer would be helpful or harmful to his case. For example, the interrogator may find helpful a claim by the witness not to remember what was said at a meeting between himself and the interrogator's client. Having so testified, the witness is not in much of a position to deny at trial the version of the meeting given by the interrogator's client.

Again, the interrogator must decide whether to persist in nailing down this claimed lack of knowledge. He may ask: "Do you have any recollection at all of what was said?" Or go further: "Do you recall if Mr. Hart's severance pay was discussed at that meeting?" Or further yet: "Do you deny that Mr. Hart's severance pay was discussed?" Or finally: "Do you deny that Mr. Simon said to you at that meeting that the company was obliged to give Mr. Hart severance pay or do you just not recall?" If the interrogator seeks an answer to the effect that the witness does not recall, he may want to end the question by specifically suggesting that option to the witness in a slightly more emphatic tone of voice. Note that the last suggested question in the example above ends with the words, "or do you just not recall?" Having heard that option last, the witness may find it the most attractive.

In questioning the witness about his recollection of such a meeting, the interrogator may sometimes ask only the first suggested question, but in other instances, he will push all the way. This is a result-oriented exercise, and the interrogator's decision will be judged by the answers he receives.

If the interrogator decides that an answer claiming lack of knowledge would damage his case, he should structure the questioning to avoid that answer. Once given, such an answer is not likely to be withdrawn, no matter how effective the subsequent questioning.

Consider a personal injury case in which the defendant has raised the defense of and carries the burden of proof on the statute of limitations. Assume that counsel for the defendant plans to depose the plaintiff's treating physician to show that, contrary to the plaintiff's contention, the physician told the plaintiff during the period of limitations that his rare hematologic disorders were probably due to exposure to certain toxic fumes generated by the defendant corporation. The doctor may be the only one who can testify that the plaintiff was so advised; without such testimony, the statute of limitations defense will be substantially weakened and possibly destroyed. Anticipating that the plaintiff's physician may be inclined to say that he does not recall whether he so advised the plaintiff, the defendant's attorney may ask preliminary questions designed to elicit answers, the intellectual force of which may cause the doctor to discard his original inclination to claim not to remember. Thus, before posing the key questions, the interrogator may ask:

When you suspect the cause of a patient's problem, do you generally advise the patient of your view so that he might take steps to avoid the cause?

Was there any reason not to advise plaintiff of your view as to the probable cause of his condition?

Did plaintiff ever complain to you or threaten to sue you for withholding information from him?

The interrogator should also show the doctor his own records containing statements about the suspected cause of the problem. If the doctor answers such introductory questions as expected, he may then be unwilling to make the implausible statement that although he suspected the cause of the plaintiff's maladies, he cannot recall whether he informed the plaintiff of his suspicion. On the other hand, if the doctor answers these preliminary questions in a noncommittal way, he probably will maintain that he does not recall when asked the key question. At this point, the interrogator may remind the doctor that to say that he does not remember when he does is a violation of the oath. On the other hand, such a reminder may only provoke the witness and make him more defensive than forthright, particularly if his counsel vehemently objects to the interrogator's reminder as implying that the witness is lying under oath.

A particularly difficult problem for the interrogator is the witness who was deeply involved in the underlying facts some years ago but who claims that, because of the passage of time, he is unable to give substantive answers to most questions without refreshing his recollection by reading many documents and talking to others who were involved. Such a witness may claim, for example, not to recall preparing a memorandum sent out over his name and not to remember whether the memorandum accurately reflected his views at the time, even though he will not go so far as to deny that he prepared and sent it. Unlike the typical witness who says that he cannot remember, this deponent has not ruled himself out as a possible trial witness. He has stated that reviewing many documents and talking to others might refresh his recollection. The interrogator has no idea what this witness will say at trial.

The interrogator is thus presented with two choices. First, he can ask the witness to confirm that he would so testify with respect to each of the major topics in the litigation. The interrogator might then recess the deposition and advise opposing counsel that he will object to any more specific testimony by the witness at trial unless advised sufficiently in advance of trial so that he may resume the deposition.

Second, the interrogator can attempt to refresh the recollection of the witness. He might begin with each of the more important documents in chronological order and ask the witness whether he recalls sending or receiving it, discussing its contents before it was sent or after it was received, expressing agreement or disagreement with it, or taking action as a result of the document. He might also paraphrase for the deponent the statements by other witnesses about the key underlying events and ask whether that helps him to recall. If the witness's recollection is refreshed by such questioning, the interrogator may obtain useful information because the witness presumably has not discussed the underlying events with his own lawyer in much detail. If the witness's recollection is not refreshed by the interrogator's review of the documents and other testimony, the jury may not believe a claim that upon further review of the documents after the deposition, it all came back to him.

K.   The Deponent Who Says Too Much

Often the interrogator will happily allow the deponent to talk. Given enough rope, the witness may hang himself. On the other hand, the interrogator who seeks admissions may be frustrated by a verbose, argumentative witness. Consider these exchanges:

Q.   Did you ever complain to the defendant that its pricing policies were unfair?

A.   Knowing the defendant's unsavory reputation and the vindictive temperament of its management, we decided that complaining would only provoke it to take further action to crush us.

* * *

Q.   Did you attend the meeting of December 14, 1987?

A.   We were trying to deal with a cancer, that is, defendant's illegal business practices, and we met on that day to examine the limited options open to us.

The interrogator cannot read such deposition segments to the jury. What should he do? First, the interrogator should move to strike the answer insofar as it is unresponsive to the question. Otherwise, if the witness should later become unavailable, the interrogator's opponent may attempt to read the full answer into the record at trial.[28]

---

28   See FED. R. CIV. P. 32(a)(3).

How does the interrogator make the witness give direct factual responses? If the witness were to give argumentative testimony at trial, the judge would undoubtedly reprimand him, and the jury would soon become impatient if he persisted. But the interrogator may be justifiably reluctant to raise this kind of problem with the court at the discovery stage, particularly where the answer includes the information requested. Judges resist becoming embroiled in the parties' pretrial squabbling, especially when asked not just to rule on the propriety of a specific question, but to peruse a transcript to determine whether the witness should be directed to give more responsive answers.

However, the interrogator may gain control over the witness by using the force of his own personality and manner. For example, he may say:

> Please listen carefully to the next question. You will see
> that it can fairly be answered yes or no or that you don't
> remember. Please answer it that way.

Of course, counsel for the witness will not likely sit back and allow the interrogator to instruct the witness. He may object to such instructions, note that the question has been answered, and request that the interrogator ask his next question.

If the witness remains quarrelsome, the interrogator may say:

> Mr. Bruton, I am asking you questions to learn certain
> facts. Please answer those questions directly. Leave it
> to your lawyer to ask whatever supplemental questions
> he believes should be put to you and, at the appropriate
> time, to make whatever arguments should be advanced.
> Now, listen carefully to the next question, and you will
> see that it can be answered fully by giving a date or by
> saying that you do not know or remember. Please
> answer it that way.

The interrogator should then sharpshoot the next several questions to call for precise, limited information. If the witness persists in giving rambling, argumentative answers, the interrogator may make one final plea:

> I suggest that we take a break here. I would ask counsel
> for the witness to confer with him during the break to
> advise him of his duty to answer questions directly
> without making speeches. If the witness continues to
> give the same kinds of answers, I intend to seek the aid
> of the court.

Consistent with the notion that the interrogator should not take a position and then retreat from it, the attorney should not make this threat unless he plans to act on it should the witness remain obdurate. If the witness still refuses to give directly responsive answers, the interrogator may apply to the judge who, although annoyed, may issue a general instruction that the parties should proceed in good faith and that the witness should do his best to be responsive. With most witnesses, even such a tepid direction will be adequate to correct the problem.

L.   The Deponent Who Fights the Objective of the Interrogator

Sometimes the deponent will try to guess the interrogator's objective and give answers at odds with the objective. The interrogator should respond by strategically structuring questions and inflecting his voice to disguise his objective. The interrogator may even be able to make the deponent think his objective is the opposite of what it really is. For example, suppose the plaintiff alleges that the defendant engaged in predatory pricing in violation of the antitrust laws by setting its price below average variable cost in an attempt to monopolize the market. Counsel for the defendant may know from his own expert's analysis of accounting records that, if the defendant's price had been 15 percent higher, it could not be found to be below average variable cost. Suppose the defendant's counsel wants to establish that even if the defendant's price was below cost, such pricing had no impact upon the plaintiff. Defense counsel who senses that the plaintiff is shaping answers to defeat the interrogator's perceived objectives may word questions this way:

> You would agree, would you not, that if defendant's price were 15 percent higher during the years in question, your company would have received a lot more business?

If the witness is fighting the apparent thrust of the question, he may deny that a 15 percent price increase would have resulted in much additional business. The interrogator may then ask:

> Are you trying to tell me that even if defendant's price had been 15 percent higher, your company would not have received any additional business?

If the deponent again fights the question by saying that he would have received no additional business even with the increase, he may have great difficulty establishing at trial that he suffered damages — even if the defendant's price was below cost. In short, the deponent who fights the interrogator instead of simply answering the questions truthfully may find he has crippled his own case.

M.   The Lawyer Who Says Too Much

Sometimes the witness's counsel will disrupt the interrogator's examination by interjecting comments after difficult questions before the witness starts to answer. Few comments are more infuriating to the interrogator than "If you know," or "If you remember." Predictably, such comments are almost invariably followed by an answer that the witness does not know or remember.

These comments are rarely justified, although the witness's counsel will realize on occasion that the witness has slipped into the school-examination mode of answering questions, that is, guessing when he does not know the answer in the hope that he will receive extra points if he is right.

The interrogator should not tolerate such remarks. As in dealing with the witness who talks too much, the interrogator may stop such prompting by saying:

> As I told the witness at the start of the deposition, if he does not know or remember the answer to a question, he should say so. That instruction applies to every question in this deposition. I would ask counsel not to interrupt this examination with such comments in the future. If that practice persists, I assure you that I will recess this deposition and apply to the court for relief.

In the face of this kind of threat, the witness's counsel will usually terminate or severely restrict the use of these comments, since a judge would be likely to frown upon them.[29]

Although somewhat more provocative, another possibility is to ask the witness, "Did you take your lawyer's comment, 'If you know,' to be a signal to say that you don't know?" Once in a while the witness will answer "Yes" before his lawyer reacts.

More difficult problems may arise from comments in which the witness's counsel purports to be seeking clarification of the question. For example: "Do you mean before October 13, 1987, or at any time?" or, "Do you mean besides what he told you an hour ago when he said . . . ?" Speaking objections, such as, "Objection on the grounds that it is not clear whether the witness is

---

29   *See* E.D.N.Y. STANDING ORDERS, *supra* note 11, ¶ 12 (objections "in the presence of the witness which are used to suggest an answer to the witness are presumptively improper").

being asked . . . ," present the same problems. Again, the interrogator may reprimand opposing counsel and give another stern warning. But opposing counsel knows that the interrogator will hesitate to trouble the court with this sort of objection, especially since the judge would probably have to read a good portion of the deposition to determine whether the interrogator has a legitimate grievance. Nonetheless, at some point, the interrogator will conclude that such remarks have become so intrusive as to interfere with his right to examine the witness. At this point, in spite of his reluctance, he should apply to the court.

N.   The Deponent Who Needs Time

Sometimes the deponent may say that he could answer a question if given some time. This is not uncommon when the answer involves mathematical calculations made in connection with a damage claim. The interrogator should ask how much time the deponent would need to make such calculations. If the time is not too long, the interrogator may recess the deposition for 20 minutes or so to give the deponent the time necessary to make the computations. On the other hand, the lawyer may be satisfied with a detailed description by the witness of the exact procedure he would follow in making the calculations. The interrogator can fill in the blanks for himself later.

Counsel for the witness may instruct him not to make the detailed calculations requested by the interrogator.[30] He may fairly contend that the witness should not be required to perform such work in the pressurized environment of the deposition and may offer to provide the information in writing later. Otherwise, the witness may make a mistake in his calculations which will come back to haunt him. The interrogator is not likely to press the point by seeking a ruling from the court, particularly if opposing counsel has promised to provide the information later. Moreover, the court is not likely to require that such calculations be made immediately at the deposition.

Apart from mathematical calculations, a deponent may well assert that he will be able to provide an exact answer to a pending question if permitted to consult the documents that have been produced in the case. If the documents are few in number and readily available, and if the interrogator believes he would benefit from a precise answer, he may choose to give the witness time to look at the documents. In many instances, however, the interrogator can determine details, such as the precise date of a meeting, by reviewing the documents himself, and does not need confirming testimony from the witness. He should not waste everyone's time by having the witness pore over documents.

---

30   Deep South Oil Co. v. Metropolitan Insurance Co., 25 F.R.D. 81, 82 (S.D.N.Y. 1959) (deponent should not be required to make calculations from documents at deposition).

O.   Going Off the Record

As a matter of practice, if any lawyer at the deposition asks to go off the record, the reporter will stop recording. The transcript should show that an off-the-record colloquy occurred at that point. If, however, another lawyer says he wants to stay on the record, the reporter will continue to record the proceedings.[31] Tactically, the attorney asking to go off the record should inquire whether there is any objection. If no one objects, opposing counsel cannot complain later that the lawyer went off the record to disrupt the questioning of the witness on a critical point.

The reporter should not honor a request by the witness to go off the record unless an attorney endorses that request and no one objects. Sometimes the witness, having heard the lawyers say, "Off the record," will himself preface some candid remarks with "Off the record," assuming that his subsequent comments will in fact be off the record, and will be embarrassed to discover later that the reporter (properly) has recorded everything he said.[32]

Counsel for the witness should explain to him that nothing is really off the record. Even if everyone agrees to go off the record, one of the lawyers may later ask the witness to confirm on the record whatever he said off the record.

P.   Starting and Ending Times and Breaks

Typically, the deposition will start at 10 a.m. and run to 4 or 5 p.m., with an hour for lunch and one or two breaks of five to ten minutes each session. However, the interrogator may be wise to designate a 9 or 9:30 a.m. starting time. The lawyer for the witness may not object upon receiving the notice but may run short of preparation time if the witness arrives late on the morning of the deposition.

There is usually not much advantage to working without breaks or lunch. The lawyer for the witness should be particularly cautious about agreeing to do so since the deponent may tire and make mistakes. Even if the witness insists that he feels fine, his attorney should ultimately make the decision on such matters. The same caveat applies to continuing the deposition much past 5 p.m. Tired witnesses make mistakes. Counsel for the witness should oppose working past that time unless the other lawyers make a commitment, or at least a strong affirmative statement, that they expect to finish by 7 or 8 p.m.

---

31   *See* R. HAYDOCK & D. HERR, *supra* note 14, § 3.3.5.

32   One lawyer tells with relish the story of a witness who, during a lull in the questioning, told the reporter to go off the record and then said to him, "Are you getting down all of this [expletive]?" The reporter dutifully recorded the comment, and at trial the witness was asked to read aloud his foulmouthed characterization of his own testimony.

Q.   Counsel's Reactions to Answers — Good or Bad

In poker, the admonition is, "Don't wag your tail." It is good advice for the deposition game, too.

Normally the interrogator will not reveal to the opposing party that he believes the witness has just given a helpful admission. If he does react, the witness may modify his answer or his lawyer may try to repair the damage by asking the witness whether he understood the question. Consequently, the interrogator should not pause, grin, pass a note to a colleague or his client, announce that it is time to take a break, or ask the reporter to read back the answer. He may switch to a different subject to reduce the risk that the deponent will withdraw or modify his answer, but he should do so naturally and continue to question at the same pace and with the same tone of voice. If he is taking notes while questioning the witness, the interrogator should do so at an even pace so that he does not inadvertently signal to his opponent those answers he considers important.

Similarly, counsel for the witness should not concede to the interrogator that a point has been scored against him. He should not groan, grimace, tense up, make notes, or change his position on settlement at the next break. He may consider interrupting to inquire whether the deponent understood that the interrogator was asking, for instance, what color the light was for him, not for the other driver. The danger in interrupting is that the witness may reaffirm harmful testimony, making it even more difficult to explain at trial. Additionally, the interrogator will probably object strenuously to such an interruption and may even complain to the court. Notwithstanding these risks, counsel for the witness may decide that the interruption is necessary to get the testimony straight.

Perhaps the most difficult time for the witness's counsel is when he realizes that the interrogator is close to hitting pay dirt. He should avoid defensive antics (moving to the front of his chair, objecting on flimsy bases, quarreling with the question, and the like), which the interrogator will interpret as meaning that he is on to something. A stifled yawn or a humorous aside is more likely to lead the interrogator off the track. Occasionally, counsel for the witness may try to put down a false scent by seeming concerned and protective in response to questions that he knows will be unproductive.

R.   Documents and Drawings

As with the rest of his questioning, the interrogator who is considering using a document should know his objectives. Will he be using it only to authenticate it? Or primarily for discovery purposes, that is, to refresh recollection and thus develop a more complete account of the facts? Or to obtain admissions? Or to impeach the witness, either at the deposition or at trial? The interrogator's objective will affect how and whether he uses the document, as discussed below.

In determining these objectives, the interrogator should consider whether the court's pretrial procedures require identification and exchange of trial exhibits.[33] If the court so requires, the interrogator cannot expect to surprise the witness at trial with a document, even if it was not marked as an exhibit at deposition.

1.   Mechanics

Effective handling of the documents can save the lawyer's time and the client's money. Ordinarily, if the interrogator intends to show the document to the witness, the reporter marks it as an exhibit before the lawyer hands the document to the witness.[34] The interrogator can save time by marking exhibits in advance of the deposition, that is, by placing exhibit stickers or stamps on the documents he plans to use as exhibits and numbering them, for example, 1 through 48; the reporter need only add his initials at the deposition. Alternatively, the interrogator may have the reporter mark all of the exhibits at one time before the deposition begins. If at the deposition the interrogator decides not to use Exhibits 19, 27 and 38, he can just skip them and note for the record that those numbers will not be used.

Even if the exhibits are all premarked, ordinarily the interrogator should show them to the witness one at a time, rather than giving the witness and his counsel the entire set of exhibits at the outset of the deposition. Doing so might give the witness and his counsel a preview of the deposition questioning. If that is not a significant concern in a particular case, the interrogator may decide to give a complete set of copies of all exhibits to the deponent and all counsel at the start. Things will move much faster that way.

Where numerous documents are expected to be marked at depositions, the attorney should consider how best to number them. Rather than using initials ("Exhibit P1" or "D3") or the name of the deponent ("Exhibit Kendall 5"), the interrogator may start with "Exhibit 1" at the first deposition and number the exhibits consecutively through all the depositions (so that if Exhibit 48 is the last number of the first witness's deposition exhibits, Exhibit 49 will be the first number of the next one). This approach eliminates confusion since only one exhibit will bear, for example, the number 48. In preparing the pretrial memorandum, the interrogator can give Exhibits 1 through 463, as marked at depositions, the same numbers for trial. If there are 100 exhibits that he will not use,

---

33   *See* Fᴇᴅ. R. Cɪᴠ. P. 16. Some districts require such identification and exchange by local rule. *E.g.,* E.D. Pᴀ. R. 21(c)(5) and 21(d)(1)(a).

34   *See* Fᴇᴅ. R. Cɪᴠ. P. 30(f)(1).

he can just drop those numbers. If there are additional documents to be marked for trial, he can start at Exhibit 464. Meanwhile, if opposing counsel wants to keep separate track of exhibits marked at his depositions, he may use the same system by starting at Exhibit 1001 or 2001.

An important advantage of this approach is that if the lawyer reads into the record at trial the witness's deposition testimony about what has been marked Exhibit 296 for trial, he will not encounter the problem of repeatedly explaining that the same document was marked Exhibit 221 at deposition.

A minor disadvantage of this approach is the need to keep track of the last exhibit number from deposition to deposition. This problem is compounded when a number of lawyers are taking depositions in the same case or when depositions in a case take place simultaneously.

Using the name of the witness in marking exhibits may be confusing. Suppose a key question in the case is whether Mr. Greenberg saw a certain document marked "Exhibit Greenberg 3." Even if Mr. Greenberg steadfastly denies that he ever saw the document, the jury may mistakenly conclude that since it is marked "Exhibit Greenberg 3," Mr. Greenberg must have had something to do with it.

In cases with multiple defendants, the parties may use a system of labeling the exhibit with the name of the party marking it (*e.g.*, "Megacorp Exhibit 3"). This system may also confuse the jury since it places a particular defendant's name on a document with which that party may have no connection. In addition, counsel for a particular defendant may hesitate to mark exhibits in this manner for fear that putting his client's name on many documents may give the name greater prominence before the jury.

Although the interrogator should generally be free to choose his own system of marking exhibits, opposing counsel should be alert to object to efforts to connect, by the numbering system, documents which are not obviously related to one another. For example, in a suit alleging wrongful termination of employment, counsel for the employee may try to mark as Exhibit 7A an internal memorandum from the defendant employer's records reporting that the employee will be absent from work for three weeks for jury duty. Then, marked as Exhibit 7B, rather than Exhibit 8, may be the employer's letter of termination to the employee, thereby suggesting that Exhibit 7B was sent as a result of the information contained in Exhibit 7A.[35]

Counsel for the witness should also review each exhibit to be certain that all of the pages in fact belong to a single document and have not been erroneously stapled together. In addition, he should note any pages that are missing or attachments referred to in the document that are not attached to the exhibit.

---

[35]   Establishment of such a connection would support a cause of action for wrongful termination. *See* Nees v. Hocks, 272 Or. 210, 536 P.2d 512 (1975); Reuther v. Fowler & Williams, Inc., 255 Pa. Super. 28, 386 A.2d 119 (1978).

Counsel for the witness should place on the record any such observations about each exhibit, both to protect the record and to serve as an extra caution to the witness against assuming that the document is complete or an accurate copy merely because it has been marked as an exhibit.

The interrogator should have available copies of each exhibit for all counsel and the witness, as well as a working copy for himself. The deposition will move much faster if those copies have been made in advance of the deposition.

In the absence of any other agreement, the originals of the exhibits marked during a deposition will be entrusted to the court reporter to be attached to the original of the transcript. However, usually counsel will agree that the originals of the exhibits may remain in the custody of the lawyer who requested that they be marked. That way, during the couple of weeks while the transcript is being prepared, they will be more readily available to counsel who may request that additional copies be made. Besides, some reporters tend to charge at relatively high rates to make copies of exhibits, perhaps to discourage counsel from asking that they take custody of the exhibits in the first place.

2.   *The Traditional Approach*

Some interrogators lapse into handling all documents the same way at deposition without giving thought to whether the approach is appropriate to their objective for that particular document. Thus, some interrogators always ask about the event referred to in the document before marking it or showing it to the deponent. The resulting transcript may read something like this:

> Q.   In April 1985, did your executive committee meet to discuss how your company would respond to the defendant's new marketing strategy?

> A.   There was a meeting in the spring of that year on that subject. I can't say for sure whether it was March, April or May.

> Q.   Did Mr. Hileman attend that meeting?

> A.   I think so. He's on that committee. If he wasn't there, the results would have been reported to him.

> Q.   Were minutes of that meeting prepared?

> A.   They usually are. I assume they were here. But I can't be 100 percent sure.

[And so on for another 5 pages, followed by. . .]

Q. I show you what has been marked Exhibit 218, which is the minutes of a meeting of the executive committee on April 7, 1985, showing Mr. Hileman present. Does that refresh your recollection that there was in fact a meeting of the committee in April 1985, that Mr. Hileman attended that meeting, and that minutes were prepared?

A. Yes, sure. I told you there was a meeting in the spring of that year and that I thought Mr. Hileman attended and that we normally prepare minutes.

What is the point of such belabored interrogation? If challenged, often the interrogator will defend this protracted and seemingly pointless questioning by saying that he is entitled to test the recollection of the witness independent of the document. Maybe so. But what use can be made of a series of such deposition segments? Unless there is some point in testing the recollection of the witness, why waste time?

3. Objective: Authentication

To eliminate potential problems of proof at trial, the interrogator should be careful to authenticate or establish a foundation for each document marked as an exhibit at the deposition. (One possible exception is a harmful document that the other side may not be able to authenticate.) Thus, the interrogator may ask the deponent to confirm that the document is what it purports to be (e.g., a letter to Mr. Smith) and that it was mailed on or about the date it bears.[36] If seeking to authenticate a document as a business record, counsel should be careful to ask the custodian or other qualified witness the questions necessary to establish the four elements of such a record:

(a) that it was made at or about the time of the event to which it refers;

(b) that it was prepared by a person with knowledge (or from information transmitted by such a person);

(c) that it was kept in the course of a regularly conducted business activity; and

---

36 FED. R. EVID. 901(b)(1).

    (d)   that it was the regular practice of the business activi-
ty to prepare such a document.[37]

    If the interrogator's objective is authentication, it may be wise to show
the document to the witness before asking any questions about it. If the interrogator lapses into the format of asking about the document before showing it to
the witness, he may create, rather than resolve, authentication problems.
    For example, suppose the interrogator's client has a file copy of a letter
sent by one of his employees (since deceased) to the deponent, that it would be
helpful to the interrogator's case to show that the letter was in fact received by the
deponent, and that the letter was not included in the opposing party's document
production. If, before showing the copy of the letter to the deponent, the interrogator asks whether any such letter was received, the deponent may say no,
either because that is his recollection or because he is dishonest and believes that
the interrogator cannot prove that the letter was sent. He may stand by this
answer even when shown this file copy of the letter. If he does, the interrogator
may be unable to prove at trial that the original of the document was received by
the deponent. On the other hand, if the interrogator first shows the document to
the witness and then asks whether he received it, the witness will be more likely
to answer affirmatively, because he recalls the letter, because he thinks that he
must have received it, or because he thinks that a lie would be unconvincing.

    4.   Objective: Discovery
    If the interrogator's objective is discovery, documents are fertile
sources for questions. If the document was sent out over the name of the deponent, the interrogator may ask a series of questions:

- Who drafted it?

- From whom was the information in the document obtained?

- How many drafts were prepared?

- Where are those drafts now?

- Who reviewed the document before it was sent out?

- To whom were copies sent?

---

37   Fed. R. Evid. 803(6).

- Did anyone who received a copy express agreement or disagreement with its contents?

- What reply, oral or written, was made to the document?

If the deponent received the document, the interrogator may ask:

- What response did you make to the document or, if none, why not?

- Did you draft a response (even if not sent)?

- To whom did you show the document?

- Who was consulted concerning its contents?

- What action, if any, did you take in response to the information set forth in the document?

The interrogator should not lapse into asking these questions as a matter of rote as to every document. As with the rest of his questioning, the interrogator should choose his questions to achieve his objectives.

5. Objective: Admissions or Impeachment

The interrogator who seeks to extract admissions or impeach the witness may elect to question the witness about the information in a document without showing it to him or even indicating that he has the document. The interrogator may include some of the exact words of the document in his question. For example, if the deponent prepared an internal memorandum dated January 22, 1987, the interrogator might ask, "As of January 1987, wasn't it true that [add words of memorandum]?" The advantage of using the exact words of the deponent's memorandum in the question is that should the deponent deny that those were the facts in January 1987, he cannot later reconcile the apparent contradiction on the basis of some small but supposedly meaningful difference between the wording of the memorandum and that of the question. The interrogator may use the same technique by taking language from pleadings, responses to requests for admissions, answers to interrogatories and judicial decisions.

When the deponent denies that the facts in January 1987 were as suggested by the interrogator, how should the attorney use the document? The answer depends on the objective. The interrogator seeking admissions may mark the document as an exhibit, confront the witness, and ask him to confirm that it says what it says and that the deponent accurately stated the facts when he prepared it. If the same scenario is repeated with another set of facts, the deponent may become gun-shy and hesitate to deny further requested admissions. The interrogator may then be able to push further and seek admissions on matters not confirmed in the documents.

For example, if the interrogator has another memorandum dated October 13, 1987, prepared by the deponent, the interrogator may, without marking the document as an exhibit or presenting it to the witness, ask, "As of October 1987, wasn't it true that . . . ?" The interrogator may conclude this question with various facts stated in the memorandum. He may then complete the question with a fact he believes to be true, even though not specifically stated in that memorandum. In response, the deponent may confirm that the fact is true, fearing that the interrogator has a document authored by the deponent which contains the specific information at issue. (This skirts the edge of permissible questioning; certainly the interrogator could not ask, "Did you not prepare a memorandum stating . . . ." if the interrogator knows of no such memorandum, nor should he flash a document, pretending that it is such a memorandum.)

On the other hand, the interrogator whose objective is to destroy the credibility of the deponent at trial will probably not confront the witness with documents contradicting his testimony as the deposition proceeds. Indeed, confronting the witness with each contradiction as it occurs may prompt the witness to give more carefully qualified answers — not a desirable development if the interrogator wants to attack the deponent's credibility at trial.

After completing the basic examination of a witness whose testimony is contradicted by documents, the interrogator may be tempted to confront the witness at the deposition with those documents, particularly where the court's procedures require a pretrial exchange of trial exhibits (which makes it harder to surprise the witness with the document at trial). The disadvantage of doing so is that the witness is provided with a practice round at harmonizing the contradictions. The interrogator may accept this disadvantage if he senses it is more beneficial to obtain helpful testimony at the deposition than postpone his questions until trial. Even if the witness is unaware of the contradictions, the interrogator must assume that opposing counsel will alert the witness before trial. The interrogator must rely more on intuition than logic in making this judgment.

6.   Work Copy of Document

It is often easier to mark one's questions about a document on a copy of the document itself than to list them on a separate paper, and to use that work copy of the document in questioning the witness. The words "WORK COPY" should be written in the upper right-hand corner to eliminate the risk that that copy will be mistakenly handed to other counsel or the witness if counsel has not made any notes on the first page. An example of such a work copy is included in the Appendix under "Practical Tips."

7. The Deponent's Drawing or Diagram

Sometimes the interrogator will ask the witness to make a drawing or diagram to assist in understanding his testimony. For example, a witness may be asked to draw the intersection where the accident occurred and to mark with an arrow the direction his car was traveling. Or a witness may be asked to diagram the layout of the building where a fire destroyed documents kept in various offices. The interrogator will then have the drawing or diagram marked as an exhibit and will have the witness refer to it during testimony.

Often opposing counsel will not object to such a request. The witness may testify more clearly and quickly with such a drawing available for reference. If, however, counsel for the witness is doubtful about the witness's ability to make a reasonably accurate drawing, he should instruct the deponent not to comply with the interrogator's request. A significant error or omission in the drawing may return to haunt the deponent. In some instances, the interrogator will have available a prepared drawing. If the witness can confirm that the drawing is accurate according to his recollection, the interrogator should be permitted to use it and to ask the witness to mark the drawing (e.g., showing where he fell).

If it is likely that the witness will be asked to draw a diagram, his lawyer should have the witness practice drawing it before the deposition to be certain that it is accurate and complete. Counsel may offer the pre-drawn diagram to the interrogator at the deposition so that the witness does not have to draw one anew. The witness should be prepared to respond to questions about the circumstances in which the diagram was prepared or, if he draws a new diagram at deposition, to respond to questions about whether he was coached. He should, of course, freely admit that he practiced but add that the purpose was solely to assure accuracy, not to conform the diagram to counsel's instructions on what to include and what to leave out.

8. Moving Into Evidence

There is no requirement that exhibits used at a deposition be moved into evidence. But, assuming that the interrogator is sure that he wants such exhibits admitted into evidence, he may consider so moving if the deponent is beyond the subpoena power of the court so that his deposition is likely to be his trial testimony. If opposing counsel plans to object to the admissibility of such exhibits on grounds that might be obviated by further questioning of the deponent, he should state his objection; otherwise the court may rule that it has been waived.[38]

---

[38] See FED. R. CIV. P. 32(d)(3); see also Section D.4 supra.

9. *Following Up*

Finally, the deponent will sometimes mention a document, and the interrogator will request its production. Often counsel for the witness will answer that he will consider the request and the matter ends there because the document is never produced and the interrogator forgets that he requested it. To ensure that he obtains the document, the interrogator should make a note to confirm his oral request with a formal written one. And he should send a confirming letter or supplemental document request to opposing counsel immediately after the deposition.

S. Objections

As noted in Section D.4 of this chapter, unless all objections except as to form have been reserved, counsel must object at the deposition if the ground for the objection is one that might be remedied if the objection is made at that time. Otherwise, he may be precluded from interposing the objection at trial if another party seeks to use the transcript.[39] When in doubt, prudent counsel should make the objection. On the other hand, counsel gains little by making an objection at the deposition which may properly be saved until trial (*e.g.*, an objection on grounds of relevance), and probably only prolongs the deposition by making such objections.

A question may be objectionable as to form for several reasons. First, it may be a leading question to a deponent to whom a leading question is not proper.[40] Second, it may be a double question, that is, a structurally single question which asks two separate things. For example, "Did you attend the meeting of December 14, 1987, and participate in the decision to terminate Ms. Woodruff's employment?" The question asks (a) did the deponent attend the meeting? and (b) did he participate in the decision to terminate the plaintiff's employment?

Third, a question may be objectionable as to form because it contains an assumption to which the deponent has not yet testified. For example, the interrogator may ask, "After you and Ms. Swirsky decided to terminate Ms. Woodruff's employment, how did you go about communicating that to her?" The assumption, of course, is that Ms. Swirsky and the deponent are the ones who made the decision to terminate. If the lawyer defending the deponent

---

39   *See* FED. R. CIV. P. 32(d)(3).

40   Rule 30(c) permits examination of a deponent "as permitted at the trial under the . . . Federal Rules of Evidence." FED. R. CIV. P. 30(c). These rules permit examination by leading questions of "a hostile witness, an adverse party, or a witness identified with an adverse party." FED. R. EVID. 611(c).

knows very well that the assumption is true, he may decide not to voice any objection. If he does object, the interrogator will simply ask, "Who made the decision to terminate Ms. Woodruff's employment?" and the deponent will answer, "Ms. Swirsky and I." Thus, the lawyer making the objection may look a bit foolish — either he did not know the facts (which is not good) or he knew them but made a pointless objection anyway. Further, the objection results in a more complete transcript for the interrogator.

A question may be objectionable as to form because it is argumentative ("Following your wrongful termination of Ms. Woodruff . . ."); or because it contains an ambiguous reference ("What did you do after that?" when it is not clear whether "that" refers to a telephone call or a meeting); or because it is so convoluted that it is unclear what fact it calls upon the deponent to supply.

Should the lawyer making the objection state his grounds? In light of the underlying rationale of Rule 32(d)(3) (A), as well as the general preference for requiring that grounds be stated,[41] he would be wise to do so at least in a general way (*e.g.*, "Objection; form"). If the interrogator requests a statement of the grounds, it should be given if the objection may be cured at that time by the interrogator. If the objection cannot be cured, the attorney need not state the grounds. Again, in this situation objecting at the deposition is unnecessary in the first place.

After hearing the objection and the grounds, the interrogator may remain satisfied with the question and decline to rephrase it or take other corrective action. He must balance the risk of not being able to use that question and answer at trial against the danger that rewording the question will lead to a less useful answer. Additionally, the pace of his questioning may be badly disrupted if he attempts to eliminate every picayune objection.

The deponent's lawyer should avoid the temptation to object too often. It is true that frequent objections may distract the interrogator and adversely affect the quality of his questioning, but they may also force him to sharpen his questions and do a better job. Further, objections may have a harmful impact on the deponent. Every objection breaks the concentration of the deponent whose focus is properly on the question. Too many objections may undermine the witness's confidence as he begins to fear that the questions must contain hidden traps which he is missing. Such objections often lead to bickering between counsel which may unnerve the witness further.

Thus, even if a question is technically objectionable in some small way, counsel for the deponent may decide to remain silent, or to make the objection unobtrusively, and allow the deponent to answer. The deponent will gain confidence dealing with such questions.

A deponent who is a skillful and experienced witness may be given very free rein. Indeed, the deponent's ability to take care of himself may cause

---

41   *See* FED. R. EVID. 103(a).

the interrogator to conclude that the deponent will be an effective witness at trial. This conclusion will affect his view of the settlement value of the case, making a favorable settlement more likely.

If there is a limited amount of time for the deposition (for example, if it is being taken out of town and the deponent and lawyers have allocated only one day for it), the defending attorney may elect not to quarrel about completely irrelevant but harmless questioning. Why remind the interrogator that he is wasting precious time on irrelevancies?

Finally, the deponent may occasionally answer before his lawyer has a chance to interpose an objection. In that event, the attorney should state his objection, move to strike the answer, and state for the record that the deponent answered so quickly that a more timely objection was not possible.

T.   Instructions Not To Answer

The Federal Rules of Civil Procedure say nothing about going beyond simply objecting to a question at a deposition and instructing a deponent not to answer the pending question. Indeed, Rule 30(c) provides that evidence objected to "shall be taken subject to the objections." However, in practice it is considered entirely proper to instruct a witness not to answer when the answer would reveal information protected by a privilege or trade secrets.[42] An instruction not to answer because the question is irrelevant is a different matter.

Generally, as discussed at Section S above, relevance is not even a ground for objection, much less for an instruction not to answer. Judges are impatient with lawyers who persist in instructing deponents not to answer solely because they deem questions to be irrelevant; technically, the proper procedure if a lawyer thinks that questioning is in bad faith, harassing or greatly outside the bounds of proper discovery is to halt the deposition and apply for a protective order.[43]

But, as a practical matter, when questioning goes beyond any conceivable relevance, counsel for the deponent will often instruct the deponent not to answer as an informal means to get the deposition back on track. Suppose, for example, that the driver in a right-angle collision case were asked at deposition

---

[42]   *See, e.g.,* International Union of Electrical, Radio & Machine Workers v. Westinghouse Electric Corp., 91 F.R.D. 277, 279 (D.D.C. 1981) ("Rule 30(c) should not mandate disclosure of trade secrets or privileged information merely because such information is sought through a question asked on deposition.").

[43]   FED. R. CIV. P. 30(d); *see* Ralston Purina Co. v. McFarland, 550 F.2d 967, 973 (4th Cir. 1977); Lloyd v. Cessna Aircraft Co., 74 F.R.D. 518, 520 (E.D. Tenn. 1977); Preyer v. United States Lines, Inc., 64 F.R.D. 430, 431 (E.D. Pa. 1973); Shapiro v. Freeman, 38 F.R.D. 308, 311 (S.D.N.Y. 1965) ("if counsel were to rule on the propriety of questions, oral examination would be quickly reduced to an exasperating cycle of answerless inquiries and court orders").

to give the names of all of his college professors, to list the subjects each of them taught him, and the grades they gave him. It would be difficult to quarrel with an instruction not to answer on grounds of relevance.

There is often a good deal of gamesmanship in giving and testing an instruction not to answer, particularly in the first few depositions of a case in which many depositions will be taken. If the instruction is raised with the court, the prevailing party gains an edge. If the court orders the deponent to answer, counsel for the deponent may be reluctant to give another such instruction. He will not want to give the court an early impression that he is attempting to obstruct discovery. On the other hand, if the court sustains the instruction, the interrogator may hesitate to press subsequent instructions with the court. He will not want the court to think that he does not know the proper scope of discovery or how to ask a question.

1.   Making the Record

As a prerequisite to seeking a ruling from the court, the interrogator should have a clearly worded instruction not to answer on the record. The deponent will follow such an instruction from his own attorney but not from other counsel.

Often counsel for the witness will avoid giving an instruction not to answer; instead, he may ask for clarification or narrowing of the question. Alternatively, the witness's counsel may make a speaking objection, following which the witness may say nothing. If the interrogator proceeds to the next question, the transcript may appear as if he abandoned the original question. He should ask opposing counsel whether he is instructing the witness not to answer and make certain that the response is clear on the record.

Opposing counsel may occasionally respond by sidestepping the interrogator and saying that he is instructing the witness not to answer the question "in that form," while adding that he would allow the witness to answer a proper question. The interrogator must then decide whether to rephrase the question to eliminate opposing counsel's objection and accompanying instruction not to answer. Although the interrogator may decide that the question is proper in its original form and refuse to reword it, more often he will rephrase the question.

Sometimes, regardless of his phrasing of a question, the interrogator will be met with an objection "as to form" and an instruction not to answer. He may try the question several ways so the record will show that, in spite of opposing counsel's characterization, the objection is really to the substance of the question and not to the form. At this point, some interrogators will ask the witness to confirm for the record that he will follow his lawyer's instruction not to answer. The witness may be unnerved by suddenly being drawn into a dispute between counsel.

The interrogator who meets with an instruction not to answer should make an adequate record before seeking relief from the court. In many instances, opposing counsel will allow the witness to answer enough of the follow-up questions so that the interrogator will not seek a ruling on the original instruction.

Consider, for example, a case in which the plaintiff brings suit for damage to a cello in an accident allegedly caused by the defendant's negligence. Assume that the plaintiff sold the cello in its damaged condition a year later and that counsel for the defendant asks the plaintiff at his deposition the price he obtained for that sale. Suppose that the plaintiff's attorney instructs his client not to answer on the ground that since the plaintiff's damages were fixed at the moment of the accident, the subsequent sale price is not admissible,[44] nor is that information reasonably calculated to lead to discovery of admissible evidence.[45]

If the interrogator drops the subject, he has no assurance that the court will later order the deponent to answer the question. At the least, the interrogator should request the name and address of the buyer. He may decide to stop there, hoping to obtain more information from the buyer. If, however, he is not sure that the buyer will be a friendly witness, the interrogator may continue questioning and ask the deponent whether he brought the damage to the buyer's attention, how he described it, and what he said, if anything, about its effect on the cello's value. The interrogator is surely entitled to answers to these questions, and the court will so order if necessary. If the witness is permitted to answer, the interrogator may decide he has sufficient information and that he need not seek a ruling on the original question about the sale price.

2.   *Overcoming the Instruction*

In many instances, rewording the question will eliminate the instruction not to answer. For example, if an insurance carrier disclaims coverage on the ground that the insured made misrepresentations in applying for the policy, the insured's counsel may ask the underwriter at the deposition whether he claims that the alleged misrepresentations were material. Although the chances of a favorable answer are slim, the interrogator may ask the question so that he knows what he must meet at trial.

Counsel for the deponent may instruct him not to answer such a question on the dubious ground that it "calls for a legal conclusion." The interrogator may circumvent this instruction by explaining:

> I am not asking you to give your view of the proper
> legal conclusion. I am asking you only to give facts.
> As a matter of fact, was this information material to you

---

44   *See generally* II J. WIGMORE, A TREATISE ON THE ANGLO-AMERICAN SYSTEM OF EVIDENCE IN TRIALS AT COMMON LAW, § 437 (Chadbourn rev. 1979).

45   FED. R. CIV. P. 26(b)(1).

in deciding whether to cover this risk in the sense that it played a part in your decision?

A question which asks the witness what he would have done *if* certain information had been reported to him will often be met with an instruction not to answer on the ground that the question is "hypothetical and calls upon the witness to speculate." Some hypothetical questions are undoubtedly proper, and if petitioned, the court will order the deponent to answer.[46] However, the interrogator may avoid or eliminate such an instruction by carefully structuring his questioning. For example, the interrogator should avoid using the word "if" in his question. A question which begins "If you had known . . ." tends to provoke a Pavlovian instruction not to answer. Instead, the interrogator might ask, "Had you known that information in July 1987, would you . . . ?" This small difference in wording may prevent an instruction not to answer.

If the instruction is given, the interrogator should ask follow-up questions which persuasively demonstrate that he is entitled to discover the information sought. For example, he may ask:

> Without saying how such information would have affected your decision, please answer this question: Would you have taken such information into account in reaching your decision?

If the deponent answers this question affirmatively, the interrogator may ask:

> Are you able to say whether your decision would have been the same or different had you known that information?

With an affirmative answer to this question, the deponent's attorney will probably permit his client to explain how his decision would have been affected. If not, with that foundation, the court probably will order the witness to answer the question.

---

46   Although it has been said that only experts may answer "hypothetical" questions, Teen-Ed, Inc. v. Kimball Int'l, Inc., 620 F.2d 399, 404 (3d Cir. 1980), nonexperts are entitled (and may, therefore, be compelled) to give opinion answers in response to questions in the vein: "What would have happened if X had been different?" Thus, an accountant, as a nonexpert, may give his opinion as to what profits would have been earned if a contract had not been breached, *id.*, and an automobile driver may give his opinion as to what would have happened had he pursued a different course of action prior to an accident, Fullerton v. Sauer, 337 F.2d 474, 478-79 (8th Cir. 1964). This is the sense in which the term "hypothetical" is used here. For citations to older state cases on this issue, see 3 F. BUSCH, LAW AND TACTICS IN JURY TRIALS § 338, at 285 n.21 (1960).

If the deponent claims that he would not have considered such information, the interrogator may ask him to explain why such information would have been unimportant to his decision. Or, if the deponent admits that he would have considered such information, but cannot say whether his decision would have been different, the interrogator may follow up by asking the deponent to list, first, the factors that would have pointed to the decision reached, and second, the factors that would have led to a different decision. The interrogator may also ask the deponent to list the options available to him when making his decision. With answers to these questions, the interrogator probably will not need a ruling on the original instruction not to answer.

As an alternative to asking individual follow-up questions, the interrogator may ask counsel for the witness to confirm that he would object to all questions on the subject. Such an invitation contains dangers for both parties. If the interrogator intends to seek a ruling from the court, he will create a more compelling record if he asks his questions (at least generally) and receives a series of instructions not to answer. If, for example, counsel for the witness instructs him not to answer a question pertaining to a certain meeting, the interrogator can ask in just a few minutes who attended, how long the meeting lasted, what subjects were discussed, if subject A was discussed, if anyone took notes, what action was decided upon, and how things were left at the end of the meeting.

Counsel for the witness, too, may hesitate to say that he would instruct the witness not to answer all questions on a certain subject. To avoid this apparently arbitrary stance, the witness's attorney should state that he would have to hear the questions and decide individually. If he then allows some questions to be answered in whole or in part, he may appear to the court to be reasonably cooperative. Additionally, he will deprive the interrogator of a short transcript of 20 clear instructions not to answer, which the court might quickly review and rule upon.

If opposing counsel gives an instruction not to answer a certain question, the interrogator may ask the witness whether he possesses the information necessary to answer that question. If the witness says no, the interrogator may decide that it is pointless to seek a ruling on the instruction. If, however, the witness admits knowledge of the information sought, the court will be inclined to rule that he must reveal it to the interrogator.

The instruction not to answer may be obviated in some cases by the offer of a protective order. When it is not feasible to recite extemporaneously the precise terms of such an order, the interrogator may circumvent the problem by agreeing to keep the answers confidential (perhaps not even revealing them to his own client) until the parties can concur on the wording of the order or, if no agreement is reached, until the court enters its own order. Counsel should consider instructing the reporter to type as a separate transcript the portion of the deposition in which confidential information is revealed.

3. Asserting a Privilege

If counsel for the witness objects to a question on the ground that it invades some privilege (for example, the attorney-client privilege or the Fifth Amendment privilege against self-incrimination), he will usually have no choice but to give an instruction not to answer and leave it to the interrogator to seek a ruling. Counsel may, however, decide to permit the witness to answer the question with the express understanding that an answer to a single question does not constitute a general waiver of the privilege.[47]

Moreover, the interrogator should be aware that, through his questioning, he may waive his own client's privilege.[48] For example, if the plaintiff alleges that he was defrauded by the purchaser in a certain real estate transaction, the plaintiff's litigation counsel may depose the plaintiff's original real estate counsel (whose interest at this point may be adverse to that of the plaintiff). If the interrogator asks real estate counsel about his conversations with the plaintiff, the court will likely rule that the plaintiff has thereby waived the attorney-client privilege as to all communications between him and his real estate counsel.

Finally, counsel for the deponent should remember that he will be bound at trial by the instructions given at the deposition. Thus, he will not be permitted to elicit from his own witness at trial any information that he instructed the witness not to reveal at the deposition.[49]

4. Confidential Information

As discussed earlier in this section and at Section S above, generally speaking, objections and instructions not to answer on the grounds of relevance are neither necessary nor appropriate at deposition. However, if the information sought would invade privacy interests or elicit confidential information, counsel may not only object, but also instruct the witness not to answer. Courts have upheld such limitations on discovery, particularly from nonparty witnesses.[50]

---

47   Ordinarily, if a witness discloses a privileged attorney-client communication, it constitutes a waiver of the privilege as to all other such communications on the same subject, whether or not the witness intended a waiver. *See, e.g.,* Weil v. Investment/Indicators, Research and Management, Inc., 647 F.2d 18, 24 (9th Cir. 1981), and cases cited therein.

48   *See* A.H. Robins Co. v. Fadely, 299 F.2d 557, 560-61 (5th Cir. 1962); C. WRIGHT & A. MILLER, *supra* note 13, § 2016, at 130-31. *Cf., e.g.,* Nick Istock, Inc. v. Research-Cottrell, Inc., 74 F.R.D. 150-51 (W.D. Pa. 1977) (accountant-client privilege may not be asserted to prevent depositions of accountants listed as trial witnesses).

49   *See* 4 J. MOORE & J. LUCAS, MOORE'S FEDERAL PRACTICE, ¶ 26.60[2] (2d ed. 1981) at 26-203 to -236; C. WRIGHT & A. MILLER, *supra* note 13, § 2016, at 130-31.

50   *See, e.g.,* Westmoreland v. CBS, Inc., 584 F. Supp. 1206, 1212-13 (D.D.C. 1984), *aff'd in part, rev'd in part on other grounds,* 770 F.2d 1168 (D.C. Cir. 1985); Oliver v. Committee for Re-Election of the President, 66 F.R.D. 553, 555 (D.D.C. 1975).

Suppose, for instance, that a former employee of the defendant was fired for sexual harassment of subordinates, that the reason for the firing is not widely known, and that the former employee is subpoenaed for deposition by the plaintiff, a supplier of the defendant, in a breach-of-contract action. If the plaintiff's counsel begins to question the former employee about why he is no longer employed by the defendant, counsel for the former employee may decide to object and instruct him not to answer. In order to avoid a dispute, counsel should be prepared to permit the witness to answer questions as to whether his leaving the defendant's employment had anything to do with the contract dispute at issue.

Examples of similar questions that may be declined on confidentiality grounds if they are not relevant to the subject matter of the litigation are inquiries into the deponent's salary, details about his personal life, details about his past, gossip about fellow employees, and his medical and psychological history.[51] Certainly, the interrogator should be required to demonstrate the claimed relevance of such questions before the deponent should have to answer them.

U.   Obtaining Rulings on Instructions Not To Answer

The interrogator seeking an order from the court directing the deponent to answer must decide:

(a)   whether to apply to the court in which the action is pending or to the court in the district where the deposition is being taken;

(b)   whether to seek immediate relief (by placing a telephone call to the court) or to file a written motion later; and

(c)   whether to continue with the deposition if an immediate ruling cannot be obtained or recess the deposition pending such ruling.

1.   Where to Apply

If the deponent is not a party, the interrogator must apply to the court in the district where the deposition is being taken.[52] If the deponent is a party,

---

51   Eggleston v. Chicago Journeymen Plumbers' Local Union, 657 F.2d 890, 903 (7th Cir. 1981), cert. denied, 455 U.S. 1017 (1982) (instruction not to answer appropriate on sensitive racial questions); In re Folding Carton Antitrust Litigation, 83 F.R.D. 132, 135 (N.D. Ill. 1979) (appropriate where "argumentative and misleading questions" are pressed to point of harassment).

52   FED. R. CIV. P. 37(a)(1).

the interrogator may apply either to the court in the district where the action is pending or to the court in the district in which the deposition is being taken.[53]

Typically, the interrogator will seek a ruling from the court where the action is pending if that court has an individual calendar program assigning the case to a particular judge. The judge who is already familiar with the case should rule more quickly and surely than one selected at random in another district. The judge may consider the case his own and prefer to maintain control of discovery. If the case has not been assigned to a judge, the interrogator will usually apply to the court whose internal procedures will yield the most speedy ruling.

2. *When to Apply*

In a case involving a complex factual dispute, the interrogator will often decide to submit a written motion to the court. In some jurisdictions, however, it is possible to obtain a ruling by telephoning either the chambers of the judge to whom the case is assigned or the court clerk who will assign the case to a judge.[54] This procedure is expeditious and inexpensive. Ordinarily, an oral motion is as likely to succeed as a written one. Indeed, given the appropriate predisposition of most judges to direct that the question be answered, the interrogator's chances of a favorable ruling may be better with an oral motion than a written one, which will necessarily require more reflection on the part of the judge.

The interrogator should be prepared to give the judge:

(a) his name;

(b) the caption of the case including the civil action number;

(c) his client's name;

(d) the names of opposing counsel and their clients;

(e) a brief description of the nature of the case;

---

53 FED. R. CIV. P. 37 (a)(1).

54 *See* E.D.N.Y. STANDING ORDERS, *supra* note 11, ¶ 6(b)(i) (providing for telephone conference with court to resolve disputes during depositions); Deposition Protocol Order in *In re Washington Public Power Supply System Securities Litigation*, MDL No. 551 (W.D. Wash. June 7, 1984) (ordering parties to seek immediate telephone ruling from court on any direction not to answer except on grounds of privilege).

(f)   the name of the deponent;

(g)   the subject and the question as to which the instruction not to answer has been given;

(h)   the stated basis for the instruction; and

(i)   a brief argument in favor of the propriety of the question.

Counsel for the deponent will then make a short argument in support of the instruction. Following any brief supplemental comments, the court will rule (or request that the matter be briefed).

This approach of making an immediate oral motion is particularly advantageous to both parties when the deponent lives elsewhere. Counsel for the deponent can avoid the expense and inconvenience of an additional trip should the instruction be overruled later, and the interrogator may feel that the court would be reluctant to order the question answered after briefing if such an order would require the witness to make another trip. Additionally, the ruling is very likely to be sound since trial judges regularly make on-the-spot rulings on objections to questions.

The principal disadvantage to this approach is that, if abused, it may become an imposition upon the court. However, litigators learn that the judge who is frosty the first time may be chilling the next.

3.   *Whether to Recess*

Generally, the interrogator will continue to question the witness while awaiting (whether for hours or weeks) a ruling on the instruction. However, the interrogator should exercise his right to recess the deposition [55] if, first, the information sought by the question at issue is critical to further examination of the witness, or second, the instruction is one which is likely to recur at numerous points. In either of these circumstances, the interrogator will gain little by continuing with his examination and may, by persisting, reveal much of his script to opposing counsel.

V.   Questioning One's Own Witness

After the initial interrogator has completed his examination, other counsel (usually in the order in which their clients appear in the caption) may

---

[55]   *See* FED. R. CIV. P. 37(a)(2).

question the witness.[56] When they have concluded their questioning, counsel for the witness must decide whether to ask his own questions. Most frequently, counsel for the witness will elect not to question the deponent. The rationale for choosing that course is sound.

First, counsel for the witness may expect the witness to be available to testify at trial and to clarify his deposition testimony at that time. Second, the witness may give harmful answers to his own lawyer's questions. Third, the greatest danger is that such questioning will lead to another round of questioning by opposing counsel. The witness who is unscathed after his own attorney's questioning may be bloodied by opposing counsel's subsequent examination.

Nonetheless, counsel for the witness will decide in certain instances to ask questions at the deposition. He should consider the following factors:

    (a)   the possibility that the witness will be unavailable at trial;

    (b)   the extent to which the witness has been damaged by opposing counsel's questioning;

    (c)   the danger that needed clarifications may sound disingenuous if initially made at trial; and

    (d)   the attorney's sense of his witness's ability to defend the clarifications made in answering his questions if then subjected to further questioning by other counsel.

In evaluating the second factor, if opposing counsel has badly damaged the witness (perhaps giving rise to the spectre of summary judgment), the witness's attorney may decide to risk an attempt to rehabilitate the witness through his own questioning.

In evaluating the fourth factor, counsel for the witness may want to request a break after opposing counsel have finished their questioning so he can confer with the witness about the additional questions he proposes to ask and determine how the witness will respond to those questions. The witness may also point out some areas of testimony that he believes could usefully be clarified at that time. However, even after such consultation, the witness may continue to testify poorly and make a bad situation worse. The decision whether to question one's own witness is based more on intuition than reason.

---

56   FED. R. CIV. P. 30(c).

W.   Recessing or Concluding

At the close of the testimony, the interrogator may attempt to keep the deposition open by remarking that he has "no more questions for now," by declaring the deposition "recessed," or by adding that he may need to recall the deponent after the opposition has complied with an open discovery request (*e.g.*, by producing documents). In many instances, counsel for the witness will state for the record an objection to leaving the deposition open. When such an objection is made, the witness's attorney may persuade the court that he should not have to produce the witness for another deposition session.[57] In any event, counsel representing the deponent should press the interrogator to complete the deposition before producing the next deponent. Otherwise he may find that after, say, 15 witnesses have given not-fully-completed depositions, the interrogator wants to start at the top of the list again — by which time areas of possible supplemental questioning will have proliferated.

X.   Videotaping

1.   *Why Videotape?*

Normally a videotaped deposition is a trial deposition, that is, it is taken by the party which would call the witness at trial as part of its direct case. Counsel should consider videotaping the deposition if the testimony of the witness is important to his case, if there is a substantial risk that the witness will be unavailable at trial, and if the demeanor of the witness will enhance his testimony in a material way.[58] The Prefatory Note to the Uniform Audio-Visual Deposition [Act] [Rule] lists several advantages to a videotaped deposition:[59]

---

57   *See* FED. R. CIV. P. 26(c).

58   FED. R. CIV. P. 30(b)(4). *See generally* R. HAYDOCK & D. HERR, *supra* note 14, §§ 3.3.2-.3. For practical suggestions on how to conduct a videotaped deposition, see Eble, *Videotape Depositions in Federal Court*, 93 CASE & COMMENT, January-February 1988, 3 (including sample order under Rule 30(b)(4) authorizing videotaped deposition); Frederick, *Videotaped Depositions - A Primer for Defense Trial Counsel*, FOR THE DEFENSE, November 1987, 8; Balabanian, *Medium v. Tedium: Video Depositions Come of Age*, LITIGATION, Fall 1980, 25, 26-27.

59   The Uniform Audio-Visual Deposition [Act] [Rule] was approved by the National Conference of Commissioners on Uniform State Laws in 1978. It has been adopted in two jurisdictions, North Dakota and Virginia. *See* 12 U.L.A. §§ 1-10 (Supp. 1987); N.D.R. Civ. P. 30.1; VA. CODE ANN. §§ 8.01-412.2 to 8.01-412.7(1950). A copy of the Uniform Act is included in the Appendix under "Rules."

95

(a) A method of presenting deposition testimony superior to reading a transcript of a deposition into the record.

(b) The presentation of visual and oral testimony of witnesses otherwise unavailable by reason of distance, illness, death, etc.

(c) Alleviation of problems associated with scheduling witnesses, particularly medical experts, in a visual and oral form.

(d) Presentation of visual and oral evidence in logical progression without respect to scheduling requirements.

(e) A shorter trial by enabling the judge to delete objectionable testimony before its presentation to the jury.

(f) Immediate availability and greater accuracy than that of stenographic transcriptions.

(g) Opportunity to take the court on location, thereby visually showing, for example, the surroundings in which an incident occurred.

A principal use of videotape is to capture the testimony of an ill party in a more vivid manner than a transcript, even read aloud, could convey. Counsel for a very sickly plaintiff should consider videotaping his client's deposition.[60] If the plaintiff should then die before trial, the jury can still view him as a person. If the case presents a sharp credibility dispute, the plaintiff's personal characteristics, as depicted on the videotape, may help to persuade the jury to accept his version of the facts. Opposing counsel should be alert to object if the plaintiff, or any other witness, behaves unnaturally or in a manner calculated to elicit sympathy.[61] On the other hand, not every plaintiff is attractive and

---

60 *See, e.g., In re* "Agent Orange" Product Liability Litigation, 28 Fed. R. Serv. 2d (Callaghan) 993 (E.D.N.Y. 1980); United States v. LaFatch, 382 F. Supp. 630 (N.D. Ohio 1974).

61 One court has ordered: "During the videotape deposition, the deponent shall in no way act unnaturally in answering questions or give an appearance in such a fashion which elicits sympathy." *In re* Asbestos-Related Litigation, No. MDCP-82-1, at 9 (M.D.N.C. Feb. 2, 1982) (order coordinating proceedings).

believable, and, in a given case, counsel for the plaintiff may be better off with only the dry transcript of his client's testimony.

Another reason to take a videotaped deposition is that the witness can be asked to demonstrate or operate something. For instance, in a suit alleging that the defendant manufactured a defective pistol that injured the plaintiff when it fired while he was cleaning it with the safety on, counsel for the defendant may want to videotape the plaintiff demonstrating (with an unloaded pistol) how he put the safety on and how he began to clean the gun.

An effective videotaped deposition may be filmed "on location," for example at the site of the accident so that the plaintiff can demonstrate how he operated the machine that he claims injured him.[62] Or the expert may run a test or re-create the accident on videotape.

If counsel deposes his own expert prior to trial, he will usually videotape the deposition. If a dispute among the experts arises at trial and the expert is not available to testify in person, the videotape will usually impress the jury more than a transcript, which will appear even drier than usual due to its technical content.

In some jurisdictions, the videotaped deposition of an expert witness may be used at trial even if the witness is available to testify in person.[63] Indeed, in some instances, a party may be barred from presenting the live testimony of an expert witness whose videotaped deposition was taken expressly for use at trial.[64] Obviously, opposing counsel's questioning will differ significantly when he is not merely attending a regular discovery deposition, but cross-examining the witness for use at trial.

2. Special Considerations

Although jurors may be quite interested in the first few minutes of the first tape, they may quickly lose interest.[65] Videotaped depositions tend to be boring, perhaps because they are recorded rather than live. Some litigators say

---

62   Roberts v. Homelite, 109 F.R.D. 664 (N.D. Ind. 1986) (granting manufacturer-defendant's motion for videotaped deposition, including reenactment of accident, over plaintiffs' objection); Carson v. Burlington Northern, Inc., 52 F.R.D. 492 (D. Neb. 1971) (granting motion for videotaped deposition to demonstrate operation of machine, subject to condition that plaintiff not be requested actually to touch or operate machine).

63   E.g., PA. R. CIV. P. 4017.1(g).

64   Reber v. General Motors Corp., 669 F. Supp. 717 (E.D. Pa. 1987); Keil v. Eli Lilly & Co., 88 F.R.D. 296 (E.D. Mich. 1980).

65   See Attorneys Interview Jurors Regarding $1 Million Mississippi Verdict, ASBESTOS LITIGATION REP., Aug. 27, 1982, at 5409 ("Jurors were unanimous in their criticism of videotaped depositions. . . .").

that it is unrealistic to expect jurors to concentrate on a videotape for more than about 25 minutes — the length of the average television show. Thus, it is particularly important to get to the point quickly.

For example, in taking the videotaped deposition of their own expert, some lawyers shorten their preliminary questions as to his credentials, eliciting only the most important and most basic information to qualify him as an expert. They then move directly to his opinions and the support therefor. Supplemental questions about his qualifications can be asked toward the end of direct examination.

The interrogator should also proceed at a crisp pace. A pause at a videotaped deposition may seem much longer than one at trial since the jury will see only the inexpressive face of the witness for several seconds as he waits for the next question.

Lawyers should be aware that a deponent who comes across well in person may be transformed by videotape into a seemingly dull, lifeless individual. Conversely, an unappealing deponent may be fine on tape. One lawyer remembers being at a videotaped deposition of an expert witness, a surgeon, and concluding that the expert's impassive, icy manner would turn off the jury. When the videotape was played to the jury at trial, however, the ice had melted and the surgeon made a fine and convincing appearance.

It is important to review the tape before trial to pick up not only how the witness projects, but also any technical problems that may hinder a smooth showing to the jury. The lawyer who will be responsible for showing the tape at trial should also ensure that the appropriate equipment is available and in functioning order in the courtroom. Counsel can thus avoid the embarrassment of a television monitor that does not work or a tape that goes blank three minutes into a replay of the deposition for the jury.

3.   Notice

The Federal Rules do not require special notice for a videotaped deposition because the parties must either agree to videotape the deposition or obtain a court order to do so.[66] Some jurisdictions, however, require special advance notice.[67] If a deponent refuses to have his deposition videotaped, the interrogator must obtain a court order. Even if the parties have agreed to videotaping, a nonparty deponent has the right to refuse unless a court orders him to be videotaped.[68]

---

66   *See* FED. R. CIV. P. 30(b)(4).

67   *See, e.g.*, PA. R. CIV. P. 4017.1(b) and UNIF. AUDIO-VISUAL DEPOSITION [ACT] [RULE], 12 U.L.A. § 3 (Supp. 1987).

68   *See* Westmoreland v. CBS, Inc., 770 F.2d 1168 (D.C. Cir. 1985).

A lawyer served with notice of a videotape deposition that will probably be shown at trial as the testimony of the witness may seek to take a regular "discovery" deposition in advance.[69] Thus, the attorney will be in the same position to cross-examine the witness at the videotape deposition as he normally would be at trial.

4. Mechanics

Several technical arrangements require attention prior to the deposition. The lawyer scheduling the videotaped deposition may elect to film it in color rather than in black and white. The color tape will be more attractive visually but is more expensive. The tape operator may have helpful suggestions about dress and staging for color tapes. The operator will decide what microphones (boom, table or lapel) are necessary and should be instructed to alert counsel if a problem arises with sound. Counsel should review the quality of the tape and check on how the witness appears on the tape before beginning the deposition. (This preview should eliminate staging problems, such as flowers that appear to be growing out of the deponent's head.)

Counsel should consider the physical setting in which the videotaped deposition will be taken. For example, counsel may object to the opposing party deposing its expert witness in his office with his various academic degrees hanging on the wall behind him.

Finally, the deposition should be timed to the second by a digital clock which will show inconspicuously on the tape.[70]

Counsel should reach a clear understanding on several points at the start of the deposition. First, how are the expenses to be apportioned? Normally, the lawyer scheduling the deposition pays for the originals of the videotape and the stenographic transcript, and counsel ordering copies pay for those.[71] It might be advisable, however, to agree with opposing counsel that if

---

69   For examples of orders granting the right to take such "discovery depositions," *see In re* Asbestos-Related Litigation, No. MDCP-82-1, at 8 (M.D.N.C. Feb. 2, 1982) (order coordinating proceedings); *In re* Asbestos-Related Litigation, No. CP-81-1, at 6-7 (E.D.N.C. Sept. 15, 1981) (first pretrial order); *In re* Asbestos Cases, at 3 (S.C. Cir. Ct. 1982) (order) (if witness critically ill). *Cf. In re* "Agent Orange" Product Liability Litigation, 96 F.R.D. 587 (E.D.N.Y. 1983) (prohibiting defendants from conducting discovery depositions before videotaping does not deprive them of meaningful opportunity for cross-examination).

70   PA. R. CIV. P. 4017.1(d) (required); UNIF. AUDIO-VISUAL DEPOSITION [ACT] [RULE], 12 U.L.A. § 4(6) (Supp. 1987).

71   *See* UNIF. AUDIO-VISUAL DEPOSITION [ACT] [RULE], 12 U.L.A. 1(a), 1(c) and 5 (Supp. 1987). *See also* Tsesmelys v. Dublin Truck Leasing Corp., 25 Fed. R. Serv. 2d 465 (E.D. Tenn. 1977); *In re* Rhode Island Asbestos Cases, R.I.M.L. No. 1, at 9 (D.R.I. Mar. 15, 1982) (pretrial order No. 2); *In re* Asbestos-Related Litigation, No. MDCP-82-1, at 10-11 (M.D.N.C. Feb. 2, 1982) (order coordinating proceedings); *In re* Asbestos-Related Litigation, No. CP-81-1, at 7 (E.D.N.C. Sept. 15, 1981) (first pretrial order).

the length of his examination equals or exceeds that of the lawyer scheduling the deposition, he will have to pay a ratable portion of the costs of the original videotape and transcript.

Second, counsel should understand the practice of the videotape operator (that is, where he will be focusing and when) — this is particularly important if the videotape operator is an employee of opposing counsel and there is no local rule governing these things — and should act at all times as if the jury were in the room.[72] Third, the attorneys should agree on the site where the completed tapes will be stored and preserved.[73]

In some jurisdictions a stenographer is required to be present at a videotape deposition; in others no such requirement exists. There are advantages to engaging a stenographer even though one is not required, which will sometimes outweigh the disadvantage of the additional expense.[74] Often counsel will agree that a lawyer desiring to make an objection will state only that he wants to go off the record. The videotape will be stopped, but the stenographic record will continue. Thus, the videotape will be free of any objections and arguments by counsel; the tape may then be played before the jury without the necessity of editing objections and arguments. If the court overrules an objection, the tape can be shown without interruption or editing; even if the court sustains the objection, the interruption (to delete the question and answer) will be much shorter if the arguments of counsel are not included on the videotape.[75]

---

[72]   The operator may be restricted to a still camera permanently focused on a frontal view of the witness with no zoom lens. In Matter of Daniels, 69 F.R.D. 579 (N.D. Ga. 1976). One pretrial order provides: "At the beginning of the examination by any counsel, counsel shall identify himself or herself by name within the camera's field of vision. The camera will thereafter focus exclusively on the deponent at all times during the deposition, except for identification of exhibits, and will not zoom in or out on a witness or any other person at the deposition. The camera shall not 'pan' other than to include exhibits, and the field of view should, to the extent possible, consist of a plain background." (M.D.N.C. Feb. 2, 1982) (order coordinating proceedings). See also No CP-81-1, at 7 (E.D.N.C. Sept. 15, 1981) (first pretrial order).

[73]   "Unless otherwise stipulated by the parties, the original audio-visual recording of a deposition, any copy edited pursuant to an order of the court, and exhibits must be filed forthwith with the clerk of the court." UNIF. AUDIO-VISUAL DEPOSITION [ACT] [RULE], 12 U.L.A. § 4(9) (Supp. 1987).

The original tape may also be kept by a court reporter who transcribes the deposition. See In re Asbestos-Related Litigation, No. MDCP-82-1, at 10 (M.D.N.C. Feb. 2, 1982) (order coordinating proceedings) (so ordering); In re Asbestos-Related Litigation, No. CP-81-1, at 7 (E.D.N.C. Sept. 15, 1981) (first pretrial order) (same).

[74]   "A party may arrange to have a stenographic transcription made at his own expense." FED. R. CIV. P. 30(b)(4).

[75]   See Kelly v. GAF Corp., 115 F.R.D. 257 (E.D. Pa. 1987) (where defense counsel's multiple objections required substantial editing after court overruled them and resulting edited version of videotape was a "hodge-podge," court reversed defense verdict on ground that jury was not able to base verdict on full and fair consideration of evidence).

Additionally, if counsel later wants to check exactly how the witness responded to a particular question, it is much easier to read the transcript than to run the videotape. Moreover, with the transcript in hand, the judge can more easily rule on objections before playing the tape for the jury. Finally, the stenographic record will provide a useful description of changes or interruptions on the videotape, as well as descriptions of mechanical and technical problems.[76]

At the start of the videotape, the operator should state his name, the caption of the case, the name of the deponent, the date, the time, the place and any stipulations. Then, each lawyer should identify himself by giving his name and the name of the party he represents, and counsel taking the deposition should ensure that the administration of the oath is recorded on the videotape so the jury will be sure to see it.[77] At the start of questioning, each attorney should again state his name so that even if the videotape operator does not focus on him, the jury will know who is interrogating the witness.[78] The operator should announce on the audio recording portion the end of one tape and the start of the next.

At the conclusion of the questioning, the lawyers should remain silent until certain that the videotape equipment is off. Otherwise, the jury may hear a chorus of sighs and the start of banter among the attorneys. Such conduct may detract from the force of the testimony.

Editing, which is troublesome and often expensive, may be accomplished in several ways. First, the operator can black out the audio portion only. This method works well for short deletions and is not expensive. However, the jury will grow bored and inattentive if forced to watch several minutes of the tape without sound. A second editing method is to block out both the audio and video portions and move at fast-forward through the deleted segment. This method works well unless the operator resumes the tape at the wrong point.

---

76   The order coordinating proceedings in *In re* Asbestos-Related Litigation, No. MDCP-82-1, at 10 (M.D.N.C. Feb. 2, 1982) provides: "It shall be the duty of the person who records the deposition stenographically to accurately record during the course of the deposition as to when a tape is changed, when examination by each of the various counsel commences and ends, and whenever there is an interruption of the continuous tape exposure for the purposes of off-the-record discussions, mechanical failure of the machine, or other similar technical problems. Before the video recorder is turned off for any reason, the video operator shall allow all parties to briefly state their positions, agreement, or disagreement with that action for the record."

77   *See* UNIF. AUDIO-VISUAL DEPOSITION [ACT] [RULE], 12 U.L.A. §§ 4(1), 4(3), 4(22) (Supp. 1987); *see also In re* Asbestos-Related Litigation, No. MDCP-82-1, at 9 (M.D.N.C. Feb. 2, 1982) (order coordinating proceedings) (ordering same).

78   *See In re* Asbestos-Related Litigation, No. MDCP-82-1, at 9 (M.D.N.C. Feb. 2, 1982) (order coordinating proceedings) (ordering such identification); *In re* Asbestos-Related Litigation, No. CP-81-1, at 7 (E.D.N.C. Sept. 15, 1981) (first pretrial order) (same).

The best, but most expensive, method is to create a second tape with all objectionable material deleted.[79]

Y.   Summarizing the Testimony

Immediately upon conclusion of the deposition (or at the end of the day if the deposition is to be continued), the interrogator and the lawyer defending the deposition should each dictate a memorandum to his file summarizing the testimony given. The longer such dictation is delayed, the more the product will suffer.

Before starting dictation, the lawyer should decide what purpose the summary is to serve. In some cases, this memorandum will serve as the attorney's summary of the deposition for all purposes prior to trial. In other cases, particularly in complicated litigation, a legal assistant will prepare a detailed summary of the deposition as soon as the transcript is received. Both the lawyer's time and the client's money would be wasted by dictating a comprehensive summary which will shortly be superseded. In that situation, the lawyer may dictate a memorandum describing only the highlights of the deposition. The interrogator's memorandum might include:

(a)   the principal points that the deponent would make on direct examination if called as a witness at trial by the opposition;

(b)   the interrogator's evaluation of the deponent as a possible trial witness;

(c)   the principal points that the interrogator would develop if he were to cross-examine the witness at trial based on his current knowledge; and

(d)   what further investigation or discovery should be initiated in light of this deposition testimony.

The lawyer for the deponent might want to include the following in his highlights memorandum:

---

79   *See* Note, PA. R. CIV. P. 4017.1; R. HAYDOCK & D. HERR, *supra* note 14, § 3.3.3, at 171-72. Section 4(8) of the Uniform Audio-Visual Deposition [Act] [Rule] provides: "If the court issues an editing order the original audio-visual recording must not be altered." 12 U.L.A. § 4(8) (Supp. 1987); *see also In re* Asbestos-Related Litigation, No. MDCP-82-1, at 11 (M.D.N.C. Feb. 2, 1982) (order coordinating proceedings) (ordering same).

(a)   his evaluation of the deponent as a possible trial witness;

(b)   what damage, if any, the deponent's testimony did to the case and what was helpful about the testimony;

(c)   what the interrogator's questioning revealed about what he considered important issues in the case;

(d)   what subjects the interrogator is likely to pursue with other deponents based on what he asked and what he learned at this deposition; and

(e)   what further investigation of his client's documents or other witnesses should be instituted in light of this deposition testimony.

One of the principal problems facing a lawyer preparing to try a large or complicated case is too much information. A highlights memorandum allows the trial lawyer to take a quick hold on the most important points that he will seek to make in questioning the witness. With that framework in mind, the trial lawyer can then tackle more detailed materials which may suggest additional lines of inquiry. In this context, note that some court reporters are capable of retrieving "key words" in the transcript by computer, thus providing the interrogator with a guide to passages he thinks may be important.

Generally, the lawyer will forward a copy of his highlights or summary memorandum to his client. He should carefully consider whether to send such memoranda to a person who may testify at deposition or trial since opposing counsel may ask that person what materials he has reviewed in connection with the litigation; there is the danger that opposing counsel may then seek discovery of such memoranda.[80] Finally, the highlights memorandum may provide a more meaningful and useful report to the client than a summary including every detail.

Z.   Reading and Correcting the Transcript

Ideally, counsel who attended the deposition should read the transcript immediately upon receipt. Reporters occasionally make mistakes. In transcribing, the reporter may skip a fold of paper and inadvertently omit testimony from

---

80   *See* generally FED. R. EVID. 612; *cf.* Sporck v. Peil, 759 F.2d 312 (3d Cir.), *cert. denied*, 474 U.S. 903 (1985) (holding that counsel's designation and compilation of documents to prepare a witness for deposition is opinion work product and balancing the privilege against Fed. R. Evid. 612). This subject is discussed at Chapter 9, Section E.3, *infra*.

the transcript. Also, the reporter may be interrupted while completing the transcription and may neglect to include the last few questions and answers in the transcript. Counsel is more likely to detect and correct such errors if the transcript is read upon receipt.

Counsel for the deponent should confer with him to decide what corrections should be made to the transcript. Rule 30(e) provides that changes "shall be entered upon the deposition by the officer with a statement of the reasons given by the witness for making them." In practice, however, lawyers in many jurisdictions simply prepare a correction sheet to append to the transcript with columns for the page and line numbers, the existing version of the answer to be corrected, the corrected version, and, in some cases, the reason for each correction. If the opposing lawyer objects to this method of correction, however, the court may direct strict compliance with Rule 30(e) so that the transcript itself is amended by the reporter to reflect the changes and reasons for them.[81] The original answers remain on the transcript with the corrections and may be read at trial,[82] although their impact may be diminished by the pretrial corrections.

One disadvantage of using a separate sheet for corrections is that the transcript and the correction sheet may become separated. That is not likely to be a problem for the witness who will give only one deposition in a single case. But what about the witness who has been deposed more than once in a series of toxic tort cases? Suppose in the next deposition or at trial he is confronted with an answer he gave on page 363 of his fourteenth deposition. If his lawyer had insisted that all corrections be made by the reporter on the transcript itself, the witness could look at the transcript and point out that he had corrected the original answer or could note for himself that he had not done so. On the other hand, if that practice was not followed, the correction sheet might well not have been attached to the copy of the transcript that the interrogator showed to the witness. And the witness is not likely to be able to remember whether he made a correction, or, if so, precisely what the correction was.

The deponent has the right to make changes of substance in the transcript under Rule 30(e).[83] For example, he may say that he erred at the deposition by testifying that the light was red, and that it was really green. The reason for making the change may be that he simply misstated a fact or that his memory has improved. If the deponent makes a fundamental change in his testimony, the interrogator may ask to resume the deposition to question him concerning

---

81   See Lutgig v. Thomas, 89 F.R.D. 639, 641 (N.D. Ill. 1981).

82   Usiak v. New York Tank Barge Co., 299 F.2d 808 (2d Cir. 1962); Allen & Co. v. Occidental Petroleum Corp., 49 F.R.D. 337, 340 (S.D.N.Y. 1970).

83   See R. HAYDOCK & D. HERR, supra note 14, §§ 3.8.4.5; Lugtig v. Thomas, supra note 81; Allen & Co. v. Occidental Petroleum Corp., supra note 82.

the change. The deponent may decide not to correct minor typographical errors that do not affect meaning. If at trial he claims that he misstated one of his deposition answers, opposing counsel may bring out that the deponent not only made the statement, but failed to amend it even though he read the transcript and corrected several minute errors.

Sometimes if the deponent's testimony was particularly harmful to his position, he and his counsel will decide for tactical reasons that he should not make corrections and sign. He may not be able to correct his most harmful testimony (that is, it may be true). And by making some small corrections and then signing the transcript, he has made things worse for himself. Bad enough that he said it; now he has added his imprimatur.

There is some question whether corrections may properly be made to the transcript of the interrogator's questions or the defender's objections. Although there appears to be no authority for the proposition, the witness should be able to correct a question if his answer depended on the wording of the question and the question was erroneously transcribed. For example, suppose the transcript reads as follows:

Q.   Was the letter accurate as sent?

A.   Yes.

In fact, the letter was not accurate as sent, and the dialogue at deposition (as the deponent and his counsel understood it) was as follows:

Q.   Was the letter *actually* sent?

A.   Yes.

Rather than changing the "Yes" answer to a "No," it would be more appropriate and accurate to correct the question.

Similarly, if an objection is inaccurately transcribed, the objecting lawyer may want to correct it so that the grounds are properly stated rather than take the chance that the judge will bind him to the objection as transcribed. This is particularly important if the parties have not stipulated to reserve objections except as to form until trial. Suppose, for instance, that a lawyer objected to a question on the dual grounds that the question was irrelevant [not an "obviable" ground under Rule 32(d)(3)(A)] and there was no foundation for the question (an "obviable" ground, waived if not made at deposition), but the transcript shows merely the relevancy objection. The interrogator ignored the objection and did not establish a foundation. The objecting lawyer should correct the transcript so that the fully stated objection, as made at the deposition, is reflected.

If the deponent does not sign the transcript within 30 days, the reporter may then file the unsigned transcript in jurisdictions where filing is permitted.[84] If the interrogator wants the transcript signed to eliminate the risk that the deponent will claim at trial that the transcript is erroneous, the only remedy specified in the Federal Rules is a motion to suppress the deposition or some part thereof.[85] This remedy fails to satisfy the needs of the lawyer who wants to ensure his use of the deposition at trial without surprise.

---

[84]   FED. R. CIV. P. 30(e).

[85]   *See id.*; FED. R. CIV. P. 32(d)(4).

CHAPTER EIGHT

DEPOSITIONS OF EXPERTS

A.   Can the Expert Be Deposed?

1.   The Expert Consultant

Not all experts may be deposed. Under the Federal Rules of Civil Procedure, discovery is not permitted of facts known or opinions held by an expert who is retained as a consultant in anticipation of litigation or in preparation for trial and who is not expected to testify at trial, unless the expert made a medical examination of a party or "upon a showing of exceptional circumstances under which it is impracticable for the party seeking discovery to obtain facts or opinions on the same subject by other means."[1] Of course, if a party is himself an expert and his alleged improper exercise of professional skills is at issue, he is subject to full discovery.[2]

As noted, discovery may be obtained of an expert who is not expected to testify if the expert has made a medical examination of a party. For that reason, before requesting a medical examination of the plaintiff, prudent counsel for the defendant will forward copies of all hospital and medical records and reports to a proposed examining physician with the request that the physician advise whether in his judgment there is any point to such an examination. Sometimes after reviewing these materials, the physician will respond that the strong likelihood is that an examination would only confirm the conclusions of the plaintiff's physicians. In that case, counsel for the defendant will probably decide not to request such an examination. Otherwise, the report of the examination results might only cause the plaintiff's counsel's settlement position to harden. Or, if the case should go to trial, the plaintiff's counsel would be able to prove that the plaintiff was examined by a physician selected by the defendant. The jury could conclude from the fact the defendant did not call the physician to testify at trial that the results of the examination did not help the defendant's position.

2.   The Trial Expert

The Federal Rules of Civil Procedure treat the expert who is identified as an expected-to-testify-at-trial witness altogether differently from the expert

---

1   FED. R. CIV. P. 26(b)(4)(B).

2   See PROPOSED AMENDMENTS TO THE FEDERAL RULES OF CIVIL PROCEDURE RELATING TO DISCOVERY, 48 F.R.D. 487, 503 (1970) [hereinafter 1970 ADVISORY COMMITTEE NOTES].

who is not. The trial expert's opinions and factual knowledge, and the grounds for each opinion, may be elicited by interrogatory.[3] And, upon motion, the court may permit a deposition of the expert.[4]

For several reasons, counsel will often agree that each side may depose the other's expert without the need to resort to a motion. First, in spite of the natural reluctance to expose an important witness to a deposition, counsel will be interested to see how his expert stands up to the adversary's questioning. The expert's performance at trial will be better by reason of the dress rehearsal that the deposition affords. Second, counsel will usually want to depose the other side's expert and knows that opposing counsel is unlikely to agree to such a deposition unless he has the same right to depose his adversary's expert. Third, counsel may know that the judge handling the case routinely grants motions for expert depositions and may conclude that opposing such depositions will be not only futile, but also irritating to the court.

If counsel cannot agree, a court is likely to order depositions, particularly from experts on liability issues. On the other hand, if an expert will be testifying only on damages (for example, a medical doctor in a personal injury case) and has provided a comprehensive report or answers to expert interrogatories, a court may be more reluctant to allow a pretrial deposition.

A court will usually direct the party seeking to depose an opponent's expert to pay a reasonable fee for the time the expert spends responding to discovery, including time spent in preparation and travel as well as in the deposition itself.[5] The court may even make the privilege of deposing a party's expert contingent upon compensation to that party of a "fair portion" of the fees and expenses incurred by that party in obtaining facts and opinions from the expert.[6] This compensation, which is in addition to that paid to the expert for his time, may be ordered by the court either before or after discovery from the expert is completed.[7]

B.   Should the Expert Be Deposed?

Counsel who feels reasonably well prepared to cross-examine the other side's expert at trial may elect to forgo the expert's deposition. While the

---

3   FED. R. CIV. P. 26(b)(4)(A)(i).

4   FED. R. CIV. P. 26(b)(4)(A)(ii).

5   FED. R. CIV. P. 26(b)(4)(C)(i).

6   FED. R. CIV. P. 26(b)(4)(C)(ii).

7   See 1970 ADVISORY COMMITTEE NOTES, supra note 2, 48 F.R.D. at 505.

interrogator will learn something about the expert at the deposition, the expert will also learn something about the interrogator. The questions asked necessarily reveal something of counsel's thinking about the case and the tack he is likely to take at trial. Hence, counsel must balance the value of the information to be learned through a deposition against the detriment of educating the other side about his theories of the case.[8]

There are two not-so-obvious pitfalls that the lawyer who deposes the other side's expert should bear in mind:

1. The Risk of Destroying the Expert

The interrogator should consider whether it would be wise to destroy the other side's expert at deposition. Although, as discussed below, the deposition may be the interrogator's only opportunity to score points (since the expert may not be available at the time of trial), the interrogator should be aware that if the expert is mortally wounded at deposition, the other side may simply obtain a new expert unless the case is too close to trial for it to do so. Few experiences in litigation are more frustrating than completely undercutting the other side's expert at deposition, only to find that he has been replaced. It is then difficult to gain any advantage from the first expert's deposition transcript, particularly if the new expert has not read it.

There is support for a party's right to subpoena the opponent's former expert witness and to force him to express an opinion at trial,[9] but there are obviously practical problems in attempting to extract opinion testimony from a hostile expert. An alternative approach is to argue that the opponent's expert's deposition should be admissible under Rule 801(d)(2)(D) of the Federal Rules of Evidence as a statement by an agent of the opponent concerning a matter within the scope of his agency, made during the existence of the relationship, thus avoiding the need to call the opponent's expert as a live witness at trial.[10]

2. The Deposition Transcript May Be the Trial Testimony

The interrogator should keep in mind that, although he may desire the deposition for discovery purposes only, his opponent may use the deposition

---

8   *See* Graham, *Discovery of Experts Under Rule 26(b)(4) of the Federal Rules of Civil Procedure: Part Two, an Empirical Study and a Proposal,* 1977 U. ILL. L.F. 169, 186 ("Occasionally an attorney will forego deposing an expert because of a fear that the deposition will result more to educate the expert and the opponent about the examining attorney's trial strategy and prospective cross-examination than to provide the examining attorney with information that will assist in impeaching the expert or aid the examining attorney's case.").

9   Kaufman v. Edelstein, 539 F.2d 811 (2d Cir. 1976).

10   Hely, *Opponent's Expert Can Work For You,* TRIAL, Sept. 1985.

transcript in place of live testimony by the expert. Rule 32(a)(3) of the Federal Rules of Civil Procedure permits any party to use the deposition of a witness "for any purpose" if the witness becomes unavailable to testify at trial. Thus, if an expert witness is unavailable to testify at trial because he is beyond 100 miles from the courthouse or for other reasons identified in Rule 32(a)(3), the party who retained the expert may be allowed to introduce his deposition at trial against the party who took the expert's deposition.[11] As a consequence, an interrogator who saves some of his best ammunition for cross-examining the expert at trial may never have an opportunity to use it.

To improve the chances of the court's ruling the deposition transcript inadmissible in the event an opposing expert is unavailable for trial, the interrogator may want to omit questions about the expert's qualifications if there is no real doubt that the expert has the qualifications to testify.[12] Just as an expert is not permitted to testify in person without being qualified, so, too, his deposition testimony cannot be admitted if he has not been qualified. Of course, the opposing party's lawyer whose expert is being deposed may (and should) supply the qualifications by examining the expert after the interrogator's examination. In that event, the interrogator should be certain to state any objection to the expert's qualifications or he may be deemed to have waived it.[13]

Because of the possibility that an expert may be unavailable at the time of trial, some lawyers will examine their own experts after opposing counsel finishes his questioning. For example, suppose the defendant's counsel takes the plaintiff's expert's deposition in a medical malpractice case. Although the expert, in responding to the defendant's counsel's questions, may have said everything he would say at trial in support of the plaintiff's case, his testimony may be disjointed and spread over many pages of the transcript. Consequently, after the defendant's counsel has completed his interrogation, the plaintiff's counsel might ask several questions in order to obtain a compact, to-the-point statement of the expert's views. If the expert's deposition transcript is then used instead of live testimony, the plaintiff's counsel can start by reading his readily

---

11   Comment, *Twisting the Purposes of Discovery: Expert Witnesses and the Deposition Dilemma*, 36 VAND. L. REV. 1615, 1617, 1625 (1983) ("Today, parties frequently hire expert witnesses who live and work more than 100 miles from the place of trial . . . . [B]ecause experts are very costly and often live outside the 100 mile zone, parties who hire them are more likely to abuse the 100 mile requirement by not paying the expert to return for trial than parties who seek attendance of nonexpert witnesses.") *See also* Gill v. Westinghouse Electric Corp., 714 F.2d 1105, 1107 (11th Cir. 1983) (where defense expert died before trial, defendant at trial was permitted to introduce discovery depositon of expert taken by plaintiff).

12   *See* McNamara & Sorensen, *Deposition Traps and Tactics*, LITIGATION, Fall 1985, 48, 51-52.

13   Cordle v. Allied Chemical Corp., 309 F.2d 821, 826 (6th Cir. 1962).

understood examination of the expert and supplement that with portions of the testimony elicited by other counsel.

Of course, when the plaintiff's counsel begins to question his own expert at deposition, the defendant's counsel must consider whether to ask some or all of the damaging questions he had intended to save for the expert's cross-examination at trial. He may correctly take the plaintiff's counsel's interrogation of his own witness to be a signal that the plaintiff's counsel is not expecting to bring the expert in for trial and conclude that the deposition will be the only opportunity for cross-examination. Thus, if opposing counsel questions his own expert after the interrogator finishes his examination, the balance for the interrogator may tip in favor of asking the expert some or all of his telling cross-examination questions at the deposition and not saving them for trial.

At times, counsel may want to take a deposition of his own expert for use at trial. (See Chapter 7, Sections X.1 and X.2 for a discussion of videotaping the expert's deposition.) If the deposition does not go well or if for some other reason counsel decides not to use the deposition at trial, opposing counsel may be permitted to introduce it for his own purposes even if the expert is, strictly speaking, available (for example, within 100 miles of the courthouse) at the time of trial because the parties intended it to be a trial deposition.[14] Thus, counsel should not assume that a deposition of his own expert is just a dress-rehearsal or that, once taken, he retains control of its use at trial.

C.   Preparing for the Deposition

Obtaining technical assistance before deposing an expert is often crucial. The interrogator should give consideration to meeting with his own expert, or an employee of his client with the necessary technical background, before the opposing expert's deposition to obtain a full understanding of the expert's report or answers to interrogatories and to assist him in developing questions for the expert. The interrogator may also want to have his own expert or a knowledgeable employee of his client present when deposing the other side's expert. Such a person can suggest useful follow-up questions that might otherwise be overlooked. See Chapter 2, Section E.

The interrogator must always keep in mind that the deposition transcript will probably be his most important tool for cross-examining the expert and may even be used in place of the expert's live testimony at trial, as discussed at Section B, Part 2 of this chapter.

---

14   *See, e.g.*, Reber v. General Motors Corp., 669 F. Supp. 717 (E.D. Pa. 1987).

D.   The Expert's File

Deposing counsel should *always, always, always* ask to see the expert's file and should ask whether it is the complete file. The expert's correspondence and notes will often be fertile sources of inquiry. For example:

1.   Retention Letter

- What does the letter from counsel retaining the expert say?

- Does it set forth counsel's theory of the case? Or limit the expert's assignment in some way?

2.   Materials Reviewed

- What materials were made available to the expert to review in forming his opinion?

- Did he know there were other materials?

- Did he ask to see them?

- If not, why not?

- If so, what was he told?

3.   Notes

- In reviewing materials, did the expert make notes only of things helpful to his side of the case?

- Why was he interested only in one side of the story?

- Or did he also note harmful facts?

- Did he take notes on the basis of what he perceived to be important?

- If so, what importance does he attach to each fact noted?

- Do the notes include the name of opposing counsel? Why was that of interest to him?

- Do the notes include instructions from counsel as to pitfalls to be avoided in expressing his opinion? Was he not able to form his opinion on his own without counsel's aid?

- Counsel should ask the witness to read each note and to say what it means.

The interrogator should give thought to serving a subpoena on the expert approximately 10 days before the deposition requiring him to produce his complete file at the deposition. Otherwise the expert may leave a portion of the file in his office or, in reviewing the file a couple of days before the deposition, may purge it of potentially harmful notes on the rationale that, in the absence of a subpoena, he is free to discard materials that are no longer of use to him. Additionally, some lawyers argue that serving a subpoena on an expert has the desirable effect of impressing upon him that the interrogator is and will be in charge.

But, deposing counsel who suspects the expert is a scoundrel may have second thoughts about serving a subpoena. If the expert is dishonest, the subpoena may only remind him to purge his file; whereas, if not served with a subpoena, the same expert may unsuspectingly appear at the deposition with the full file in his briefcase, particularly if the file has not been requested at other depositions. Thus, one of the interrogator's first questions to the expert should be, "What documents do you have with you?"

E.   Topics To Be Covered

Generally, the interrogator will want to cover the following topics with an expert at his deposition:

- qualifications;

- compensation;

- experience as an expert witness;

- what his assignment was;

- what work he has done in connection with that assignment;

- what opinions he has formed as a result of his work;

113

- the basis for each such opinion, including any tests he or his staff may have performed;

- what further work he plans to do on the case and for what purpose;

- by what date he expects to complete his work; and

- whether changing any particular facts would cause him to change his opinions.

Counsel deposing an expert must grapple with many of the same strategic and tactical considerations that apply to any other witness, which have been discussed at length in the preceding chapters of this book. But there are certain aspects of deposing an expert that merit comment here.

F.   The Order of Topics

As discussed in Chapter 6, Section B.1 above, with respect to varying the expected order of questioning, the interrogator should not lapse into starting with the expert's qualifications simply because most lawyers do that most of the time. There are advantages to moving directly to the heart of the expert's anticipated testimony.

In deposing an expert witness, some lawyers may spend the first two hours (or even two days if the case is a major one that turns on expert testimony) on the expert's qualifications. An expert will usually feel relatively comfortable while discussing his credentials and will become more so as he establishes eye contact with the interrogator and grows accustomed to the cadence of his voice and mannerisms. The same expert, however, may be surprised and flustered if asked in rapid succession whether he has been hired by the defendant as an expert, whether he has formed any expert opinions, what they are, and then, in greater detail, the bases for each of those opinions. The expert's qualifications can be explored toward the end of the deposition. The expert may be unnerved by the simple fact that the interrogator is not playing by "the rules" as the expert knows them from past experience.

G.   The Expert's Qualifications

The interrogator should leave the deposition with a clear understanding of every line of the expert's curriculum vitae unless the amount involved does not warrant such detailed questioning. (But see the discussion at Section B.2 of this chapter about foregoing questioning on qualifications to improve the chances of blocking the use of the expert's deposition transcript as his trial testimony.) An expert's overstatement of his credentials, which occasionally occurs, can form the basis for withering cross-examination at trial.

1.   Professional Societies

If the expert claims membership in a professional society, what are the requirements for membership? More than to pay dues? What, if anything, does he do as a member of the society?

2.   Seminars

If the expert lists participation in a seminar in his credentials, what did such participation entail? How long did it last? Was it a difficult, demanding course? Who sponsored it? What topics were covered? Where was it held? (At a well-known resort?)

3.   Degrees

Did the expert actually receive a degree from the university listed on his resume or did he take some courses there but receive his degree from some other college or university? What courses did he take for the degree?

4.   His Firm

If the expert operates a consulting firm, how many employees does it have? Often the expert will hold himself out as a representative of a consulting firm with an impressive name — e.g., Megadynatech, Ltd. — of which he is the sole shareholder and only employee. If he has employees, what are their qualifications and what input have they provided to the expert in this case?

5.   Publications

What is the nature of the publications in which the expert's work has appeared? Are they scholarly journals or merely popular magazines written for a lay audience?

6.   Disqualification

Has any court ever ruled that the expert was not qualified to speak as an expert? That ruling and the transcript leading to it, if it exists, could be important tools for challenging the expert's credentials.

7.   Other Testimony

How many times has the expert testified?[15] Has he consistently been on the same side of an issue? That is, has he always testified for plaintiffs, or

---

15   See Bockweg v. Anderson, 9 Fed. R. Serv. 3d (Callaghan) 386 (M.D.N.C. 1987) (compelling plaintiff's expert witnesses to answer deposition questions concerning their involvement in other past or pending medical malpractice actions).

always for defendants? Has he always found that the product in question, whatever it was, was defective?

Even if the expert is well qualified and there is no doubt that he will be permitted to testify as an expert witness at trial, it may still be worthwhile to ask questions to show that there are some things lacking from his background. For example:

- If the expert comes from industry, has he ever taught a course at any college or university? Or given a series of academic lectures?

- Even if he has written many papers, has he written on the issue involved in this case?

- Has the expert done substantive work in the field recently, rather than simply providing expert consultation services?

- Has he attended seminars, or does he subscribe to publications in the field, in order to keep abreast of the latest developments in the field?

If the witness answers "no" to half a dozen such questions, the cross-examiner at trial can ask just those six questions as to his qualifications, hope that he has somewhat tarnished the expert's image, and move on to other subjects. (Of course, the cross-examiner might well decide not to question the expert's qualifications at trial if he has only a few minor points to raise.)

It may also be helpful to ask the expert in what subject areas he considers himself to be an expert, either by an open-ended question or by identifying possible areas of expertise. The interrogator will want to explore specialized fields where lack of expertise might disqualify the expert from rendering an opinion. Thus, he may ask an engineer who is the other side's causation expert in a case involving the failure of a metal component at high temperatures, "Do you consider yourself an expert in the field of metallurgy? In the field of high-temperature alloys?" Or a medical causation expert in toxic tort litigation may be asked, "Do you consider yourself an expert in epidemiology?" Such questions may elicit an interruption from opposing counsel ("What do you mean by 'expert'?"), and the interrogator should be prepared to elaborate on the definition of "expert" as, for example, one with specialized knowledge in a recognized field, and possibly to define further the specialty mentioned.

H.   The Expert's Work on the Case

The interrogator should ask not only what work the expert has done on the case, but also what approaches he considered and then rejected and how far he went with each such approach before discarding it. What results was he getting with each approach? Did he discuss those results with the lawyer who retained him before rejecting an approach?

What information did the expert request from the party that retained him? For what purpose? Was it provided? If not, what was the expert told? (Sometimes the interrogator will have been seeking the same information through written discovery and the fact that the other side's expert also requested that information will be helpful support for a motion to compel.)

I.   Understanding the Expert's Views

The interrogator should arrive at the deposition with a clear understanding of the expert's report or answers to interrogatories and should leave with a clear understanding of his testimony. That is, he should not allow himself to be "snowed" by a barrage of jargon. Rather, the interrogator should press the expert to simplify and explain until he has a clear understanding of what the expert is saying, no matter how long it takes.

J.   Asking Open-ended Questions

Normally the interrogator should ask an expert a series of open-ended questions followed by a question designed to summarize the expert's position on an issue. For example, the interrogator may ask, "Is there any other basis for your opinion that the chain saw was defective?" until the answer is "No." The interrogator may then close by asking, "You base your opinion that the chain saw was defective on the facts that the guard was removable and that a warning against removing the guard was affixed only to the guard and not to the body of the saw, and nothing else, is that correct?"

The purpose of the open-ended questions is to obtain a complete statement of the grounds for the expert's opinion, without alerting him to the ways counsel will cross-examine him at trial. The purpose of the final, summarizing question is to obtain a compact statement of the expert's position that can be read to the court or jury if the expert's testimony at trial should differ from his deposition testimony.

Although the interrogator often starts a deposition with the objective of exploring the grounds for an expert's opinion without cross-examining him, the interrogator will sometimes decide to ask additional questions to be sure of being prepared to deal with the expert at trial. For example, suppose the plaintiff's expert in a product liability case says the product should have been accompanied by a certain warning. After asking the expert to state the bases for that opinion, should the defendant's counsel ask whether the expert can identify any literature that supports his view? Or whether he can identify any other expert who takes the same position? Or any other manufacturer who gives such a warning?

The interrogator who does not ask these questions at the deposition will not know what answers the expert would give at trial in response to such questions. But by asking them at the deposition, the interrogator creates the danger that the expert may do more work to buttress his opinion after the deposition, and give answers damaging to the defendant's case if asked the same questions at trial. Most lawyers tend to resolve this tension in favor of pressing the questions at the deposition on the ground that they must know what they will face at trial; they worry about the expert's doing more work and coming up with better answers if and when that happens.

K.   Questioning Beyond the Scope of Answers to Interrogatories

If the answers to expert interrogatories state that the expert witness will be testifying about subjects A and B, the interrogator may face a difficult choice in deciding whether to ask about subject C. If the answers to interrogatories do not mention C and the subject is not mentioned at the expert's deposition, the court may refuse to allow expert testimony on C at trial unless subject C is a fair extrapolation from A and B.[16] But if subject C was covered at the expert's deposition, the court will almost certainly allow trial testimony on that subject even if it was not included in answers to interrogatories.

Thus, a good argument can be made that the interrogator should steer clear of subject C at the deposition. But, as is so often true, there is also an argument for the opposite side. The interrogator may perceive that sooner or later his opponent is likely to wake up and realize that expert testimony on subject C is essential or helpful to his case. The interrogator can decide to wait and hope that his opponent does not wake up. On the other hand, he may obtain some helpful answers by questioning on subject C before the expert has thought through his position on it or discussed it with counsel.

Further, the court may decide not to exclude testimony on subject C at trial despite its omission from answers to expert interrogatories. It may instead

---

16   *See* Weiss v. Chrysler Motors Corp., 515 F.2d 449 (2d Cir. 1975) (exclusion of testimony because defendant did not supplement responses to expert interrogatories to disclose new defense theory and its basis). *Cf.* Stacey v. Bangor Punta Corp., 107 F.R.D. 786 (D. Me. 1985) (scope of expert witness's testimony not strictly limited to contents of pretrial expert report unless expert's testimony will include data or opinions not previously disclosed in discovery, other side will be prejudiced by the testimony, and no remedy short of exclusion will suffice).

permit the testimony, throwing counsel the sop of taking a supplemental deposition of the expert on subject C some evening during trial, by which time the expert will be very well prepared on it.

Of course, if the interrogator decides to question the expert about subject C, opposing counsel may object to questions on that subject as beyond the scope of the expert's report and may instruct him not to answer. If this happens, the interrogator should probably drop the subject. Unless opposing counsel's position changes well in advance of trial, the interrogator will encounter great difficulty in convincing the court that the expert should be permitted to testify on subject C.

L.   Reading Back the Perfect Question

Some experts have learned to dodge difficult questions by asking the questioner to rephrase them in the hope that the interrogator will not ask the question quite so well the second time. A phrase may be omitted, a word changed. Thus, before rewording the question, the interrogator should ask whether the expert understands the question as originally worded. If the expert concedes that he does, then the interrogator should ask him to answer it and direct the court reporter to read the question back. If the expert says that he does not understand it, the interrogator should determine what is confusing and repeat the question in the original form with the required clarification.

A final note: Although this chapter earlier discussed the risk of destroying the expert at deposition, the interrogator would be unrealistic if he set as his goal in the deposition the destruction of the expert:

> "As a general thing, it is unwise for the cross-examiner
> to attempt to cope with the specialist in his own field of
> inquiry. Lengthy cross-examinations are disastrous and
> should rarely be attempted."[17]

---

17   F.L.Wellman, The Art of Cross-Examination 82 (1903).

CHAPTER NINE

PREPARING THE DEPONENT TO TESTIFY

A.   Introduction

Although this handbook has focused primarily upon the interrogator, the most challenging task is performed by opposing counsel — in preparing the deponent to testify. Counsel for the deponent must anticipate every subject of consequence on which the interrogator may question, the various ways in which the questioning is likely to be structured, and the phrasing of the individual questions. Counsel must then decide, based on the knowledge, intelligence, personality and temperament of the deponent, how to prepare for such questioning.

Some lawyers make the mistake of assuming that while it takes a high degree of skill to take a deposition, even a very junior lawyer should be able to prepare the witness and sit through the deposition. Before deciding to delegate the assignments of preparing and representing the deponent, the senior attorney should give some thought to how crucial the deponent is and what he will say to the client about that delegation if the deponent performs badly.

B.   Attorney-Client Privilege

Before meeting with the deponent, counsel should give thought to whether an attorney-client privilege will exist between them. If it will, then their preparation session will be protected from discovery and at the deposition counsel may instruct the deponent not to answer where appropriate. Conversely, if the privilege does not apply, then at the deposition the deponent must answer questions about conversations with counsel, and counsel cannot instruct the witness not to answer questions on that subject or any other.[1] See Chapter 7, Section T, above.

Counsel should advise the deponent whether the privilege exists and the implications of that fact — that is, that their conversation is (or is not) protected from discovery and that counsel can (or cannot) give the deponent an instruction not to answer at the deposition. The deponent will be more relaxed knowing that he need not answer questions about his conversations with counsel. And if their conversation will not be protected, the deponent should know that from the start so that, for example, he does not make flippant remarks

---

1   Counsel can nevertheless advise, rather than instruct, the witness not to answer. *See* Perrignon v. Bergen Brunswig Corp., 77 F.R.D. 455, 461 (N.D. Cal. 1978).

during the preparation session which he would not want to repeat later at the deposition.

One recurring problem is the situation of the former employee who continues to be friendly with his former employer. Suppose the plaintiff in a lawsuit brought against the former employer serves a notice for the deposition of the former employee to delve into his knowledge of events which occurred during his employment with the corporate defendant.

Should counsel for the former employer attempt to create an attorney-client privilege between him and the deponent and, if so, how should he go about that?[2] The principal advantage of establishing the privilege is one of control: as noted above, if the privilege is present, counsel's conversations with the deponent are protected and counsel may give appropriate instructions not to answer. There is no completely satisfying answer to how to establish the privilege. Probably the best way is for the former employer to offer to have its lawyer represent the former employee at the deposition. Otherwise counsel for the former employer may find himself in the awkward position of offering his services to the former employee when they first meet.

But counsel must balance the short-term advantage of control at the deposition against the long-term disadvantage of how such representation will affect the fact finder's perception of the former employee at trial. Often at trial counsel can portray a former employee as an essentially independent witness, with nothing to gain or lose regardless of the outcome of the case. But can he plausibly maintain that characterization after opposing counsel brings out that the witness retained his former employer's lawyer at no fee to represent him at his deposition where he followed that lawyer's instructions not to answer certain questions? Indeed, there is the danger that these facts may convince the trial court to allow opposing counsel who has called the former employee as his own witness at trial to ask leading questions on the ground that the former employee has become "a witness identified with an adverse party,"under Rule 611(c) of the Federal Rules of Evidence. Any pretense that the witness is independent will then be destroyed.

Counsel should weigh these considerations carefully before agreeing to represent such a deponent.

C.   Fact Gathering Versus Witness Preparation

There is a difference between gathering facts and preparing a witness for deposition. Counsel should be careful not to confuse these two activities.

---

2   At least one appellate court has ruled that predeposition sessions between former employees and counsel for their former employers are protected by the attorney-client privilege without the need for counsel to have been retained by the employees. *In re* Coordinated Pretrial Proceedings in Petroleum Antitrust Litigation, 658 F.2d 1355 (9th Cir. 1981).

When gathering facts, counsel will want the deponent to be very forthcoming and to volunteer important information. By contrast, when preparing the deponent to testify, counsel will want to drill the deponent to answer questions as he would at the deposition: short and to the point, with nothing volunteered. If counsel switches back and forth from fact gathering to deposition preparation, the result may be a witness with little idea of what is expected of him at deposition.

To avoid these problems some litigators prefer to schedule two separate sessions with each deponent — one for fact gathering and another for deposition preparation. But not every case can stand that expense and not every deponent is that cooperative. Even if there will be only one meeting between counsel and the deponent, counsel can achieve some of the benefits of separate meetings by devoting the first half of the meeting to fact gathering and the rest to deposition preparation.

In any event, regardless of the number or structure of meetings, counsel should be sure that the deponent knows at each point what counsel is doing: gathering facts or preparing for the deposition.

D.   Preparation for Fact Gathering

Counsel should prepare for the fact gathering session for several reasons. First, if counsel is not prepared, the session will take longer and be less focused. If the deponent is the client, he will be annoyed that his time is being consumed unnecessarily (while counsel relearns the case) and chagrined to find that his lawyer does not have control of the facts. Second, by being unprepared, counsel will not be sensitive to those points on which the deponent, even if completely truthful, may testify one way or another depending upon how counsel goes about eliciting the facts from him. The account of the facts given by the deponent during the fact-gathering session may set in concrete quickly; by the time the deposition preparation session starts, it may be too late to ask the deponent to recollect whether things really happened as he first said.

Thus, in advance of this fact-gathering session, counsel should review the file so that, at the start of the session, he will have at his fingertips:

- the principal contentions of each of the parties;

- a chronology of the key events giving rise to the lawsuit;

- any statement previously taken from the deponent;

- a clear understanding of where the deponent fits into the underlying facts;

123

- copies of all documents authored by or received by the deponent plus copies of the most important documents in the case and of the deposition exhibits previously marked (whether or not authored by or received by the deponent); and

- a list of all words and actions attributed to the deponent by others in their depositions.

So armed, counsel should be in control of the fact-gathering session from the start.

E. The Fact-Gathering Session

1. Preliminary Information About Depositions

Notwithstanding the desirability of separating fact gathering from witness preparation, at the start of the fact-gathering session, counsel should give the deponent some notion of what a deposition is and what to expect. Otherwise the deponent may be preoccupied with these concerns and his concentration on the facts may suffer.

Perhaps the best way to prepare the witness is to have him attend the deposition of some other deponent. But, as noted at Chapter 7, Section C above, this will not be an option if counsel have agreed to sequester deponents or the court has ordered it. Another way to familiarize a deponent with the deposition process is to show him a deposition transcript, which is, after all, the net result of the taking of the deposition.

Counsel should also explain generally the nature of the lawsuit (the gist of the plaintiff's claim and the principal defenses), what a deposition is (an opportunity for opposing counsel to take the witness's testimony in advance of trial), and the reason why depositions are taken (to allow each party to learn more about the other's case to improve the chances of settlement or, if the case should be tried, of a just result). He should describe for the witness the atmosphere of a deposition.

In addition, counsel should give the deponent some sense of the personality of the interrogator and his style. How old is he? How experienced? Is he aggressive? Argumentative? Or methodical and matter of fact? Is it clear that he, rather than some other lawyer in his office, will take the deposition? Who is the most likely substitute? What is that lawyer like?

Counsel should also inform the witness where the deposition will be taken, who may be present (at a minimum, the interrogator, the stenographer, and perhaps the opposing party), and that the witness will be under oath. Then counsel should tell the deponent that he will instruct him later on rules of thumb to be followed in answering questions at the deposition but that he wants to start his review of the deponent's facts unless the deponent has further questions about the deposition that he is anxious to have answered immediately.

2. *Review of Contentions and Facts*

Next, the lawyer should outline in more detail for the deponent the principal contentions of the parties and review the key facts in dispute. Having provided that framework to the deponent, the lawyer may question him to learn what he knows of the underlying facts. Ordinarily the lawyer will develop the deponent's facts chronologically. That is, he will take each of the key events in order, find out what the deponent knows about it, and then move on to the next. Of course, counsel should be careful to inquire whether the deponent has knowledge of what was happening in the interim between the main events. When he has completed that exercise, counsel should make a crosscut by subject matter to be sure that nothing has been overlooked.

Counsel should be careful not to assume that a deponent lacks knowledge on a subject simply because it is outside his normal sphere of interest. For example, suppose that in a breach-of-contract case counsel for the defendant schedules the deposition of the plaintiff's controller, presumably to explore the plaintiff's claim for damages. In the fact-gathering session, counsel for the plaintiff should not overlook the possibility that the controller is knowledgeable about the liability issues, too. Even if he was not personally involved in any of the underlying dealings between the parties, he may have heard highly relevant statements about those dealings from co-employees. Thus, even in preparing a deponent with seemingly limited knowledge, counsel should review the principal subjects at issue and inquire whether the deponent has any information, first- or second-hand, about them.

The lawyer should be alert to the possibility that a lay deponent will make the erroneous determination that anything he has heard is "hearsay" and should not be repeated either in the preparation session or in the deposition; counsel should explain that he is interested in anything that the deponent might have heard from others. He should also explain that questions about what the deponent has heard or has second-hand knowledge about are generally proper at deposition.

3. *Review of Documents — Rule 612*

If there are many documents to be reviewed with the deponent, counsel must give thought to how that can best be accomplished. The most orderly and easiest approach is to arrange the documents to be reviewed in chronological order. The lawyer then has two alternatives. First, as he reviews the facts in chronological order, he can do the same with the documents, that is, as he discusses with the deponent his knowledge of subject A, he can show him the appropriate documents on that subject. The principal disadvantage of this approach is that the review of the facts becomes attenuated. The deponent may be left with a morass of detail in his head, but no overview.

125

The second approach is to show the deponent only the most important documents in the initial review of the facts, at the end of which the deponent should have a good overview of the history of the key events. Then counsel can make a separate review of the documents with the deponent, which should reinforce his recollection.

In deciding whether to show the deponent a document, particularly one not previously obtained by the other side through discovery, counsel should be cognizant of the risk that "if a witness uses a writing to refresh memory for the purpose of testifying . . . before testifying, if the court in its discretion determines it is necessary in the interests of justice, an adverse party is entitled to have the writing produced . . . ."[3] Even if the documents shown to the deponent were previously produced to the other side, normally counsel for the deponent will want to resist producing those he used in preparing the deponent because of concern that the opponent may thereby gain insight into his thinking.

Counsel for the deponent has these alternatives:

(a) Do not show the document to the deponent and do not describe it to him in such detail as to constitute use of a writing under Rule 612.

(b) Caution the deponent not to say at deposition that a document refreshed his recollection unless it did.

(c) When the interrogator requests the document at the deposition, state for the record (if it is true) that the deponent was shown only copies of documents already produced to the interrogator so that a second production is not "necessary in the interests of justice."

(d) At their meeting, show the deponent many documents already produced to the other side and then, if required to produce documents under Rule 612, produce all of them so that the interrogator will gain little insight into the thinking of opposing counsel.

The lawyer should be careful not to show his work product (summaries of prior depositions, notes of witness interviews, and the like) to a witness before the deposition unless he is willing to risk running afoul of Rule 612. By using his work product or documents ordinarily protected by the attorney-client

---

3   FED. R. EVID. 612. *But see* Sporck v. Peil, 759 F.2d 312 (3d Cir.), *cert. denied*, 474 U.S. 903(1985) (Rule 612 gives way to protection of the attorney's work product in selecting documents under certain circumstances).

privilege to refresh the witness's recollection, the lawyer may be held to have waived any work product protection or privilege.[4] See Chapter 7, Section Y above.

4.   Refreshing — or Not — the Deponent's Recollection

Sometimes the witness will remark that he does not recall whether he attended a certain meeting or, if he did, that he does not remember statements made there. Usually, deponent's counsel will press the witness to refresh his recollection. He may show the deponent minutes of the meeting or correspondence generated soon after the meeting referring to it; he may even tell the witness what others have said about that meeting. In some cases, however, the lawyer may be pleased that the witness does not recall the meeting. A deponent who does not remember a meeting cannot give harmful testimony about comments made there.

The lawyer has no duty to refresh the recollection of the deponent. However, if he does not make such an attempt, he runs the risk that the interrogator will press the deponent and will succeed in jogging his memory. Counsel for the deponent will then face the serious disadvantage of having had no opportunity to probe the deponent's recollection and to alert him to the interrogator's potential questions on this subject. On the other hand, if at their pre-deposition meeting the lawyer attempts to refresh the deponent's recollection, he may succeed and thereby unwittingly help the other side. In the absence of such preparation, the deponent's memory might not have been refreshed, even by the interrogator's thorough questioning.

Tactically, the lawyer preparing the deponent will not want him to be blind-sided by prior deposition testimony inconsistent with his own. Counsel should consider including in the preparation session information about prior

---

4   James Julian, Inc. v. Raytheon Co., 93 F.R.D. 138, 145 (D. Del. 1982) ("Those courts which have considered the issue have generally agreed that the use of protected documents to refresh a witness' memory prior to testifying constitutes a waiver of the protection."); *In re* Comair Air Disaster Litigation, 100 F.R.D. 350, 353 (E.D. Ky. 1983) (acccident reports that were trial preparation materials under Fed. R. Civ. P. 26(b)(3) discoverable because used by witness in preparation for deposition and thus "substantial need" test was met); Wheeling-Pittsburgh Steel Corp. v. Underwriters Laboratories, Inc. 81 F.R.D. 8 (N.D. Ill. 1978) (plaintiff waived attorney-client privilege for certain documents by allowing witness to review them prior to his deposition); Berkey Photo, Inc. v. Eastman Kodak Co., 74 F.R.D. 613, 616 (S.D.N.Y. 1977) (holding prospectively that under Fed. R. Evid. 612 there is powerful reason to require production of documents considered attorney work product if used to refresh a witness's memory before or during a deposition). *But see* Bloch v. SmithKline Beckman Corp., Civil Action No. 82-510 (E.D. Pa. April 9, 1987) (upholding work product protection and rejecting plaintiff's demand under Fed. R. Evid. 612 for defense counsel's summary of prior interview with deponent reviewed by deponent before deposition); Carter-Wallace, Inc. v. Hartz Mountain Industries, 553 F. Supp. 47, 52 (S.D.N.Y. 1982) (refusing to order production of documents protected by work product doctrine).

deposition testimony, particularly versions of the facts that do not square with that of the deponent. Knowing that a deponent may be questioned about how he prepared for the deposition, however, counsel should think twice about giving the deponent portions of transcripts of previous depositions to review. Rather, counsel may choose to discuss with the witness the gist of relevant prior testimony and thereby improve the chances that his selection of prior testimony that he thinks is significant for that witness will be protected from discovery.

The purpose of such preparation is not to have the deponent mechanically conform his testimony to what has gone before if his recollection is different, but rather to alert him to apparent discrepancies between his account of the facts as told to counsel and prior testimony, and to let the deponent know the background knowledge of the interrogator. Apparent discrepancies may result simply from different ways of stating the same information or from the deponent's guesswork or incomplete memory. The lawyer can work with the deponent to avoid creating apparent inconsistencies between his testimony and that of an earlier witness. Discussing prior testimony with the deponent will also assist counsel in pinpointing areas where the witnesses really do diverge and in developing an explanation for any serious discrepancies.

5.   The Deponent's Efforts To Refresh Recollection

At the conclusion of the fact-gathering session, the lawyer and the deponent should have a clear understanding as to what, if anything, the deponent plans to do to refresh his recollection further. Sometimes the lawyer will be concerned that further inquiry by the deponent (speaking to other witnesses and reviewing other documents) may make the deponent knowledgeable about harmful facts that he will be obliged to reveal at the deposition if asked appropriate questions, and so he will instruct the witness not to make such inquiries.

In other cases, the attorney will prefer that the deponent confirm his recollection of certain facts by consulting other people or documents so that, having assured himself of the accuracy of his recollection, he is then likely to testify with greater confidence. Indeed, if the point on which the deponent is somewhat uncertain is important enough, the lawyer may recess their meeting so that the deponent can make a telephone call to confirm his recollection. In any event, the deponent should not be given a roving commission to collect and verify facts; he and his attorney should agree on what questions he will ask of whom and what documents he will review.

F.   Fact Reconstruction

During both the fact-gathering session and the deposition-preparation session, counsel for the deponent should be sensitive to subjects on which the deponent's recollection is equivocal so that, even if completely truthful, the deponent may testify one way or another depending upon how his lawyer goes about developing the facts. This process might be called fact reconstruction.

1.   The Order of Asking Questions

Sometimes the order in which the attorney asks questions will affect the substance of the answers given, that is, the way in which the facts are reconstructed.

For example, suppose that A and B are brothers; A owns 49 percent of the stock of a family corporation and his wife owns 1 percent; B owns 49 percent and his wife 1 percent. Over time, the relationship between A and B has deteriorated. For many years, corporate affairs were conducted quite informally. A and B would attend annual shareholders' meetings and elect themselves directors; the wives never attended those meetings, nor did either provide a proxy. Because A and B were unable to agree, no third director was elected. Following the shareholders' meeting, A and B would hold a directors' meeting at which they would elect themselves vice presidents. Because of the brewing hostility between them, no president was elected.

In the year in question, after the shareholders' meeting starts, B's wife joins the meeting. B and his wife deny A's request for a postponement to allow time for A's wife to join the meeting. B and his wife, now holding a 50 percent to 49 percent edge, elect themselves — and not A — directors, and then move directly to a directors' meeting at which they elect themselves officers and vote to fire A. A starts a lawsuit challenging that action. His complaint alleges that there was an implied contract between him and B to vote as they had for many years unless notice were given of intention not to do so.

One question likely to be asked by B's attorney at A's deposition is whether it occurred to A before the meeting at issue that B's wife might attend and vote. If it occurred to him, he must explain why he neither inquired of B whether his wife planned to attend nor arranged for his own wife to do so or to provide a proxy. Further, if he entertained such a thought, it would undermine his claim that there was an implied contract that only A and B, and not their wives, would ever vote, absent notice of intention to change the longstanding practice.

In reviewing the facts with A before the deposition, his attorney might just ask him straight out, "Did it occur to you that B's wife might attend the meeting?" The danger in that approach is that A, considering himself an astute businessman and wanting to appear that way to others, may think that that thought (so obvious in hindsight) must have occurred to him, so he says "Yes," that it did occur to him. Once A says that, it may be difficult or impossible for his lawyer to dislodge that answer — even though it is contrary to A's interest and probably not true.

On the other hand, suppose A's lawyer, being sensitive to this risk, jumps ahead in their chronology and works backward. Their dialogue might read this way:

Q. What was your reaction when Mrs. B entered the room?

A. I was astonished.

Q. What did you say?

A. I said, "What kind of a dirty trick is this?"

Q. Why did you call it "a dirty trick"?

A. Because that's what it was.

Q. Didn't it occur to you before the meeting that B might bring his wife?

A. Of course not. Our wives had never attended these meetings. And, in spite of our disagreements, that's not the way we dealt with each other. If it had occurred to me, I would have brought my own wife.

Thus, by establishing certain preliminary facts before asking the crucial question, counsel for the deponent has prepared him to give a more favorable and, it might be argued, more truthful answer.

2. Scene Re-creation

Another important aspect of fact reconstruction is scene re-creation. Particularly where the deponent's recollection of a disputed conversation is hazy, counsel can give the deponent greater confidence in recalling what was said by asking questions to show that if the other side's version of the conversation were correct, the deponent would have taken different actions after the conclusion of the conversation than he actually did.

By way of example, suppose that A and B enter into a contract whereby B, an engineering firm, agrees to supervise the construction on A's property of a cyclator, a large cylindrical tank with a horizontal rotating arm which is to be used to separate pulp from a mixture. B takes soil borings to be sure that the ground where the cyclator is to be located is sufficiently firm so that its concrete base will not settle and shift; if the cyclator is not perfectly level, it will not function. The results of the soil borings are somewhat equivocal. B takes further soil borings which are reassuring to some extent but leave some doubt as to the suitability of the site. B's project chief and A's representative then discuss the matter.

130

The cyclator is constructed. After operating satisfactorily for two years, the foundation shifts, causing the cyclator to tilt and become inoperable. A starts suit against B for negligence in its selection of the site for the cyclator.

There is a dispute as to what was said during the preconstruction conversation. B's project chief confidently testifies at his deposition that during that conversation he reported the results of the soil borings to A's representative, and said that while they appeared to be satisfactory enough to warrant going forward, A would have to recognize and assume the risk that the concrete base might settle and shift, causing the cyclator to tilt.

A's representative does not recall the conversation very clearly, partly because of the passage of time and partly because at the time neither party expected a problem to arise. He remembers that the last results were reported to him and that he was told that they were reassuring. He recalls, too, that B's project chief said that he could not rule out the possibility that the cyclator might shift position and he thinks that he replied to the effect that this was why A had hired B, that is, to make this kind of professional judgment, and that B would have to decide whether it was appropriate to proceed. But, because his memory of the conversation is flawed, A's representative is tentative in his denial of the claim that B's project chief told him that A would have to assume the risk.

Rather than just pressing A's representative to search his memory further (which he has probably already done *ad nauseam*), counsel for A might recreate the conversation with the deponent and then press him as to what he would have done if things had happened as B's project chief claims. Thus, he might say something like this to the deponent:

> You and B's fellow are discussing the new soil boring results. He says that they look pretty good but there is still some question whether the foundation will support the cyclator. Suppose he then says that your company, A, will have to assume the risk that the cyclator might settle and tilt.
>
> If he had said that, would you have said "Fine," and gone back to work?
>
> What was the contract price for the cyclator? Wasn't $5 million a substantial investment for your company? Did you have authority to accept a $5 million risk for your company on your own?
>
> Can the cyclator be operated if it tilts? Did you know that back at the time of your conversation?

If he had really made this assume-the-risk comment, would you have agreed to accept that liability without consulting anyone else in the company? Whom would you have consulted? Did you in fact consult them?

When you first learned that the cyclator had tilted, did you say to yourself, "I'm in trouble now," or anything like that?

Think back to your conversation. Do you have any recollection of B's project chief saying that your company would have to assume the risk of this kind of a catastrophe?

Having reconstructed in his own mind what he would have done if the other side's account were accurate, the deponent should testify with greater assurance that no such thing was said during the conversation.

3. Unethical Conduct

Counsel for the deponent should be careful in fact reconstruction. There is a point at which aggressive lawyering becomes unethical conduct. It is important that the lawyer say and repeat — and mean — that his objective in preparing the witness is the truth.

G. Deposition Preparation

1. Rules of Thumb

Before their meeting, some lawyers furnish the deponent with a letter or preparation sheet outlining basic points of deposition procedure and how the deponent should behave.[5] Even so, at the start of the deposition preparation session, the lawyer for the deponent should review basic rules of thumb on how to answer questions at a deposition. Most formulations come down to this:

(a)   Listen to the question.

(b)   Be sure you hear the question.

(c)   Be sure you understand the question.

---

5   Examples are found in Block & Ferris, *Basic Techniques for Defending Depositions,* 9 ALI-ABA COURSE MATERIALS J. 115–19 (1985); D. DANNER, PATTERN DISCOVERY : ANTITRUST at 614 (1981); and A. MORRILL, TRIAL DIPLOMACY, §12.20 (2d ed. 1972).

(d)   Answer the question, nothing more. Do not volunteer.

(e)   If your first answer was truthful, stick to it.

(f)   Tell the truth.

A sample script of the lawyer's preparatory remarks to the deponent on these six basic rules and certain corollaries may be found in the Appendix under "Practical Tips."[6] To avoid undue repetition, what is set forth at length there will not be set out here as well.

Even if the deponent has been previously prepared to testify in some other case by the same lawyer and is bright and articulate, the lawyer should insist on reviewing the basic rules of thumb for testifying as if he and the witness were working together for the first time. If the witness resists, the lawyer might say, "Look, anybody can have a bad day testifying. If you have a bad day, I don't want the two of us to be wondering whether you might have done better if we had taken the time to review the basics."

The lawyer should make certain the witness understands that the deposition has been scheduled by the opposing party and that it is not the proper forum for the deponent to prove his case. It may be useful to explain to the deponent that he will be in a position comparable to that of a soccer goalie attempting to prevent the opponent from scoring. If he decides to run down the field and score by making self-serving speeches, he increases the danger of being scored upon himself.

The witness should appreciate direct advice from his attorney. The lawyer, for example, may remark:

> Look, Mr. Haley, I'm not much use to you unless I talk straight to you. You're a good salesman and I can see why. You have an engaging manner and customers must enjoy spending time with you. But we are not trying to sell a computer here. For your own good, let me tell you that your answers are much too long. Answer the question and then keep quiet.

If the lawyer senses that the deponent is not being truthful, he should press him further. The attorney might comment, for example, "Mr. Spiegel, that doesn't make an ounce of sense to me. It won't to the other lawyers or, later, to the jury." The truth is rarely as damaging as some tale concocted by the deponent.

---

6   The script is a shortened form of "Segal's Six Rules," so named because they are the product of Irving R. Segal, Esq., whom we must thank for their use here, as well as their proven usefulness in practice.

2. *Putting the Deponent "On the Stand"*

Having reviewed the facts and these rules of thumb, the attorney for the deponent will then put him "on the stand" and ask questions which he anticipates from the interrogator. From time to time, the lawyer will interrupt this exercise to caution the witness that, for example, he is giving more information than the question calls for or to ask follow-up fact questions for his own benefit.

The lawyer and the witness should agree to some system so that the witness knows whether he is supposed to answer as he would at the deposition or is "off the stand" and so should be more forthcoming in expressing his concerns and in providing supplemental information. One approach is for the lawyer to tell the witness directly whether he is on or off the stand and to use the witness's last name when he is on the stand and his first name when he is off. Thus, he might say, "You're on the stand, Ms. Kutler"; and then, "You're off the stand. Now, Marilyn . . . ." Or the lawyer and the deponent can physically move to different chairs in the conference room when the deponent is off the stand.

During the preparation session, the lawyer and the witness should not lapse into speaking colloquially about the facts or documents in the case. There is too much danger that the deponent will slip and use the same language at his deposition. For example, if there is a document that the other side appears to think is very damaging to the witness's case, the lawyer and the witness should avoid speaking of it in shorthand as "the smoking gun" lest the witness inadvertently refer to it the same way at his deposition.

The lawyer should drill the witness so that he knows and follows the rules of thumb. If the witness tends to give overly long answers, the lawyer should ask him a series of questions which can be answered with a word or two and then, after the witness has caught on, move to questions requiring longer answers.

Some deponents, particularly chief executive officers, have difficulty answering, "I don't know." Again, the lawyer should ask a series of questions to which there is no other appropriate reply and force the deponent to say it out loud so that he becomes comfortable with the idea that this is an acceptable answer.

Although it is sometimes said that the lawyer preparing the deponent should strive to be harder on him than the interrogator will be, that idea can be overdone. If the lawyer preparing the witness repeatedly drives him to his knees, the witness may enter the deposition room with little confidence in himself. Thus, the lawyer may consider interrupting his mock interrogation just after the witness has given a carelessly worded answer that ultimately can be used against him if the questioning is pursued skillfully, but before the witness has been verbally backed into a corner; the lawyer can explain to the witness how the interrogator would be able to take advantage of the way the witness has phrased his answer, but without forcing him into submission.

The lawyer must also determine the limitations of the deponent he is preparing. Infrequently, he may decide that the witness does not have the capacity to be thoroughly prepared on all subjects. The result of attempting to prepare him on all subjects may be that he will testify well on none. Consequently, the attorney may decide to cover only the most important subjects and prepare the witness to defend his ground on those topics, recognizing that the interrogator may score in other areas.

Suppose, for example, the plaintiff was injured when the car he was driving was involved in a right-angle collision. He may be completely honest and have a valid claim, but may be easily confused by detailed questioning on speeds, distances and times. His lawyer accordingly may focus his preparation almost exclusively on the crucial points (that the plaintiff had the green light, was within the speed limit, looked both ways as he entered the intersection, and that the other vehicle appeared to be slowing up) and cover the other details of the accident in a more cursory manner. Counsel may rightly conclude that if the plaintiff appears honest on the main points, he will win. If drilled on less important details, he may be unable to absorb them all, resulting in poor answers on all issues.

3.   *Preparing the Deponent To Answer Questions Aggressively*

Perhaps the most challenging aspect of preparing the deponent to testify is giving him some notion of when he should disregard the fourth rule ("Answer the question. Don't volunteer"), and be more aggressive in answering questions. Uncompromising adherence to the rule against volunteering can create significant problems.

For example, take a case in which the purchaser of a computer alleges that the manufacturer's sales representative misstated the capabilities of the computer. If the sales representative were slavishly following the fourth rule, he would testify this way:

Q.   At the meeting of January 22, when you made a sales presentation to representatives of this purchaser, did you tell them that this computer was capable of storing X amount of material with the brand Y general ledger package?

A.   Yes.

Q.   In fact, was the computer capable of doing that?

A.   No.

135

Q. When you made that statement at the meeting of January 22, did you intend the purchaser's representatives would rely upon that information in deciding whether to buy your computer?

A. Yes.

If following the fourth rule strictly, the sales representative would not "volunteer" that upon returning to the office following that meeting, he (a) discovered he had given erroneous information, and (b) immediately telephoned the purchaser's senior representative to correct this error.

Of course, counsel for the manufacturer might wait until trial to elicit this testimony. But, as noted previously in Chapter 4, Section A this delayed explanation, even though not given at the deposition because not directly asked for, may appear to the fact finder to be a feeble and disingenuous attempt to evade the force of damning deposition testimony.

Or, after counsel for the purchaser has finished interrogating, the manufacturer might ask some questions to bring out this critical information. But, again, if the deposition transcript shows breaks between the original harmful testimony and the rehabilitative questioning by counsel for the manufacturer during which the deponent may have conferred with his employer's attorney or others, the attorney for the purchaser may exploit that fact to suggest that the delayed explanation is a sorry fiction.

Consequently, the lawyer preparing the deponent to testify must give the deponent some sense of when to disregard the proscription against volunteering and take the offensive. There is no ready formula available to the lawyer or the deponent. Usually the best that the lawyer can do is to take three or so examples of possible lines of questioning (such as the one above) where, if the deponent does nothing more than answer the question, the result will be a seemingly devastating deposition segment, and hope that the deponent gains some intuitive sense of when to take the offensive.

Counsel should explain to the witness that the conflicting instructions being given ("Just answer the question" versus "You can't just let it go at that") arise from the tension between the generally recognized rule not to volunteer and the reality that unwavering fidelity to the rule may create worse problems than it avoids.

In summary, the lawyer should instruct the deponent to follow the general rule if in doubt, but to use common sense in deciding whether to say more.

4. Preparing the Deponent on Documents

Preliminarily, the concerns about the discoverability of documents reviewed in fact gathering discussed in Section E.3 of this chapter apply equally to preparation.

The attorney should advise the witness that he may be shown and questioned about specific documents at the deposition. When shown a document (even one with which he is quite familiar) at the deposition, the deponent should force himself to slow down and look at the date, the author, the addressee, and those to whom copies were sent. He should then read silently as much of the document as necessary to answer the interrogator's questions. Sometimes that will mean reading the entire document word for word; if the questioning is very limited, reading a paragraph may suffice. The deponent should follow the same routine with each document so as not to rely solely on his memory of the contents of a document in answering questions about it and so as not to betray inadvertently to the interrogator which documents he reviewed to prepare for the deposition.

The lawyer should caution the witness that there are several different tactics available to the interrogator besides just asking questions to elicit supplemental information about the contents of the document. First, the interrogator may ask broad open-ended questions, such as, "What did you mean when you said . . . in this letter?" The question is not as innocuous as it looks: If the deponent meant something other than what he said, why did he not say what he really meant? The deponent can avoid that snare by answering, if it is true, that he meant what he said. On the other hand, if the letter was not so artfully drafted, that kind of question provides a good opportunity for a skillful deponent to add an explanatory gloss supportive of his side of the case.

Similarly, the interrogator may ask, "What was your purpose in sending this letter?" The question poses risks because it is an invitation to the deponent to ramble. Often the best answer is a succinct, "To convey the information in the letter to the addressee." Again, if the contents of the letter are troublesome to the deponent's side of the case, an experienced and nimble deponent can sometimes use that kind of question to explain away seemingly harmful statements in the letter.

Second, the interrogator may go to the opposite extreme and ask narrow precise questions. Suppose the deponent sent a letter to a supplier which said:

> I am writing to renew for three years our existing contract which is to expire in six months. Please sign the enclosed copy of this letter and return it to me if that is agreeable to you.

* * *

> We shall meet within 60 days to review terms and sign a new contract.

The letter is signed and returned by the supplier but disagreements then develop between the parties so that no new contract is executed. The supplier then brings suit, contending that the letter coupled with the existing contract is sufficient to create a new contract for three more years. The deponent denies that, saying that the letter was nothing more than an unenforceable agreement to agree.

The deponent should be prepared to deal with narrow questions honed to the specific language of the letter, such as, "Did you write this letter to renew for three years your existing contract with the supplier?" Or, "Was your purpose in writing this letter to have the supplier sign if it was agreeable to him to renew the existing contract for three years?" Although these questions are focused narrowly on the exact words of the letter, the deponent's answers should not be (if it was truly not his intention to renew the contract). To defend his position, he must be prepared to respond by pointing to the last paragraph of this letter, which seems to contemplate further negotiations.

Thus, to stand on the language of the document may sometimes be the best response and at other times the worst. As with so many other aspects of deposition practice, there is no one right way to do things in all circumstances.

If the witness does not remember a document, even one which he appears to have written or received, the attorney should advise him to testify at deposition that he does not remember — and nothing more. The deponent should resist the temptation to speculate about why it was written, even if he thinks he knows.

The attorney should alert the deponent that if he has read the depositions of other witnesses, he may be asked whether he noted any inaccuracies in those transcripts. Some lawyers will object to the question as overly broad and instruct the deponent not to answer. But counsel for the deponent may want to avoid giving such an instruction and, even if given, it may be overruled. Often the deponent can answer the question truthfully by stating that he did not read every page and line of the deposition and did not read the transcripts for the purpose of appraising their accuracy.

5.   Using Videotapes

Videotapes can be used in two ways in preparing the deponent. First, particularly if the preparation session is likely to be lengthy, the lawyer can vary things — and reinforce his own instructions to the deponent — by showing him one of the professionally done tapes on witness preparation. Second, the lawyer can have an operator videotape his mock interrogation of the deponent and then use the tape in critiquing the deponent's performance. While use of the video camera in the preparation session may be a luxury for the typical deposition, it should be considered essential if the deposition itself will be videotaped. Using the camera in the preparation session will help the deponent to become more comfortable with its presence, and seeing himself on videotape beforehand may enable him to perform better at the deposition.

6.   *When To Meet the Deponent*

It is usually a mistake to postpone meeting the witness until the morning of the deposition. First, the deponent may be apprehensive about the deposition upon arriving at the lawyer's office at, say, 8:30 a.m. and there will be little time to reassure the deponent if the lawyer is working against a deadline of 9:50 a.m. (the time they must leave to go the interrogator's office for the deposition).

Second, counsel may find the witness's testimony is unexpectedly shaky on one subject or another and there may be insufficient time to reconstruct the facts. It may also turn out that the witness has knowledge, although scant, about areas that the lawyer did not anticipate, and again the lawyer will not have time to reconstruct the facts with him.

Third, the witness will have no time to verify simple facts which will allow him to testify with greater confidence. For example, suppose the witness cannot recall with certainty whether the road on which he was travelling at the time of his accident had two travel lanes or four. While he may intellectually accept his lawyer's assurance that there were only two, he will be a more comfortable deponent if there is time between the preparation session and the deposition itself so that he can revisit the scene and confirm this undisputed fact.

It is usually wise to schedule the meeting (or meetings if there will be separate sessions for fact gathering and deposition preparation) three to seven days before the deposition. If it is earlier than that, the lawyer's cautions to the witness may fade in the witness's memory; if it is later, there may be insufficient time for the witness to make inquiries to shore up his recollection where it is not firm.

Of course, the lawyer should have a brush-up meeting with the witness on the morning of the deposition to reinforce his understanding of the rules of thumb and to go over the most important substantive areas on which the attorney expects the interrogator to question. Invariably, the deponent shows up with one or two questions that have troubled him as he has mulled things over after the preparation session.

7.   *"Frisking" the Deponent*

The attorney should "frisk" the witness when they meet to prepare for the deposition. If he has in his briefcase and pockets items that have not been requested by the other side (*e.g.*, a pocket calendar), the attorney should suggest that the deponent not bring them on the morning of the deposition.

The attorney should "frisk" the deponent again on the morning of the deposition. Does he have a briefcase with him? What is in it? Anything pertaining to this case? Is he carrying a pocket calendar or any other papers containing information about this case (*e.g.*, a tout sheet noting key dates)? Should they be left in the attorney's office and retrieved after the deposition? If the deponent walks into the deposition room with a briefcase, there is a significant risk that the interrogator will ask whether it contains anything pertaining to the dispute between the parties.

Once the lawyer has prepared the witness, he cannot relax. Although a well-prepared deponent should be able to handle much of what will come his way at the deposition, his lawyer will still be called upon to be a participant and not just an onlooker at the deposition. The next chapter deals with the lawyer's role in defending a deposition.

CHAPTER TEN

DEFENDING THE DEPONENT AT THE DEPOSITION

A.   Recapitulation

In discussing the conduct of the interrogator, this handbook has, of necessity, also dealt at a number of points with that of the lawyer defending the deponent. These two, the interrogator and the defender, do not perform in separate arenas, but grapple directly in an intriguing and often protracted match of intellect, wits and bluff.

Rather than just giving general references to places in the foregoing text where the conduct of the lawyer defending a witness is discussed, the points previously made about the conduct of the defender are recapitulated as follows:

1. *The Lawyer's Manner.* The defender should strive to prevent the interrogator from taking control of the deposition. Normally the defender achieves this objective by choosing his ground carefully and not retreating simply because he has been challenged. For example, he should not withdraw an instruction not to answer just because the interrogator announces that he is recessing the deposition to seek a ruling from the court. (See Chapter 5.)

2. *Who Sits Where.* The defender should be sure that the deponent is comfortably seated in the deposition room, and not, for example, facing glare from a window behind the interrogator. (See Chapter 7, Section A.)

3. *"The Usual Stipulations."*   Ordinarily the defender should not waive reading and signing of the deposition to be sure that the deponent is afforded an opportunity to make appropriate corrections; he should not care whether certification, sealing and filing are waived; and he should welcome a stipulation reserving all objections except as to the form of the question (since otherwise he would be at greater risk of having waived any objection by not making it at the deposition). (See Chapter 7, Section D.)

4. *The Interrogator's Preliminary Instructions to the Deponent.* The defender should be prepared to respond to arguably inappropriate instructions. For example, suppose the interrogator tells the deponent that if he answers a question, the interrogator will assume that he has heard it and understood it; in response, the defender might note that the interrogator should not make that assumption since it is always possible that, notwithstanding this instruction, the deponent will misunderstand some question. (See Chapter 7, Section E.)

5. The Need To Visualize the Transcript. The interrogator should "see" the transcript as testimony is given and be alert to note for the record things that affect meaning but that will not otherwise be reflected in the transcript, such as a rising inflection indicating that the deponent is asking a question, not making a statement. (See Chapter 7, Section F.)

6. Private Conversations Between the Deponent and His Counsel. The defender should not initiate a private conversation with the deponent at any time during the deposition, particularly when a question is pending, although he may confer with him during breaks. The deponent should not initiate a private conference with his lawyer while a question is pending. One exception: if the deponent or the defending attorney is concerned that answering the question may reveal privileged information, it is appropriate for either to initiate a conference, even while a question is pending, but only for the limited purpose of making that determination as to the privilege. (See Chapter 7, Section G.)

7. The Deponent Who Says Too Much. If the interrogator chastises the deponent for "making speeches," the defender should come to his aid, note that the answer given provided the information called for by the question, and tell the interrogator to stop his efforts to intimidate the deponent. (See Chapter 7, Section K.)

8. The Lawyer Who Says Too Much. The defender is rarely justified in interjecting the comments "If you know" or "If you remember." More generally, the defender's comments should not be thinly veiled efforts to testify for the deponent or to prompt him as to how he should testify. (See Chapter 7, Section M.)

9. The Deponent Who Needs Time. If the deponent says that he would need time to answer a question (for example, to make mathematical calculations), the defender should consider instructing him not to make such calculations at the deposition. A mistake made in determining the appropriate mathematical formula or in making calculations may plague the deponent for the duration of the case. The defender should couple his instruction not to answer with an offer to provide the requested information by a supplemental letter. (See Chapter 7, Section N.)

10. Going Off the Record. The defender should remind the deponent, if necessary, that ordinarily the stenographer will not honor a request by the deponent that a comment is "off the record" and thus should not be recorded. From the point of view of the deponent and the defender, nothing is "off the record" since there is always the danger that the interrogator will ask the deponent to confirm on the record what he has just said off. (See Chapter 7, Section O.)

11. Starting and Ending Times and Breaks. The defending lawyer should be careful about suggestions that the interrogator be permitted to question the deponent without periodic breaks or a recess for lunch. The same caution applies to continuing the deposition much past 5:00 p.m. Tired witnesses make mistakes. The defending lawyer should make his own decision on such matters and not rely on the deponent's assurance that he feels fine. (See Chapter 7, Section P.)

12. Counsel's Reactions to Answers — Good or Bad. Counsel for the deponent should not react to harmful answers in a way which amounts to a concession that a point has been scored against him. He may consider interrupting to seek clarification of a seemingly harmful answer but should recognize the risk that the deponent may reaffirm such damaging deposition testimony.

The defending attorney should avoid patently defensive antics when the interrogator is close to hitting paydirt because his actions will tip off the interrogator. (See Chapter 7, Section Q.)

13. Documents and Drawings. The defending attorney should be alert to object to efforts by the interrogator to link, by the numbering system used for exhibits, documents that are not obviously related to one another. For example, if the interrogator marks two documents as Exhibits 7A and 7B (rather than 7 and 8), he is suggesting that there is a connection between them.

The defending attorney should review each exhibit to be sure that all of the pages comprise just one document and to be sure that no pages or attachments are missing. He should note for the record any such apparent irregularity in the exhibit.

If the interrogator requests that the deponent make a drawing (of the scene of the accident, for example) but the defending attorney is doubtful about the deponent's ability to do so, he should instruct him not to comply. A significant error or omission may affect the entire course of the case. On the other hand, if the interrogator has available a prepared drawing which the witness can confirm to be accurate, the interrogator should be permitted to use it in his questioning. (See Chapter 7, Section R.)

14. Objections. Generally speaking, the defending attorney must object at the deposition if the ground for the objection is one that might be removed if made then. When in doubt, prudent counsel should object and state the grounds for the objection. Certainly if the interrogator requests a statement of the grounds, it should be given so that the interrogator has an opportunity to cure the objection at that time.

Ordinarily the defending attorney should not object just because of some small but immaterial flaw in the question; he should keep in mind that every objection breaks the concentration of the deponent. Similarly, if there is a limited amount of time for the deposition, the wise defender will not object to completely irrelevant but harmless questioning that consumes time.

If the deponent answers an improper question before the defending attorney can interpose an objection, the defender should so state for the record and move to strike the answer. (See Chapter 7, Section S.)

15. Instructions Not to Answer. Instructions not to answer should be given rarely unless the basis for the instruction is that the question seeks to elicit

143

testimony about privileged communications or confidential business information or invades the deponent's Fifth Amendment right not to incriminate himself. Often the defending attorney can avoid giving such an instruction by requesting that the question be narrowed or reworded.

If the defending attorney instructs the deponent not to answer a particular question, the interrogator may ask the defender to confirm that the defender would instruct the deponent not to answer all other questions on the same subject. Rather than taking that seemingly arbitrary position, usually the defending attorney will state that he would have to hear each question and make an individual decision.

If the question is objectionable because it seeks privileged information, the defender will have no choice but to give an instruction not to answer. Sometimes the problem can be solved if counsel agree on the record that allowing the witness to answer certain questions which arguably seek privileged information will not constitute a waiver of the privilege. Similarly, an instruction not to answer a question because it calls for confidential business information may be obviated by a confidentiality agreement.

The defending lawyer should keep in mind that he may himself be bound at trial by the instructions which he gave at the deposition. Thus, upon objection by opposing counsel, he may not be permitted to elicit from his own witness at trial any information that he instructed the witness not to reveal at his deposition. (See Chapter 7, Section T.)

16. Obtaining Rulings on Instructions Not To Answer. If the interrogator seeks an immediate ruling on the instruction not to answer (by telephoning the chambers of the judge to whom the case has been assigned), the defender must be prepared to state the basis for the instruction and to make a brief argument in support of the propriety of the instruction. Alternatively, the deponent's lawyer may suggest, if appropriate, that the court defer a ruling until the matter has been briefed. (See Chapter 7, Section U.)

17. Questioning One's Own Witness. After the interrogator has completed his questioning, counsel for the deponent may ask his own questions. Usually he will not elect to do so, primarily because of the danger that it will lead to another, perhaps more damaging, round of questioning by the original interrogator. In deciding whether to question the deponent, the defender should consider (a) the possibility that the deponent may be unavailable at trial; (b) the extent to which the deponent has been damaged by opposing counsel; (c) the danger that needed clarifications may sound disingenuous if first made at trial; and (d) the defender's sense of the deponent's ability to defend the clarifications made in answering his questions if then subjected to further questioning by other counsel. (See Chapter 7, Section V.)

18. Recessing or Concluding the Deposition. Ordinarily the defending lawyer should oppose the interrogator's efforts to keep the deposition open (by, saying, for example, that he has "no more questions for now," or by declaring

144

the deposition "recessed"). The defender should object to leaving the deposition open, invite the interrogator to ask any additional questions he may have, and state that he will not produce the deponent for another session at a later time. With such a record, the court may conclude that the deponent should not be required to return for further interrogation. (See Chapter 7, Section W.)

B.   The Defending Lawyer as a Presence

The defending attorney should be a presence, "not a potted plant." In a broad sense, the defender establishes himself as a presence whenever he speaks effectively. The deponent should sense, feel and know that the defending attorney is there to protect him.

This does not mean that the defending attorney should interfere with proper questioning of the deponent. He should not make captious objections or give instructions not to answer on flimsy bases. Indeed, as previously noted, such antics may be distracting to the deponent, particularly if they lead to bickering between the attorneys, and they will not enhance the defender's standing with the interrogator.

The defender may establish himself as a presence in several ways. First, he does so when he makes a crisp business-like objection or when he confidently gives an instruction not to answer, in each case coupled with a brief statement of his grounds.

Second, the defender may establish himself as an active participant by pressing the interrogator to ask additional questions. Although the defender will normally prefer that the deponent do nothing more than answer the question, sometimes he will want the deponent to be more forthcoming, either because the answer standing alone may sound bad, or because he fears that later it may appear that the deponent was being too literal in answering the question (that is, that the deponent was being evasive). In these circumstances, the defender may say to the interrogator something like, "There's a lot more to it than that as you will find if you ask appropriate follow-up questions." Or, "If you expand your question to include telephone conversations as well as meetings, I think you'll find that there were communications on that subject."

Or the defender can exert control by reminding the deponent, where appropriate, of the rules of thumb for testifying as the following examples illustrate:

(a)   If the deponent is looking at the last exhibit as the interrogator is beginning to ask about a new subject, the defender may ask, "Are you listening to the question?"

(b)   If someone sneezes as the question is being asked, "Did you hear the entire question?"

(c)   If the question is a long and convoluted one, "Do you understand the question?"

(d)   If the deponent is beginning to give more expansive answers than the questions require, "Just answer the question; don't make speeches."   Or, "You can answer that question with a 'yes' or 'no.' "

(e)   If the question was previously answered, "Asked and answered. Are you asking whether he sticks to his earlier answer to the same question?" (Some defenders will add, "when he told you that he wasn't involved in that decision," but the court may frown on that kind of comment as an improper attempt to prompt the deponent.)

In some cases, the defender may sense that the interrogator is establishing a comfortable rapport with the deponent, perhaps even engaging in humorous banter, so that the deponent is beginning to let his guard down. If there will be no recess in the near future when he can speak privately with the deponent, the defender may reprimand the deponent with something like, "Mr. Garner, there's nothing amusing about this procedure. Keep concentrating." Even if taken aback at first, the deponent will appreciate being reminded of the seriousness of the answers he gives.

The defender can also ensure that the deponent continues to keep his eye on the ball by reminding him at breaks to listen to the questions and not to volunteer. Although the lawyer should be reassuring about the deponent's performance, he should not contribute to overconfidence. It is sometimes a mistake to tell the deponent that he is doing well before the deposition is over. Having been complimented on their performance during the first portion of their deposition, some witnesses decide that they are going to do even better when the deposition resumes — and ham things up badly. Thus, the lawyer defending the deponent may decide to tell him nothing more than, "You're doing all right so far," until the deposition is concluded. Even then it may be a mistake to compliment the deponent extravagantly; he may have to testify again at the trial.

The defending lawyer must continually remain aware of his obligation to protect the deponent from harassment and undue burden at the deposition. One instance of possible oppressive conduct is the (infrequent) practice of double-teaming in which more than one lawyer for the same party attempts to question the deponent. The defender should consider instructing the deponent not to answer questions from the second would be interrogator, particularly if his appearance is not entered in the action.[1]

A difficult problem for any defender is the skillful interrogator who asks incisive, technically unobjectionable questions and asks them quickly. The deponent may begin to race to give his answers at the same speed and then develop the sense that he is being relentlessly pursued by a merciless predator who will not let him catch his breath. Meanwhile, the defender who is looking for the opening of an objectionable-as-to-form question may see none and thus no way to aid the deponent.

Without being obstructive, the defender can break the interrogator's cadence by, for example, asking to have the question read back, by inquiring as to the last exhibit number, by asking when the interrogator next plans to take a short recess, or by saying just about anything else so long as it is not foolish. Sometimes the defender will decide that the direct approach is the best one and say to the deponent, "Look, Mr. Greene, just because Mr. Tiger asks his questions in rapid-fire fashion doesn't mean that you have to answer them that way. Slow down."

In general, it is not a bad rule to say that if 20 minutes have elapsed without the defender's saying anything, he should at least consider saying something to reassure the deponent that he is present and paying attention and prepared to come to his aid if necessary.

C.   No-Lose Opportunities for Asserting Control

In every deposition, there are certain opportunities for the defender to assert his control over the deponent where the interrogator will have no recourse but to accept that control. Depending upon the tenor of the deposition, the defender may or may not choose to take advantage of those opportunities. For example, suppose the interrogator requests immediate production of a document to which the deponent has just referred in his testimony which can probably be located without unusual effort. The defender has several options: he can produce the document; he can say that he wants to think about the request; or he can refuse to produce it and leave it to the interrogator to serve a formal request which, of course, allows 30 days for a response.

Usually the defender will take one of the first two options. He will know that discovery is a two-way street and, if he demands strict adherence to the rules, he can expect opposing counsel to do the same. But there will be instances where, because of the general course of discovery or because of the interrogator's treatment of the deponent, the defender will want to rap the interrogator's knuckles and

---

1   *See* Guy v. Rudd, 345 F. Supp. 1382, 1384-85 (W.D. Pa. 1972), *amended and remanded on other grounds,* 480 F.2d 677 (3d Cir. 1973) (prohibiting double-teaming at trial).

will simply reject the request. (Of course, the defender then runs the risk that the interrogator will attempt to resume the deposition after the document is finally produced.)

Similarly, at the end of the day, if the deposition has not been completed, the interrogator may ask the deponent, perhaps on the record, when he can be available to resume the deposition. If he represents the deponent, the defender may instruct him not to answer, reprimand opposing counsel for failing to direct such inquiries to him (rather than to the deponent), and then, when the deposition has concluded for the day, insist that he will consult privately with the deponent about his schedule and then confer with other counsel. On the other hand, if things are going more agreeably, the defending lawyer may suggest that they go off the record to discuss a new deposition date and may permit a three-way discussion among the interrogator, himself and the deponent to clear a new date.

Another control opportunity arises when the interrogator asks the deponent to read into the record a particular sentence of a document. Often the defender will not quarrel with that request and the deponent will comply; then the interrogator will ask his follow-up questions. But in some instances, the defender may instruct the deponent not to read the sentence aloud. If pressed for a reason, he may say that the deponent has appeared to testify, not to recite, and leave it to the interrogator to figure out how to proceed. Usually the interrogator will announce that he will read the sentence into the record himself, do so, and then ask his questions about what the sentence says. In one way, things have come to the same point. But in another they have not. The deponent has seen his lawyer countermand the interrogator's instruction, the interrogator get flustered, then back off, and end up doing what the defending attorney would not allow the deponent to do, that is, recite aloud.

Sometimes there is a more substantive reason for directing the deponent not to follow a request that he read a sentence or a paragraph into the record. Suppose the interrogator anticipates that although the deponent authored the document, he may now deny that certain statements in it mean what they appear to say, perhaps because of some qualification not articulated in the document. In that kind of situation, the interrogator may ask the deponent to read certain portions into the record before questioning him about them. Deponents seem to have more difficulty saying that a statement in their own document is not quite right after they have just read it aloud under oath to a court reporter. For the same reason that the interrogator will want the deponent to read the statement into the record, the defender will be opposed to it and so may instruct the deponent not to do so.

D.   Hurrying the Interrogator

Often when the lawyers are conferring to choose a convenient date and time for the deposition, the defending attorney will inquire how long the interrogator expects the deposition to last. If the interrogator is arranging to take several depositions during the same week, he will impliedly convey this information by the schedule he requests. That is, if he asks for the first deponent at 10:00 a.m. Monday morning and the second at 10:00 a.m. on Tuesday morning, he is saying that he expects to conclude the first deposition by the end of Monday.

It may be wise for the defender to press for a "commitment" that the interrogator really believes that he can complete the depositions in accordance with the proposed schedule. He may say something like:

> You want Mr. Patton on Monday and Mr. Penna on Tuesday. That's fine. I can arrange that. But Penna's schedule is impossible so don't tell me you want him Tuesday unless you're confident that you'll be finished with Patton by then because I'm not going to be able to juggle things at the last minute.

If the interrogator sticks with his schedule in spite of that caution, the defender may be able to hurry him through the first deposition. If the interrogation is proceeding at an unduly slow pace, the defender may say something like:

> Look, I've got Penna lined up for tomorrow and Mr. Levy for the next day. I told you about how difficult Penna's schedule is and you told me you could live with this schedule. If you continue this deposition into tomorrow, you'll be eating into your time with Penna and I don't know when he can next be made available.

Although the interrogator is subject to no sanction for failing to complete the first deposition as originally scheduled (other than delay in deposing Penna), having given an assurance that he could live with this schedule, he is likely to hurry his questioning to complete the deposition as originally planned. If he does so, that can only benefit the deponent and the defender unless the deponent makes the mistake of rushing his answers to keep up with the interrogator's pace.

Another type of hurrying is more provocative and, in some instances, of questionable propriety. If the defender believes that the interrogator is prolonging the deposition unnecessarily to harass the deponent, he may announce some time early in the day that since the interrogator is abusing the deposition

149

process (perhaps citing some examples of completely irrelevant topics of inquiry), he will consider the deposition concluded when it ends that day. Almost certainly the interrogator will register his strong disagreement, including a statement of his intention to seek sanctions if counsel for the deponent should follow through on his threat.

As a technical matter, the defender cannot refuse to produce the deponent on the next scheduled day for his deposition without seeking a protective order. But, if the interrogator has in fact been abusing the deposition process, there is a good likelihood that he will complete his questioning that day and the brewing dispute will become moot. Since such abuse of the discovery process should be the exception, resort to this tactic should be correspondingly rare.

E.   Note Taking

Whether to take extensive notes at a deposition is usually a matter of personal preference. The defending lawyer should be sure not to get so involved in taking notes that he becomes a stenographer and fails to listen carefully so that objectionable questions slip by him. The defender should be careful not to confine his note taking only to those items of importance to his theory of the case; the interrogator will be able to use selective note taking as a guide to his opponent's thinking.

If several witnesses are to be deposed during a short period of time, counsel should take careful notes on their testimony so that later witnesses may be advised in their preparation sessions about relevant prior testimony. As he takes notes, counsel may indicate the initials of a subsequent deponent in the margin next to notes relevant to him. By skimming these marginal notations, counsel can inform a later deponent of the words and actions attributed to him by those deposed earlier.

Once a deposition is completed and transcribed, all of the parties can use the transcript for a number of purposes. The next chapter discusses the use of the transcript, primarily for trial.

CHAPTER ELEVEN

USING THE DEPOSITION TRANSCRIPT

The deposition transcript may be used in a number of different ways at trial. If the deponent is unavailable, some or all of the deposition transcript may be read into the record as direct evidence. If the deponent is a party, opposing counsel can read the entire transcript or excerpts into the record. The deposition transcript can be used to refresh the recollection of a forgetful witness. And, of course, it can be used to impeach the witness whose trial testimony is at odds with that given at his deposition. Short of trial, the transcript provides powerful support for motions based on facts not of record and motions for summary judgment or memoranda in opposition thereto.

A.   What Rules Apply at Trial?

Both the Federal Rules of Civil Procedure and the Federal Rules of Evidence speak to the use of depositions at trial. Rule 32 of the Federal Rules of Civil Procedure sets limits on the use of the deposition transcript as direct evidence but is generally liberal with respect to its use for impeachment. Rules 802, 803 and 804 of the Federal Rules of Evidence further permit the use of deposition transcripts under certain circumstances as an exception to the hearsay rule.

1.   Federal Rule of Civil Procedure 32

Rule 32 outlines the varying ways in which depositions may be used in court proceedings, subject to the important qualification permitting the use of a deposition only "so far as admissible under the rules of evidence applied as though the witness were then present and testifying."[1] (The applicable rules of evidence will be discussed below.) Moreover, depositions may be used only against a party "who was present or represented at the taking of the deposition or who had reasonable notice thereof."[2]

Courts generally agree that Rule 32 permits the use at trial of "discovery" depositions as well as depositions explicitly taken for purposes of trial. As discussed in detail in Chapter 4, Section B.1, counsel always runs the risk that the discovery deposition will actually become the trial testimony, and courts

---

1   FED. R. CIV. P. 32(a).

2   *Id.*

151

tend to regard any decision not to examine or cross-examine accordingly to be a tactical one made with an appreciation of that risk.

Rule 32(a) sets out various prerequisites for the use of depositions, depending upon the circumstances.

        a.   *Use "for Any Purpose."* The adverse party's deposition, or the deposition of an officer, director, or managing agent of an adverse party or of a person designated to testify on behalf of an adverse party under Rule 30(b)(6), may be used "for any purpose" under Rule 32(a)(2). This is true whether or not the adverse party is available at trial and applies even if the party has appeared and testified at trial. A co-defendant or a co-plaintiff may be an adverse party for purposes of Rule 32(a)(2).[3]

A witness in the category of officer, director or managing agent of the adverse party must have occupied that position at the time of taking of the deposition. Thus, for example, the deposition of a managing agent employed by an insurance company at the time the insurance policy was issued, but who no longer held that position at the time of his deposition, may not be used "for any purpose" by the opposing party.

The deposition of an unavailable witness may be used "by any party for any purpose" under Rule 32(a)(3) if the court finds that the witness is dead, beyond 100 miles from the place of trial (unless the party offering the deposition procured the witness's absence), or unable to testify "because of age, illness, infirmity, or imprisonment," or that the offering party has not been able to subpoena the witness.

The 100-mile limit of Rule 32(a)(3) is not co-extensive with the court's subpoena power under Rule 45 of the Federal Rules of Civil Procedure. Even if a witness is within the district and thus could be subpoenaed for trial under Rule 45, his deposition may nevertheless be used at trial if he is beyond 100 miles from the place of trial.[4]

In determining whether a witness is within the 100-mile limit, courts ordinarily measure by a straight line on the map, and not by the "usual and shortest

---

3   4A J. MOORE & J. LUCAS, MOORE'S FEDERAL PRACTICE, ¶ 32.04 at 32-18—19 (2d ed. 1981) (adverse party means "a party whose interest in the case is adverse to that of another party, even though they may be both nominally aligned as co-parties").

4   *See* United States v. International Business Machines Corp., 90 F.R.D. 377, 380 (S.D.N.Y. 1981) (deposition may be used "when the deponent would be unduly inconvenienced by requiring his presence at trial, even if the deponent was subject to subpoena power"); Houser v. Snap-On Tools Corp., 202 F. Supp. 181, 189 (D. Md. 1962).

route of travel."[5] Generally, a court will look at the deponent's place of residence or business to determine whether he is within 100 miles of the courthouse.[6] Evidence as to those locations will most likely be in the deposition transcript, since the interrogator should have asked the witness routine questions about his home address and the place where he works, and the witness's deposition testimony establishes his residence or workplace.[7] If a witness who works or resides beyond the 100-mile limit actually testifies at trial, however, he is no longer considered unavailable.[8]

A witness is available if he lives or works within the 100-mile limit not only as of the time his deposition is offered at trial, but also as of any time that a trial subpoena could have been served on him during the proponent's case.[9] A witness who lives and works outside the 100-mile limit but who has contact with the proponent or his counsel within the 100-mile limit in connection with the case during presentation of the proponent's case may also be considered available for purposes of Rule 32(a)(3).[10]

Other grounds for unavailability include "age, illness, infirmity, or imprisonment," as detailed in Rule 32(a)(3)(C). These grounds must be demonstrated before the deposition can be admitted. It is not sufficient that the witness

---

5   *See* Hill v. Equitable Bank, N.A., 115 F.R.D. 184 (D. Del. 1987); SCM Corp. v. Xerox Corp., 76 F.R.D. 214 (D. Conn. 1977).

6   *See* Ikerd v. Lapworth, 435 F.2d 197 (7th Cir. 1970) ; SCM Corp. v. Xerox Corp., 77 F.R.D.16, 18 (D. Conn. 1977).

7   *See* Hartman v. United States, 538 F.2d 1336, 1346 (8th Cir. 1976) (deposition testimony concerning residence and employment outside 100-mile radius sufficient to establish deponent's unavailability at trial considering that deposition was taken less than seven months before trial and that opposing counsel made no affirmative suggestion or showing that deponent had moved or obtained employment within 100-mile radius); Ikerd v. Lapworth, *supra* note 6 (deposition testimony taken eight months before trial sufficient to establish that deponent resided more than 100 miles from place of trial in absence of challenge by opposing counsel to truth of deposition testimony). If the trial takes place several years after the deposition, the information the deponent gave at the deposition about his residence and work location may be outdated. Nevertheless, the cases cited suggest that the burden is on counsel opposing use of the deposition transcript to make some showing that the witness has relocated since the time of his deposition.

8   *See* United States v. International Business Machines Corp., *supra* note 4, 90 F.R.D. at 381-82.

9   SCM Corp. v. Xerox Corp. *supra* note 6, 77 F.R.D. at 18.

10   *See* United States v. International Business Machines Corp., *supra* note 4, 90 F.R.D. at 383 ("Such contact would indicate that presence at the courthouse would not have been unduly inconvenient.").

alone portrays himself as unable to attend. Voluntary intoxication, particularly of a party, will probably not constitute "sickness or infirmity."[11]

If the issue is a close one, courts should favor live testimony, which permits the trier of fact to observe the witness's demeanor, over deposition testimony.[12] Rule 32(a)(3)(E) clearly states a preference for live testimony.

       b.   *Use for Contradiction or Impeachment.* Any party, including the one who called the witness at trial, may use any deposition to contradict or impeach the deponent's trial testimony. Suggestions for such use appear below at Section B.

       c.   *"Exceptional Circumstances."* The court may permit the use of a deposition under Rule 32(a)(3)(E) for any purpose if it finds "upon application and notice, that such exceptional circumstances exist as to make it desirable, in the interest of justice and with due regard to the importance of presenting the testimony of witnesses orally in open court, to allow the deposition to be used."

The catchall "exceptional circumstances" language is strictly construed. Courts tend to limit the use of this provision to those circumstances where prohibiting the use of deposition testimony would result in the total exclusion of the evidence.[13]

       2.   *Federal Rules of Evidence 802, 803 and 804*

The Federal Rules of Evidence also apply to the use of depositions at trial. Rule 802 provides that hearsay, which would include deposition testimony, is not admissible "except as provided . . . by other rules prescribed by the Supreme Court" (for example, the Federal Rules of Civil Procedure).

Rule 804(b)(1) provides an exception to the hearsay rule for testimony given by a witness who is unavailable for trial "in a deposition taken in compliance with law in the course of the same or another proceeding, if the party

---

11   *See* Moore v. Children's Hospital of Philadelphia, 16 Phila. Co. Rep. 544 (C.P. Phila. 1987) (construing language identical to Fed. R. Civ. P. 32(a)(3)(C) in the Pennsylvania Rules of Civil Procedure).

12   Fed. R. Civ. P. 32(a)(3)(E); Fed. R. Evid. 607.

13   *See, e.g.,* Huff v. Marine Tank Testing Corp., 631 F.2d 1140 (4th Cir. 1980) (unexpected absence of defendant, where plaintiff's lawyer did not subpoena defendant but instead relied on defense counsel's assurances at pretrial conference that defendant would be present and available to testify); Odel v. Miller, 10 F.R.D. 528 (W.D. Mich. 1950) (return to state would subject the witness to arrest).

against whom the testimony is now offered . . . had an opportunity and similar motive to develop the testimony by direct, cross, or redirect examination."

Unavailability of a witness for purposes of Rule 804 is not coextensive with his unavailability for purposes of Rule 32(a)(3).[14] A declarant is considered unavailable under Rule 804 on the grounds of privilege, persistent refusal to testify, lack of memory, inability to be present because of death or physical or mental illness or infirmity, or absence from trial if the proponent has been unable to procure attendance by "process or other reasonable means."[15] Rule 804 does not include a 100-mile limit, and Rule 32(a)(3) does not include privilege, refusal to testify or lack of memory as grounds for unavailability.

An argument can also be made that deposition transcripts are covered under Rule 803(5) which provides an exception to the hearsay rule for recorded recollection.[16] Rule 803(5) permits the transcript to be read into evidence on matters about which the witness once had knowledge but at trial has "insufficient recollection to enable him to testify fully and accurately."

B.   Using Deposition Transcripts Effectively at Trial

The deposition transcript may be read into evidence or may be used for cross-examination, depending on the factors discussed above. This section describes how to use the transcript effectively at trial.

1.   *Impeachment — Laying the Foundation*

To prepare the groundwork for impeachment by use of a deposition transcript, the cross-examiner should pose his questions to the witness at trial in language as close as possible to that used in the deposition. Then, the witness who gives responses inconsistent with his prior deposition testimony will not be able convincingly to explain away the discrepancy on the basis of some difference in the wording of the questions. Once the witness has given trial testimony inconsistent with his deposition testimony, the cross-examiner can use the deposition transcript for impeachment.

If the deposition transcript is to be used in a jury trial, the lawyer using the transcript must first give the jury an understanding of what a deposition is. In many jurisdictions, it is customary for the judge to tell the jury about the deposition procedure. Even if the judge has given a short summary, the lawyer will probably want to establish for the jury certain fundamentals by asking the witness questions like the following:

---

14   *See* 4A J. MOORE & J. LUCAS, MOORE'S FEDERAL PRACTICE, ¶ 32.05[2] at 32-32 (2d ed. 1981).

15   FED. R. EVID. 804(a)(1)-(5).

16   McNamara & Sorensen, *Deposition Traps and Tactics,* LITIGATION, Fall 1985, 48 at 49.

- Do you remember giving testimony in this case at a deposition in my office on June 3, 1987?

- Before you began to give your deposition testimony, did you swear to tell the truth just as you did before you began your testimony in this courtroom?

- Was your lawyer present throughout the deposition?
- Was your testimony taken down by a court reporter?

- And you had an opportunity to review the transcript of the deposition?

- In fact, you corrected and signed the transcript?

Some judges also require the ritualistic laying of a foundation before the deposition may be used for impeachment. This typically involves giving the original deposition transcript to the witness, identifying the portion to be used, requesting the witness to read that portion to himself, and then asking the witness, "Are those the questions you were asked and the answers you gave?" Then counsel asks the court for permission to proceed.[17] If there is a likelihood that the witness will deny the validity or accuracy of the transcript, the cross-examiner should be prepared to call the court reporter to testify that he is a certified reporter, that he was present at the witness's deposition, that he swore the witness, that he took notes of the testimony and transcribed them, that the transcript is an accurate verbatim record of the actual testimony given, that he submitted the original to the witness or his counsel for signature, that no corrections (or only certain ones) were made to the transcript, and that the witness signed the transcript (if he did).

Whether or not he has laid a formal foundation, the cross-examining lawyer must advise his opponent and the court, by page and line number, what portion of the deposition he proposes to use. That is, he will say something like this to the witness:

> Let me direct you to your deposition testimony on this subject. I'm going to start on page 43, line 18.

The lawyer will then pause while the judge, opposing counsel, and the witness find that starting point. If he does not pause, the judge or opposing counsel may interrupt and break his control with something like:

---

17   *See* J. COTCHETT AND A. ELKIND, FEDERAL COURTROOM EVIDENCE at 355 (2d ed. 1987).

I don't have it yet. Was that page 18, or page 43?

He must then decide whether to read aloud the questions and have the witness read aloud the answers from the transcript in a reenactment of the deposition or to read both the questions and answers to the jury himself. The lawyer will probably choose to read it all himself, unless there is a particularly devastating statement that he thinks would be most effective if spoken by the witness. Reading the dialogue himself permits maximum control.

If he decides to have the witness participate in the reading, the cross-examining lawyer should be aware that he is giving the witness an opportunity to read the answers in a way that might soften the impact of the testimony through voice inflection or pauses during the reading. The witness may also interject an explanation of his testimony as he reads and thus blunt the thrust of the cross-examination. For these reasons, many lawyers advocate retaining control of the reading.

2. *"Were You Lying Then or Are You Lying Now?"*

Once the lawyer has established that the witness's trial testimony differs from his deposition testimony, should the lawyer then press on and ask the witness to reconcile the testimony or admit that he lied either at his deposition or at trial?

It does not appear that the lawyer has any obligation to offer the witness the opportunity to reconcile the testimony or to say which version is correct. He can simply establish that the witness has told two different versions of his story, each time under oath, and leave it to the trier of fact to draw the inference that the witness is not credible. In that case, the trier of fact may disbelieve both versions. This strategy may be effective if the cross-examining lawyer does not need to establish any points through the witness and simply wants to discredit him. Of course, on redirect, the lawyer who has proffered the witness may ask him to explain why he gave two seemingly different accounts of the same events and thereby rehabilitate the witness if the explanation is credible.

Even if the objective of the cross-examination is merely to undermine the credibility of the witness and not to establish which version of the facts is correct, lawyers disagree as to whether the ultimate question — "Were you lying at your deposition or are you lying now?" — should be asked. A dramatic illustration of the way in which experienced lawyers forcefully defend opposing sides of this issue can be seen in two conflicting articles which recently appeared in the same publication. In one article, the author (a judge and law professor) strongly advises lawyers to stop short of the ultimate question because it invites the witness to explain the discrepancy, and the jury may well accept the explanation.[18] In the immediately following article, a practicing lawyer equally strongly advises that the cross-examining lawyer should always compel the witness to identify which of the statements is a lie or "incorrect," particularly if the lie occurred in front of the jury at trial.[19]

In making the decision whether to ask the ultimate question, the cross-examiner should keep in mind that he can always talk to the jury about the contradiction in the closing argument. If he does not particularly care which version the jury believes, he should avoid that ultimate question. At the very least, the question should be "Which version is incorrect?" and not "When were you lying?" The latter needlessly aggressive question is as likely to inflame the jury against the cross-examiner as it is to humble the witness.

One experienced lawyer points out that a jury will more readily forgive the witness who has lied to others in the past (that is, at his deposition) than one who has lied directly to them (at trial). Thus, the lawyer should consider structuring the cross-examination so that it will be clear that the truth was not told at trial. This subject is discussed in the next section.

3. Binding the Witness to His Deposition

If the cross-examining lawyer's case was helped by what the witness testified to at deposition, and the witness alters his testimony at trial, the lawyer may not be satisfied simply to undermine the witness's credibility. Rather, his objective on cross-examination will be to have the witness reaffirm the testimony given at deposition. The jury may then conclude that the witness has retreated from his inconsistent trial testimony.

To that end, the cross-examiner's questions may go something like this:

> Mr. Cunningham, did you testify before in this case at a deposition in my office on June 3, 1986?
>
> That date — June 3, 1986 — was less than a year after the accident?
>
> So the accident was fresher and more recent in your memory on June 3, 1986, than it is today?
>
> Your recollection of the accident at the time of your deposition was clearer than it is now, two and a half years after the accident?

---

18   R. Howerton, *CAPSTAR and The Kid: Impeaching with a Prior Statement*, LITIGATION, Fall 1987, 21, 23.

19   D. Berg, *Cross-Examination*, LITIGATION, Fall 1987, 25, 27.

> Did you testify under oath to the best of your recollec-
> tion at your deposition?

It is possible that the witness will insist that his recollection at trial is actually more reliable than it was at the time of his deposition. He may explain that he has now had an opportunity to reflect and to review documents that refreshed his memory. The jury nevertheless is likely to believe that the witness's memory must have faded during the time that has elapsed between the deposition and the trial.

If the witness is not hostile and if his recollection at trial is simply faulty, opposing counsel should not automatically embark on aggressive cross-examination but rather should be nonconfrontational about the inconsistent trial testimony. Rather than attempting to have the witness recant his trial testimony, the cross-examiner might simply use the prior deposition testimony to "refresh" the witness's recollection and leave it to the jury to conclude that his deposition testimony is more reliable than the trial testimony.

Suppose the plaintiff in an automobile accident case testified at deposition that he did not see the other vehicle (a red Chevrolet) until it struck his own, but at trial testifies that he saw the Chevrolet moving erratically as it entered the intersection. Defense counsel may cross-examine like this:

> At your deposition (page 12, lines 14-16), in answer to
> the question, "When did you first see the red
> Chevrolet?" you testified, "Not until it hit my car." Do
> you see that testimony on page 12? Does that refresh
> your recollection about when you first saw the red
> Chevrolet?

Defense counsel may choose to ask one more question to negate the witness's trial testimony without forcing him to confront or explain the inconsistency:

> So you did not see the red Chevrolet until it struck your
> car?

The jury will likely decide that the inconsistent trial testimony about when the witness saw the Chevrolet has now been corrected to conform to the deposition testimony.

4.   *Deposition of Adverse Party or Unavailable Witness*

When using the deposition as original evidence in a jury trial, most lawyers have a colleague take the part of the witness, actually sitting in the witness chair and reading the witness's deposition answers in response to the trial lawyer's reading of the deposition questions. Ideally, the lawyer or legal assistant playing the part of the deponent should be the same sex and approximately the same age as the real deponent.

The person playing the role of witness should be cautioned not to turn it into an Academy Award performance; if he does not play it straight, the adverse party's lawyer may object, the trial judge may reprimand the "witness," and the jury may find the process unconvincing.

In addition, the "witness" must prepare for his role. He should be familiar with the transcript, should practice pronouncing technical terms and should rehearse with the trial lawyer so that he does not stumble or garble the testimony when he is "on the stand."

5. Reading Portions of the Transcript

Ordinarily, only a portion of a deposition transcript is read to the jury. The designation of portions of a transcript to be introduced in evidence is often accomplished in a pretrial memorandum, in which each party designates those portions that it will read into evidence. Once a party has identified the portions it intends to read into evidence, Rule 32(a)(4) provides that the adverse party may require the introduction of "any other part which ought in fairness to be considered with the part introduced." In addition, the rule provides that "any party may introduce any other parts."

Suppose the plaintiff's lawyer has designated pages 1 through 5 and 50 through 52 of the defendant's deposition transcript and the defendant's lawyer wants to have pages 40, 57 and 60 also read into the record. The defendant's lawyer should consider whether he (a) wants to have his opponent read in those additional pages when the opponent reads the pages that he has designated or (b) prefers to read the additional pages himself, waiting until after his opponent has read his designated pages into evidence, as if the additional pages were cross-examination.

Interspersing the helpful with the not-so-helpful parts and having opposing counsel read all of them may blunt the force of the harmful testimony. Or it may be most effective to save the helpful parts until after all of the potentially damaging portions have been read so that the jury hears the helpful parts all together at the end of the other side's reading.

Counsel who first reads portions of the transcript into the record should be aware that he may not have a chance to read additional portions of the deposition on "redirect," especially if opposing counsel elects not to read in "cross-examination" portions of the deposition.[20]

---

20   *See* Gates v. Shell Oil, 812 F.2d 1509, 1514 (5th Cir. 1987) (affirming district court's refusal to permit plaintiff to read in additional testimony after defendant waived "cross-examination" by not reading in any other portions).

6.   *Testimony Ruled Inadmissible*

Typically the court will rule at the final pretrial conference or, during trial, in chambers or at side bar on any objections to portions of deposition transcripts which one side or the other intends to read into the record. If the court sustains an objection, the lawyer proffering the deposition testimony should be sure that the court's ruling and the testimony excluded are part of the trial record so that the point is preserved for appeal. If the ruling is made at trial, the lawyer should read into the record outside the hearing of the jury the portions of the transcript that he wished to offer or should have them marked for identification. Unless they are offered into evidence, deposition transcripts are not automatically part of the record.

If the court sustains an objection made at the deposition, the transcript should be edited so that the objectionable question and answer will not be read to the jury. If the court overrules the objection, the question and answer, but not the objection, will be read at trial.

C.   Using the Deposition Transcript in Support of Motions

1.   *Motions for Summary Judgment*

The deposition transcript can come into play well before trial to support or defeat a motion for summary judgment under Rule 56 of the Federal Rules of Civil Procedure. Rule 56(c) contemplates that summary judgment motions may be based on depositions as well as pleadings, answers to interrogatories, admissions and affidavits. Depositions may also be used to supplement or oppose affidavits under Rule 56(e). Moreover, if affidavits are not available from the party opposing a motion for summary judgment, Rule 56(f) authorizes the court to order a continuance so that depositions may be taken.

If the interrogator hopes to use the deposition transcript to support a motion for summary judgment, he will need to have a clear idea before beginning the deposition of the legal elements of the claim at issue and, accordingly, of the facts he must elicit. For example, in defending an action for wrongful discharge on the ground of employment-at-will, the interrogator may try to establish at the plaintiff's deposition that the plaintiff did not have a written employment agreement, that no one expressly promised him employment for a fixed period, that the plaintiff was given an employee procedures manual (which should be marked as a deposition exhibit), and that the manual contained no statement about the period of employment. (The interrogator may wish to skip this last question and simply use the exhibit itself in his motion.)

Similarly, to help prepare the foundation for a motion for summary judgment in a breach of contract action, the lawyer for the plaintiff-purchaser in deposing the representative of the defendant-supplier may attempt to establish that there was a written contract for the goods, that the contract marked as a deposition exhibit is a true copy of it, that the contract was signed by the purchaser and the supplier, that the supplier did not deliver the goods, and that the only excuse the supplier can point to for its failure to deliver is that it advised the purchaser before the contract was signed that it was looking for a geographically closer market for the goods in question. Having established these facts, the interrogator is in a good position to move for summary judgment on the basis of the contract and its integration clause.

Rather than attaching an entire deposition transcript to the motion or reply, the lawyer should consider attaching only those portions on which he relies. Indeed, the lawyer might wish to prepare a succinct exhibit of only those particular questions and answers on which he relies with appropriate references to deposition pages and line numbers, instead of attaching copies of pages from the transcript with much irrelevant material interspersed. The lawyer who decides not to attach the entire transcript and who is in a jurisdiction in which deposition transcripts are not routinely filed with the court should file the complete transcript separately with the clerk for the court's reference.

2. Motions on Facts Not of Record

Under Rule 43(e) of the Federal Rule of Civil Procedure, a court may consider wholly on deposition testimony a motion based on facts not of record. Thus, some federal judges routinely direct that the parties in preliminary injunction motions under Rule 65(a) proceed by deposition, rather than by live testimony.

Depositions that will be offered to support or oppose a motion under Rule 43(e) are, in effect, trial depositions. Thus, the interrogator should not withhold his most telling questions. Nor should the opposing lawyer refrain from bringing out points favorable to his case at the deposition. Neither side will have the opportunity to ask additional questions at a later date, and the motion will be decided on the basis of the testimony elicited at the deposition.

In sum, the deposition transcript has many uses. As emphasized throughout this book, both the interrogator and the defender at the deposition should keep in mind the ultimate use of the transcript as they proceed.

CONCLUSION

To take a deposition well requires skill and thorough preparation. While there is no substitute for first-hand experience, consideration of the matters discussed here may serve to sharpen skills and improve preparation.

APPENDIX

PRACTICAL TIPS

Witness Preparation Script: Basic Rules

Checklist: Before the Deposition

Anatomy of a Document

FORMS

Form A: Notice of Deposition

Form B: Deposition Subpoena

Form C: Rule 30(b)(6) Notice

RULES

Federal Rules of Civil Procedure Applicable to Depositions

Federal Rules of Evidence Applicable to Depositions

Uniform Audio-Visual Deposition [Act] [Rule]

PRACTICAL TIPS

Witness Preparation Script: Basic Rules

1.   Listen to the question

Concentrate on every word. Wait until you hear the last word of the question before you start your answer. If you listen closely to ordinary conversation, you will see that we cut one another off quite frequently, not to be rude but to keep the conversation moving. Listening is hard work. If you listen as you should, you will be tired at the end of the day.

2.   Be sure you hear the question

If the lawyer drops his voice or someone coughs and you miss a word or two, say that you did not hear the question. Do this even if you are almost certain that you know what word you missed.

3.   Be sure you understand the question

Sometimes the question will be so long or so convoluted that you do not know what you are being asked except that it concerns subject A. You may be tempted to answer by saying something about subject A in the hope that the lawyer will then go on to some other subject. Do not do that. Just say that you do not understand.

You may not understand because the lawyer is not exact in his language. For example, he may ask you if a certain letter was sent after "that." You may not be sure to what fact or event he is referring when he says "that." Say that you do not understand the question.

You may not be certain of the meaning of a word used by the lawyer. Or you may not be sure how he is using it. Say that you do not understand the question.

If you do not understand, do not help the other lawyer in asking the question. Do not say, "If you mean this, then my answer would be such and such; if you mean that, my answer would be so and so." You may very well give the other lawyer ideas that he never had himself. Say only that you do not understand.

4.   Answer the question

After you have listened to, heard, and understood the question, then answer; answer *the question*. Some lawyers say that if you are asked your name, you should give your name but not your address. Others say that 95 percent of the questions can be answered, "Yes," "No," "I don't know," or "I don't remember." Those statements go too far but they make the point. Generally you should keep your answer short and to the point.

What you learned in taking tests in high school or college applies here. Answer what you are asked. If the question begins "Who," your answer should be a name; if "Where," a place; if "When,"a date; and so on.

If you do not know or do not remember, say that. You do not get extra points by guessing. If you are pretty sure of the answer but not 100 percent certain, say that.

If you do not know or remember, say that and then keep quiet. Do not volunteer a reference to a document, such as, "I don't know; I would have to check my desk calendar."

You do not get extra points for giving perfectly clear and complete answers. Normally if there is some ambiguity in your answer, that will be a problem for the opposing party, not for you.

Sometimes, after you give your answer there will be a silence. The other lawyer may be thinking how to word his next question. Silences sometimes make a witness uncomfortable. You may be tempted to fill the silence with words. Do not do that. Keep quiet and wait.

If a question irritates you or makes you angry, resist the temptation to argue with the other lawyer. If you get into an argument with a lawyer, you will lose. Just give whatever facts you know responsive to the question and then keep quiet.

If you are asked a question that requires a longer answer, give it. Use your common sense. Do not make the other lawyer play "Twenty Questions." But if you are in doubt, keep your answer short. Do not make speeches. Remember that every word is another target for the other lawyer.

In dealing with the other lawyer, your manner should be courteous and open, but mentally you should be on guard at all times. Even if something is said "off the record," the other lawyer can ask you about it when you are back on the record.

I may object to certain questions. Try not to be distracted by that. Listen to the objection. It may point out some hidden trap in the question. The objection is a reminder to you to keep concentrating.

I may go further and instruct you not to answer the question. If I do, follow my instruction. I may get into trouble with the court if I am wrong, but you will not.

5. Stick to truthful answers
You may hear the same question more than once. If your original answer was accurate, stick to it. The fact that the other lawyer keeps coming back to the question does not mean that you are not answering properly. You must give the facts as you know them. If you gave them right the first time, stick to your answer.

Of course, the other lawyer is an experienced and skillful questioner, and through his questions he may try to create doubt in your mind even about facts that you know very well. Take an easy example which has nothing to do with this case. Suppose he shows you a coffee cup and asks you what it is. You say a coffee cup. He then pauses, gazes at the cup, and lets you squirm. Then, after letting you wonder what he knows that you don't, he leans forward and says, "Now, Mr. Witness, is it your testimony here today — under oath — that that object is a coffee cup? Do you really mean to say that?" There is a natural tendency to back off and say, "Well, I thought it was a coffee cup." That small change in your testimony may be crucial. Suppose a witness says the first time that he had the green light and then says that he thought he had it. That would be a devastating change. So if your first answer was true, stick to it and say, "Yes, it is a coffee cup." What does the other lawyer do then? He will go on to another subject quickly when he sees that you cannot be shaken.

Of course, if you realize that your earlier answer was in error or incomplete, you should correct or supplement it. Obviously, you should not say that an earlier answer is true if you become aware that it is not.

6.   Tell the truth
You must always follow that rule. You should not interpret anything else that I have said to you to be at odds with that rule. You will undoubtedly be asked some questions that we have not covered here today. When that occurs, do not get upset. Focus on the question and, if you can, answer it. You may be asked if we met to prepare for the deposition. Tell the truth.

Checklist: Before the Deposition

Interrogator

- ☐ Arrange for court reporter

- ☐ Reserve conference room

- ☐ Obtain proper chair for reporter (that is, a stenographer's chair with no arms)

- ☐ Coffee and water

- ☐ Business card

- ☐ Caption of case

- ☐ Last exhibit number (if exhibits are sequentially numbered from deposition to deposition)

- ☐ Last transcript page number (if there are other volumes of the witness's testimony)

- ☐ Copies of exhibits (at least 4 — one to mark and show witness, one to question from, one to give opposing counsel, and one clean copy for the interrogator's file)

- ☐ Deposition subpoena or notice (if documents were requested)

- ☐ Decide whether to order copy of transcript

Defending Lawyer

- ☐ Business card

- ☐ Pleadings file (in the event of dispute about, *e.g.*, whether answers to interrogatories verified by witness were later amended)

❏ Documents responsive to deposition subpoena or notice

❏ Deposition subpoena or notice

❏ Decide whether to order copy

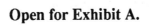

Open for Exhibit A.

M E M O R A N D U M

March 19, 1988

TO: FILE

FROM: S. D. BROWN

RE: DISCONTINUANCE OF RECORD DIVISION

At this morning's meeting, we discussed again our continuing losses in the record division and decided to discontinue that operation. The reasons for its failure include:

(a)   increasing consumer preference for compact discs;

(b)   the bankruptcy of X-Mart, our principal outlet; and

(c)   our difficulty in signing top musical artists.

I will circulate an appropriate notice.

SDB:fjt

cc: J.G. Cooney
      J.R. Horowitz

Exhibit A

Anatomy of a Document

The purpose of this section is to show how the interrogator might prepare to question a deponent about a particular document. There is no one right way to attack every document. But this analysis may be a helpful illustration.

The Document — Whether To Use It and for What Objective (Exhibit A)

Assume that the attached document, Exhibit A, has been produced by the plaintiff from its internal files in an antitrust action alleging that the defendant has attempted to monopolize the record market.

Counsel for the defendant is preparing to take the deposition of S.D. Brown, the plaintiff's vice president in charge of sales and the author of the document. He must decide whether and how to use the document in his interrogation. On its face, the document appears to be very helpful to the defendant since it seems to attribute the plaintiff's discontinuance of its record division to causes other than the defendant's conduct.

In order to decide whether to use the document and, if so, for what objective, the interrogator must first determine what questions might be asked about it — to authenticate it, to obtain discovery, to obtain admissions and to impeach the deponent.

Authentication and Discovery Questions (Exhibit A-1)

What questions must be asked to authenticate the document? Is it sufficient just to ask what it is? Or must one go further and, for example, ask the questions necessary to authenticate it as a business record under Federal Rule of Evidence 803(6)?

What questions might be asked about it to discover additional facts? Careful scrutiny of the language of the document — sentence-by-sentence, phrase-by-phrase, word-by-word — will often suggest a number of inquiries.

Open out Exhibit A-1, which is attached after page 179, to see authentication and discovery questions which might be posed about the document.

Questions Seeking Admissions (Exhibit A-2)

How does the interrogator get the most out of this document by way of admissions? To answer that question, he should force himself to articulate how the document is helpful to his side of the case. Here there are at least three helpful things about the document: (1) it makes no direct mention of the defendant's conduct as a reason for discontinuing the record division; (2) of the three reasons given, the only one that the deponent might plausibly attempt to attribute to the defendant ("our difficulty in signing top musical artists") is listed last; and (3) even that factor will not necessarily be blamed on the defendant.

With those ideas in mind, the interrogator should give thought to deciding what predicate facts he might elicit from the deponent before showing him this document. The interrogator may find that the plaintiff has produced five or six other memoranda authored by S. D. Brown with a similar format, that is, they all start with a statement of the decision reached at a meeting, followed by an enumeration of the reasons therefor. That is not too much to hope for. Many people lapse into more or less predictable patterns of expressing themselves.

If the interrogator finds other such memoranda prepared by S. D. Brown, he might ask him these questions as to one of the other memoranda:

(a)   In this memorandum, did you list all of the important reasons for the decision to [whatever it was]?

(b)   Did you omit unimportant reasons?

(c)   Did you list the reasons in the order of their importance to the decision?

It is almost impossible for the deponent to answer the first two questions with a "No." Of course, the interrogator should choose a memorandum for such preliminary questioning in which it appears that the deponent did list the reasons in the order of their relative importance. (Conversely, if reason (c) — the one that might possibly be attributed to the defendant's actions — were listed first in Exhibit A, the interrogator might use a different preliminary memorandum and seek an admission that the reasons were listed randomly.) If the deponent gives the expected answers to these preliminary questions about the memorandum, the interrogator might ask the same series of questions as to another memorandum. If the same answers are given, he might then go a step further:

> Was that your general practice when you prepared memoranda reporting decisions, that is, to list important reasons, to omit unimportant ones, and to list reasons in the order of their relative importance?

Often the deponent will answer "Yes,"perhaps because that was his conscious practice or perhaps because this review of similar memoranda demonstrates to him that it was his practice.

Open out Exhibit A-2, also attached after page 179, to see questions seeking admissions. The interrogator has marked his work copy of the critical memorandum with a note to himself in the upper right corner that, before showing this memorandum to the deponent, he should review the preliminary memoranda to attempt to obtain the desired predicate admissions. (On Exhibit A-2, the interrogator has put in brackets notes to himself and questions which he may or may not ask depending upon the deponent's testimony.) This reminder will alert the interrogator who may have deviated at some point from his original plan as to the order in which to cover subjects and, as a result, has not yet questioned the deponent about those preliminary documents.

Here the interrogator has made another note to himself in the lower left corner of possible responses the deponent might give to try to explain away the force of the document: first, that this list was not intended to be exhaustive (note the word "include" in line 3 of the memorandum); second, that reason (c) was caused by the defendant's actions; and, third, that everyone was so aware of the defendant's actions that there was no need to mention them here.

As Exhibit A-2 shows, if the interrogator has obtained the admissions sought in his questioning about the preliminary memoranda, he might then ask these questions about the critical memorandum:

> Did you follow your general practice and state the important reasons for this decision, omit unimportant ones, and list the reasons in their relative order of importance?

> [If not, why did you deviate here from your general practice?]

> Do you claim that the defendant did anything to cause the "increasing consumer preference for compact discs"?

> [*Note*: While an affirmative answer to this question and the next one is very unlikely, the interrogator should ask them to be sure that he is not overlooking anything. Indeed, if the deponent gives an affirmative answer, he may cast doubt on the plausibility of the plaintiff's case.]

> Do you claim that the defendant did anything to cause "the bankruptcy of X-Mart"?

> Do you claim that the defendant did anything to cause your "difficulty in signing top musical artists"?

[If yes, what did the defendant do to cause that? What artists? What were the details as to efforts to sign each?]

[If no, consider skipping questions as to names of artists and the details of efforts to sign; as the deponent answers those questions, he may withdraw his original admission that this problem was not caused by the defendant's conduct.]

If the deponent makes all of the admissions sought [that he followed his general practice in listing reasons and that no actions of the defendant caused (a), (b) or (c)], the interrogator may chance this further question:

Is there any statement in this memorandum that any actions by the defendant caused your company to discontinue the operations of its record division?

By asking this question, the interrogator risks losing the helpful admissions he has just won. Rather than just saying "No," the deponent may respond with something like:

Look, whether it's in the memorandum or not, it was the defendant's actions that forced us out of that business. Let me tell you what it did. . . .

Consequently, more often than not, the interrogator will stop short of that question. In any event, if he does ask it and receives another helpful answer, he should *not* ask the ultimate question:

Your company's decision to discontinue the operations of its record division was unrelated to any actions by the defendant, isn't that right?

There is virtually no chance of an affirmative answer to that question and a grave danger of provoking a jeremiad from the deponent in which he details all of the defendant's allegedly anticompetitive acts.

Impeachment Questions

Before showing this memorandum to the deponent, the interrogator might ask these questions:

176

What caused your company to discontinue the operation of its record division?

Was there any other cause?

[Ask until the answer is "No."]

Did the increasing consumer preference for compact discs have anything to do with that decision?

Did the bankruptcy of X-Mart have anything to do with that decision?

Did your difficulty in signing top musical artists have anything to do with that decision?

If the deponent says that the discontinuance of the operations of the record division was due solely to the defendant's acts (and not, for example, to the bankruptcy of X-Mart), the interrogator is in a position to impeach the deponent with the memorandum, unless he decides for tactical reasons to reserve impeachment for trial. (See "Should the Document Be Used at Deposition?" below.) Note that these questions are cast in terms of the exact language of the memorandum so that the deponent cannot explain away inconsistent testimony on the basis of some small difference between the language of the memorandum and that of the question.

Choosing Between Objectives

But is impeachment the most effective use of the memorandum? What will the deponent say if these impeachment questions are asked and he is then confronted with the document? Probably that the defendant's actions were the main cause of the demise of the plaintiff's record division, that he failed to mention that in the memorandum because it was such a given, and that on reflection he would concede that the other causes mentioned in the memorandum were factors, but of very much less importance than the defendant's actions.

The advantage of creating such an opportunity for impeachment must be balanced against the disadvantage of increasing the likelihood that the deponent will attack the contents of the memorandum — which are helpful to the defendant.

Consequently, the interrogator might decide to show the critical memorandum to the deponent without any preliminary questioning on the subject of the causes for the discontinuance of the record division. Confronted with his own written words and not having given any prior inconsistent testimony, the deponent may be less inclined to attack the contents of the memorandum. That is, while he may still claim that the defendant's actions were an important factor in causing the destruction of this business (even though not mentioned in the memorandum), he is more likely to concede the significance of the other reasons listed.

While experienced litigators might disagree about how this memorandum should be used (some preferring to take advantage of the impeachment opportunity and others not), the important point is that the interrogator should make an advertent decision as to how and for what purpose he intends to use each document.

Structuring the Order of Questions About the Document To Achieve the Interrogator's Objectives (Exhibit A-3)

Assume that the interrogator has decided to forgo the impeachment opportunity and, instead, opted to use the memorandum to obtain admissions and discovery. Having written on his work copy of the memorandum the questions he might ask, he must then settle on an order in which to ask them.

Three observations might be made about the order of the questions suggested on Exhibit A-3, attached after page 179. First, immediately after asking the deponent to identify the document, the interrogator intends to ask the key question: whether the deponent followed his usual practice in listing reasons. (See question 2 on Exhibit A-3.) That way the deponent will have little time to ponder the significance of the document before answering perhaps the single most important question about it.

Second, the interrogator will then be following an in-and-out approach, switching back and forth from questions directed to discovery to ones seeking admissions. Thus, he will ask about what other meetings there were on the same subject (question 7 — discovery), then whether the deponent claims that the defendant's actions caused reasons (a), (b) or (c) (question 8 — admissions), and then about the notice to be circulated (question 9 — discovery). It may be harder for the deponent to rationalize the statements in the memorandum when the interrogator is shifting back and forth from the substance of the memorandum, to questions seeking additional detailed fact information, to substance, and so on.

Of course, some litigators might argue that the interrogator should blitz through all of the most important questions right at the start before the deponent has much chance to think about the document. And others might argue that the deponent is most likely to have his guard up when first shown the document and, therefore, the questions seeking admissions should be deferred until the interrogator has asked those seeking discovery, by which time the deponent may have relaxed his guard. Again, the important point is that the interrogator give conscious thought to how he believes he can best achieve his objectives with this deponent and this document.

A third noteworthy point about the suggested order on Exhibit A-3 is that it ends with a discovery question. (Question 13 asks whether Mr. Brown or others took notes during the meeting.) Suppose it were otherwise, that is, that the last question about the document sought an admission. Suppose, too, that the deponent makes that admission. There is then the danger that, during the pause that almost inevitably follows the end of interrogation about a document, the deponent may modify or withdraw the admission. That is much less likely to happen if his attention has been diverted immediately from that admission to some unrelated fact question.

Should the Document Be Used at Deposition?

If confident of his ability to savage the witness if he should attempt to explain away the apparent thrust of the memorandum, a highly skilled interrogator might decide to postpone his questioning about it until trial so that the witness does not have the benefit of a dress rehearsal. But few litigators can be so sure of their ability to parry any explanation the witness might give. Suppose, for example, the witness says:

> At our meeting the next week, both Mr. Cooney and Mr. Horowitz commented that my memorandum had neglected to mention the most important reason for our decision: the defendant's relentless efforts to put us out of business. I told them that the defendant's conduct was such a given that I had not even thought to mention it. I told them that I would revise the memorandum accordingly, but they told me not to bother, that we had more pressing problems than editing internal memoranda.

Is the interrogator certain that on-the-spot at trial he can counter that answer or *any* other the witness might give? If not, he should inquire about the document at the deposition.

Open for Exhibit A-1.

Open for Exhibit A-2.

Open for Exhibit A-3.

FORMS

Form A

MEGADYNATECH, INC., 25 Paradise Industrial Park Fort Washington, PA 19042	:	
	:	
Plaintiff,	:	
	:	
v.	:	CIVIL ACTION NO. 88-142
	:	
X-MART CORPORATION 5 Benjamin Franklin Parkway Philadelphia, PA 19103	:	
	:	
Defendant.	:	

NOTICE OF DEPOSITION

TO: William Stout, Esquire
     Stout & Short
     5 Fidelity Building
     Philadelphia, Pennsylvania 19102
     Attorney for Plaintiff

PLEASE TAKE NOTICE THAT defendant X-Mart Corporation will take the deposition upon oral examination of Brenda Kinney, Executive Vice President of plaintiff Megadynatech, Inc., pursuant to Rule 30 of the Federal Rules of Civil Procedure, before a notary public or some other officer authorized to adminster oaths under law, at the offices of Schnader, Harrison, Segal & Lewis, 1600 Market Street, Suite 3600, Philadelphia, Pennsylvania 19103 on

June 20, 1988 commencing at 10:00 a.m. and continuing from day to day thereafter until completed. You are invited to attend and participate in the examination if you so desire.

The deponent shall bring with her to the deposition all documents in her possession that relate or refer to X-Mart Corporation or purchases of parts for Superpro printers from X-Mart Corporation in the period from January 1, 1985, to the present.

Dennis R. Suplee
Diana S. Donaldson
Attorneys for Defendant
X-Mart Corporation

SCHNADER, HARRISON, SEGAL & LEWIS
Suite 3600, 1600 Market Street
Philadelphia, Pennsylvania 19103

Of Counsel.

Dated: June 1, 1988

Form B

A.O 90 (Rev. 5/85) Deposition Subpoena

𝕌𝕟𝕚𝕥𝕖𝕕 𝕊𝕥𝕒𝕥𝕖𝕤 𝔻𝕚𝕤𝕥𝕣𝕚𝕔𝕥 ℂ𝕠𝕦𝕣𝕥

_____ DISTRICT OF _____

V.

DEPOSITION SUBPOENA

CASE NUMBER:

SUBPOENA FOR	
☐ PERSON	☐ DOCUMENT(S) or OBJECT(S)

TO:

YOU ARE HEREBY COMMANDED to appear at the place, date, and time specified below to testify at the taking of a deposition in the above case.

PLACE	DATE AND TIME

YOU ARE ALSO COMMANDED to bring with you the following document(s) or object(s):*

☐ Please see additional information on reverse

Any subpoenaed organization not a party to this suit is hereby admonished pursuant to Rule 30(b)(6), Federal Rules of Civil Procedure, to file a designation with the court specifying one or more officers, directors, or managing agents, or other persons who consent to testify on its behalf, and setting forth, for each person designated, the matters on which he will testify or product documents or things. The persons so designated shall testify as to matters known or reasonably available to the organization.

R CLERK OF COURT   MICHAEL E. KUNZ   DATE

(BY) DEPUTY CLERK

This subpoena is issued upon application of the:

☐ Plaintiff   ☐ Defendant   ☐ U.S. Attorney

QUESTIONS MAY BE ADDRESSED TO:

ATTORNEY'S NAME, ADDRESS AND PHONE NUMBER

*If not applicable, enter "none"

183

AO 90 (Rev. 5/85) Deposition Subpoena

RETURN OF SERVICE [1]			
RECEIVED BY SERVER	DATE	PLACE	
SERVED	DATE	PLACE	

SERVED ON (NAME)	FEES TENDERED
	☐ YES ☐ NO AMOUNT $_____

SERVED BY	TITLE

STATEMENT OF SERVICE FEES

TRAVEL	SERVICES	TOTAL

DECLARATION OF SERVER [2]

I declare under penalty of perjury under the laws of the United States of America that the foregoing information contained in the Return of Service and Statement of Service Fees is true and correct.

Executed on _____
                      Date

_____
Signature of Server

_____
Address of Server

ADDITIONAL INFORMATION

(1) As to who may serve a subpoena and the manner of its service see Rule 17(d), Federal Rules of Criminal Procedure, or Rule 45(c), Federal Rules of Civil Procedure.

(2) "Fees and mileage need not be tendered to the deponent upon service of a subpoena issued on behalf of the United States or an officer or agency thereof (Rule 45(c), Federal Rules of Civil Procedure; Rule 17(d), Federal Rules of Criminal Procedure) or on behalf of certain indigent parties and criminal defendants who are unable to pay such costs (28 USC 1825, Rule 17(b) Federal Rules of Criminal Procedures)".

Form C

MEGADYNATECH, INC.,   :
25 Paradise Industrial Park   :
Fort Washington, PA 19042   :
    :
        Plaintiff,   :
    :
      v.   :   CIVIL ACTION NO. 88-142
    :
X-MART CORPORATION   :
5 Benjamin Franklin Parkway :
Philadelphia, PA 19103   :
    :
        Defendant.   :

NOTICE OF DEPOSITION

TO: William Stout, Esquire
      Stout & Short
      5 Fidelity Building
      Philadelphia, Pennsylvania 19102
      Attorney for Plaintiff

PLEASE TAKE NOTICE THAT defendant X-Mart Corporation, pursuant to Rule 30(b)(6) of the Federal Rules of Civil Procedure, will take the deposition upon oral examination of plaintiff Megadynatech, Inc., on the following matters:

1.   Communication to and from customers of Megadynatech, Inc., concerning Superpro printers during the period from January 1, 1985, to the present;

2.   Quality control in the manufacture of Superpro printers since January 1, 1985; and

3.   The decision to purchase parts for the Superpro printer from X-Mart.

The oral examination will take place on July 6, 1988, at the offices of Schnader, Harrison, Segal & Lewis, 1600 Market Street, Suite 3600, Philadelphia, Pennsylvania 19103 at 10:00 a.m. and will continue from day to day until completed. The depositions will be taken before a notary public or some other officer authorized to administer oaths under the law. You are invited to attend and examine the witnesses if you so desire.

Megadynatech, Inc., is requested to designate one or more officers, directors, or managing agents, or other persons who consent to testify on its behalf, and to set forth, for each person designated, the matters on which the person will testify.

> Dennis R. Suplee
> Diana S. Donaldson
> Attorneys for Defendant
> X-Mart Corporation

SCHNADER, HARRISON, SEGAL & LEWIS
Suite 3600, 1600 Market Street
Philadelphia, Pennsylvania 19103

Of Counsel.

Dated: June 1, 1988

RULES

Federal Rules of Civil Procedure
Applicable to Depositions

Rule 26. General Provisions Governing Discovery

(a) DISCOVERY METHODS. Parties may obtain discovery by one or more of the following methods: depositions upon oral examination or written questions; written interrogatories; production of documents or things or permission to enter upon land or other property, for inspection and other purposes; physical and mental examinations; and requests for admission.

(b) DISCOVERY SCOPE AND LIMITS. Unless otherwise limited by order of the court in accordance with these rules, the scope of discovery is as follows:

(1) *In General.* Parties may obtain discovery regarding any matter, not privileged, which is relevant to the subject matter involved in the pending action, whether it relates to the claim or defense of the party seeking discovery or to the claim or defense of any other party, including the existence, description, nature, custody, condition and location of any books, documents, or other tangible things and the identity and location of persons having knowledge of any discoverable matter. It is not ground for objection that the information sought will be inadmissible at the trial if the information sought appears reasonably calculated to lead to the discovery of admissible evidence.

The frequency or extent of use of the discovery methods set forth in subdivision (a) shall be limited by the court if it determines that: (i) the discovery sought is unreasonably cumulative or duplicative, or is obtainable from some other source that is more convenient, less burdensome, or less expensive; (ii) the party seeking discovery has had ample opportunity by discovery in the action to obtain the information sought; or (iii) the discovery is unduly burdensome or expensive, taking into account the needs of the case, the amount in controversy, limitations on the parties' resources, and the importance of the issues at stake in the litigation. The court may act upon its own initiative after reasonable notice or pursuant to a motion under subdivision (c).

(2) *Insurance Agreements.* A party may obtain discovery of the existence and contents of any insurance agreement under which any person carrying on an insurance business may be

187

liable to satisfy part or all of a judgment which may be entered in the action or to indemnify or reimburse for payments made to satisfy the judgment. Information concerning the insurance agreement is not by reason of disclosure admissible in evidence at trial. For purposes of this paragraph, an application for insurance shall not be treated as part of an insurance agreement.

(3) *Trial Preparation: Materials.* Subject to the provisions of subdivision (b)(4) of this rule, a party may obtain discovery of documents and tangible things otherwise discoverable under subdivision (b)(1) of this rule and prepared in anticipation of litigation or for trial by or for another party or by or for that other party's representative (including the other party's attorney, consultant, surety, indemnitor, insurer, or agent) only upon a showing that the party seeking discovery has substantial need of the materials in the preparation of the party's case and that the party is unable without undue hardship to obtain the substantial equivalent of the materials by other means. In ordering discovery of such materials when the required showing has been made, the court·shall protect against disclosure of the mental impressions, conclusions, opinions, or legal theories of an attorney or other representative of a party concerning the litigation.

A party may obtain without the required showing a statement concerning the action or its subject matter previously made by that party. Upon request, a person not a party may obtain without the required showing a statement concerning the action or its subject matter previously made by that person. If the request is refused, the person may move for a court order. The provisions of Rule 37(a)(4) apply to the award of expenses incurred in relation to the motion. For purposes of this paragraph, a statement previously made is (A) a written statement signed or otherwise adopted or approved by the person making it, or (B) a stenographic, mechanical, electrical, or other recording, or a transcription thereof, which is a substantially verbatim recital of an oral statement by the person making it and contemporaneously recorded.

(4) *Trial Preparation: Experts.* Discovery of facts known and opinions held by experts, otherwise discoverable under the provisions of subdivision (b)(1) of this rule and acquired or developed in anticipation of litigation or for trial, may be obtained only as follows:

(A)(i) A party may through interrogatories require any other party to identify each person whom the other party expects to call as an expert witness at trial, to state the subject matter on which the expert is expected to testify,

188

and to state the substance of the facts and opinions to which the expert is expected to testify and a summary of the grounds for each opinion. (ii) Upon motion, the court may order further discovery by other means, subject to such restrictions as to scope and such provisions, pursuant to subdivision (b)(4)(C) of this rule, concerning fees and expenses as the court may deem appropriate.

(B) A party may discover facts known or opinions held by an expert who has been retained or specially employed by another party in anticipation of litigation or preparation for trial and who is not expected to be called as a witness at trial, only as provided in Rule 35(b) or upon a showing of exceptional circumstances under which it is impracticable for the party seeking discovery to obtain facts or opinions on the same subject by other means.

(C) Unless manifest injustice would result, (i) the court shall require that the party seeking discovery pay the expert a reasonable fee for time spent in responding to discovery under subdivisions (b)(4)(A)(ii) and (b)(4)(B) of this rule; and (ii) with respect to discovery obtained under subdivision (b)(4)(A)(ii) of this rule the court may require, and with respect to discovery obtained under subdivision (b)(4)(B) of this rule the court shall require, the party seeking discovery to pay the other party a fair portion of the fees and expenses reasonably incurred by the latter party in obtaining facts and opinions from the expert.

(c) PROTECTIVE ORDERS. Upon motion by a party or by the person from whom discovery is sought, and for good cause shown, the court in which the action is pending or alternatively, on matters relating to a deposition, the court in the district where the deposition is to be taken may make any order which justice requires to protect a party or person from annoyance, embarrassment, oppression, or undue burden or expense, including one or more of the following: (1) that the discovery not be had; (2) that the discovery may be had only on specified terms and conditions, including a designation of the time or place; (3) that the discovery may be had only by a method of discovery other than that selected by the party seeking discovery; (4) that certain matters not be inquired into, or that the scope of the discovery be limited to certain matters; (5) that discovery be conducted with no one present except persons designated by the court; (6) that a deposition after being sealed be opened only by order of the court; (7) that a trade secret or other confidential research, development, or commercial information not be disclosed or be disclosed only in a designated way; (8) that the parties simultaneously file specified documents or information enclosed in sealed envelopes to be opened as directed by the court.

If the motion for a protective order is denied in whole or in part, the court may, on such terms and conditions as are just, order that any party or person provide or permit discovery. The provisions of Rule 37(a)(4) apply to the award of expenses incurred in relation to the motion.

(d) SEQUENCE AND TIMING OF DISCOVERY. Unless the court upon motion, for the convenience of parties and witnesses and in the interests of justice, orders otherwise, methods of discovery may be used in any sequence and the fact that a party is conducting discovery, whether by deposition or otherwise, shall not operate to delay any other party's discovery.

(e) SUPPLEMENTATION OF RESPONSES. A party who has responded to a request for discovery with a response that was complete when made is under no duty to supplement the response to include information thereafter acquired, except as follows:

(1) A party is under a duty seasonably to supplement the response with respect to any question directly addressed to (A) the identity and location of persons having knowledge of discoverable matters, and (B) the identity of each person expected to be called as an expert witness at trial, the subject matter on which the person is expected to testify, and the substance of the person's testimony.

(2) A party is under a duty seasonably to amend a prior response if the party obtains information upon the basis of which (A) the party knows that the response was incorrect when made, or (B) the party knows that the response though correct when made is no longer true and the circumstances are such that a failure to amend the response is in substance a knowing concealment.

(3) A duty to supplement responses may be imposed by order of the court, agreement of the parties, or at any time prior to trial through new requests for supplementation of prior responses.

(f) DISCOVERY CONFERENCE. At any time after commencement of an action the court may direct the attorneys for the parties to appear before it for a conference on the subject of discovery. The court shall do so upon motion by the attorney for any party if the motion includes:

(1) A statement of the issues as they then appear;

(2) A proposed plan and schedule of discovery;

(3) Any limitations proposed to be placed on discovery;

(4) Any other proposed orders with respect to discovery; and

(5) A statement showing that the attorney making the motion has made a reasonable effort to reach agreement with opposing attorneys on the matters set forth in the motion.

Each party and each party's attorney are under a duty to participate in good faith in the framing of a discovery plan if a plan is proposed by the attorney for any party. Notice of the motion shall be served on all parties. Objections or additions to matters set forth in the motion shall be served not later than 10 days after service of the motion.

Following the discovery conference, the court shall enter an order tentatively identifying the issues for discovery purposes, establishing a plan and schedule for discovery, setting limitations on discovery, if any; and determining such other matters, including the allocation of expenses, as are necessary for the proper management of discovery in the action. An order may be altered or amended whenever justice so requires.

Subject to the right of a party who properly moves for a discovery conference to prompt convening of the conference, the court may combine the discovery conference with a pretrial conference authorized by Rule 16.

(g) SIGNING OF DISCOVERY REQUESTS, RESPONSES, AND OBJECTIONS. Every request for discovery or response or objection thereto made by a party represented by an attorney shall be signed by at least one attorney of record in the attorney's individual name, whose address shall be stated. A party who is not represented by an attorney shall sign the request, response, or objection and state the party's address. The signature of the attorney or party constitutes a certification that the signer has read the request, response, or objection, and that to the best of the signer's knowledge, information, and belief formed after a reasonable inquiry it is: (1) consistent with these rules and warranted by existing law or a good faith argument for the extension, modification, or reversal of existing law; (2) not interposed for any improper purpose, such as to harass or to cause unnecessary delay or needless increase in the cost of litigation; and (3) not unreasonable or unduly burdensome or expensive, given the needs of the case, the discovery already had in the case, the amount in controversy, and the importance of the issues at stake in the litigation. If a request, response, or objection is not signed, it shall be stricken unless it is signed promptly after the omission is called to the attention of the party making the request, response, or objection, and a party shall not be obligated to take any action with respect to it until it is signed.

If a certification is made in violation of the rule, the court, upon motion or upon its own initiative, shall impose upon the person who made the certification, the party on whose behalf the request, response, or objection is made, or both, an appropriate sanction, which may include an order to pay the amount of the reasonable expenses incurred because of the violation, including a reasonable attorney's fee.

(As amended Dec. 27, 1946, eff. Mar. 19, 1948; Jan. 21, 1963, eff. July 1, 1963; Feb. 28, 1966, eff. July 1, 1966; Mar. 30, 1970, eff. July 1, 1970; Apr. 29, 1980, eff. Aug. 1, 1980; Apr. 28, 1983, eff. Aug. 1, 1983; Mar. 2, 1987, eff. Aug. 1, 1987.)

Rule 27. Depositions Before Action or Pending Appeal

(a) BEFORE ACTION.

(1) *Petition.* A person who desires to perpetuate testimony regarding any matter that may be cognizable in any court of the United States may file a verified petition in the United States district court in the district of the residence of any expected adverse party. The petition shall be entitled in the name of the petitioner and shall show: 1, that the petitioner expects to be a party to an action cognizable in a court of the United States but is presently unable to bring it or cause it to be brought, 2, the subject matter of the expected action and the petitioner's interest therein, 3, the facts which the petitioner desires to establish by the proposed testimony and the reasons for desiring to perpetuate it, 4, the names or a description of the persons the petitioner expects will be adverse parties and their addresses so far as known, and 5, the names and addresses of the persons to be examined and the substance of the testimony which the petitioner expects to elicit from each, and shall ask for an order authorizing the petitioner to take the depositions of the persons to be examined named in the petition, for the purpose of perpetuating their testimony.

(2) *Notice and Service.* The petitioner shall thereafter serve a notice upon each person named in the petition as an expected adverse party, together with a copy of the petition, stating that the petitioner will apply to the court, at a time and place named therein, for the order described in the petition. At least 20 days before the date of hearing the notice shall be served either within or without the district or state in the manner provided in Rule 4(d) for service of summons; but if such service cannot with due diligence be made upon any expected adverse party named in the petition, the court may make such order as is just for service by publication or otherwise, and shall appoint, for persons not served in the manner provided in Rule 4(d), an attorney who shall represent them, and, in case they are not otherwise represented, shall cross-examine the deponent. If any expected adverse party is a minor or incompetent the provisions of Rule 17(c) apply.

(3) *Order and Examination.* If the court is satisfied that the perpetuation of the testimony may prevent a failure or

delay of justice, it shall make an order designating or describing the persons whose depositions may be taken and specifying the subject matter of the examination and whether the depositions shall be taken upon oral examination or written interrogatories. The depositions may then be taken in accordance with these rules; and the court may make orders of the character provided for by Rules 34 and 35. For the purpose of applying these rules to depositions for perpetuating testimony, each reference therein to the court in which the action is pending shall be deemed to refer to the court in which the petition for such deposition was filed.

(4) *Use of Deposition.* If a deposition to perpetuate testimony is taken under these rules or if, although not so taken, it would be admissible in evidence in the courts of the state in which it is taken, it may be used in any action involving the same subject matter subsequently brought in a United States district court, in accordance with the provisions of Rule 32(a).

(b) PENDING APPEAL. If an appeal has been taken from a judgment of a district court or before the taking of an appeal if the time therefor has not expired, the district court in which the judgment was rendered may allow the taking of the depositions of witnesses to perpetuate their testimony for use in the event of further proceedings in the district court. In such case the party who desires to perpetuate the testimony may make a motion in the district court for leave to take the depositions, upon the same notice and service thereof as if the action was pending in the district court. The motion shall show (1) the names and addresses of persons to be examined and the substance of the testimony which the party expects to elicit from each; (2) the reasons for perpetuating their testimony. If the court finds that the perpetuation of the testimony is proper to avoid a failure or delay of justice, it may make an order allowing the depositions to be taken and may make orders of the character provided for by Rules 34 and 35, and thereupon the depositions may be taken and used in the same manner and under the same conditions as are prescribed in these rules for depositions taken in actions pending in the district court.

(c) PERPETUATION BY ACTION. This rule does not limit the power of a court to entertain an action to perpetuate testimony.

(As amended Dec. 27, 1946, eff. Mar. 19, 1948; Dec. 29, 1948, eff. Oct. 20, 1949; Mar. 1, 1971, eff. July 1, 1971; Mar. 2, 1987, eff. Aug. 1, 1987.)

Rule 28. Persons Before Whom Depositions May Be Taken

(a) WITHIN THE UNITED STATES. Within the United States or within a territory or insular possession subject to the jurisidiction of the United States, depositions shall be taken before an officer authorized to administer oaths by the laws of the United States or of the place where the examination is held, or before a person appointed by the court in which the action is pending. A person so appointed has power to administer oaths and take testimony. The term officer as used in Rules 30, 31 and 32 includes a person appointed by the court or designated by the parties under Rule 29.

(b) IN FOREIGN COUNTRIES. In a foreign country, depositions may be taken (1) on notice before a person authorized to administer oaths in the place in which the examination is held, either by the law thereof or by the law of the United States, or (2) before a person commissioned by the court, and a person so commissioned shall have the power by virtue of the commission to administer any necessary oath and take testimony, or (3) pursuant to a letter rogatory. A commission or a letter rogatory shall be issued on application and notice and on terms that are just and appropriate. It is not requisite to the issuance of a commission or a letter rogatory that the taking of the deposition in any other manner is impracticable or inconvenient; and both a commission and a letter rogatory may be issued in proper cases. A notice or commission may designate the person before whom the deposition is to be taken either by name or descriptive title. A letter rogatory may be addressed "To the Appropriate Authority in [here name the country]." Evidence obtained in response to a letter rogatory need not be excluded merely for the reason that it is not a verbatim transcript or that the testimony was not taken under oath or for any similar departure from the requirements for depositions taken within the United States under these rules.

(c) DISQUALIFICATION FOR INTEREST. No deposition shall be taken before a person who is a relative or employee or attorney or counsel of any of the parties, or is a relative or employee of such attorney or counsel, or is financially interested in the action.

(As amended Dec. 27, 1946, eff. Mar. 19, 1948; Jan. 21, 1963, eff. July 1, 1963; Apr. 29, 1980, eff. Aug. 1, 1980; Mar. 2, 1987, eff. Aug. 1, 1987.)

Rule 29. Stipulations Regarding Discovery Procedure

Unless the court orders otherwise, the parties may by written stipulation (1) provide that depositions may be taken before any person, at any time or place, upon any notice, and in any manner and when so taken may be used like other depositions, and (2) modify the procedures provided by these rules for other methods of discovery, except that stipulations extending the time provided in Rules 33, 34, and 36 for responses to discovery may be made only with the approval of the court.

(As amended Mar. 30, 1970, eff. July 1, 1970.)

Rule 30. Depositions Upon Oral Examination

(a) WHEN DEPOSITIONS MAY BE TAKEN. After commencement of the action, any party may take the testimony of any person, including a party, by deposition upon oral examination. Leave of court, granted with or without notice, must be obtained only if the plaintiff seeks to take a deposition prior to the expiration of 30 days after service of the summons and complaint upon any defendant or service made under Rule 4(e), except that leave is not required (1) if a defendant has served a notice of taking deposition or otherwise sought discovery, or (2) if special notice is given as provided in subdivision (b)(2) of this rule. The attendance of witnesses may be compelled by subpoena as provided in Rule 45. The deposition of a person confined in prison may be taken only by leave of court on such terms as the court prescribes.

(b) NOTICE OF EXAMINATION: GENERAL REQUIREMENTS; SPECIAL NOTICE; NON-STENOGRAPHIC RECORDING; PRODUCTION OF DOCUMENTS AND THINGS; DEPOSITION OF ORGANIZATION; DEPOSITION BY TELEPHONE.

(1) A party desiring to take the deposition of any person upon oral examination shall give reasonable notice in writing to every other party to the action. The notice shall state the time and place for taking the deposition and the name and address of each person to be examined, if known, and, if the name is not known, a general description sufficient to identify the person or the particular class or group to which the person belongs. If a subpoena duces tecum is to be served on the person to be examined, the designation of the materials to be produced as set forth in the subpoena shall be attached to or included in the notice.

(2) Leave of court is not required for the taking of a deposition by the plaintiff if the notice (A) states that the person to be examined is about to go out of the district where the action is pending and more than 100 miles from the place of trial, or is about to go out of the United States, or is bound on a voyage to sea, and will be unavailable for examination unless the person's deposition is taken before expiration of the 30-day period, and (B) sets forth facts to support the statement. The plaintiff's attorney shall sign the notice, and the attorney's signature constitutes a certification by the attorney that to the best of the attorney's knowledge, information, and belief the statement and supporting facts are true.

The sanctions provided by Rule 11 are applicable to the certification.

If a party shows that when the party was served with notice under this subdivision (b)(2) the party was unable through the exercise of diligence to obtain counsel to represent the party at the taking of the deposition, the deposition may not be used against the party.

(3) The court may for cause shown enlarge or shorten the time for taking the deposition.

(4) The parties may stipulate in writing or the court may upon motion order that the testimony at a deposition be recorded by other than stenographic means. The stipulation or order shall designate the person before whom the deposition shall be taken, the manner of recording, preserving and filing the deposition, and may include other provisions to assure that the recorded testimony will be accurate and trustworthy. A party may arrange to have a stenographic transcription made at the party's own expense. Any objections under subdivision (c), any changes made by the witness, the witness' signature identifying the deposition as the witness' own or the statement of the officer that is required if the witness does not sign, as provided in subdivision (e), and the certification of the officer required by subdivision (f) shall be set forth in a writing to accompany a deposition recorded by non-stenographic means.

(5) The notice to a party deponent may be accompanied by a request made in compliance with Rule 34 for the production of documents and tangible things at the taking of the deposition. The procedure of Rule 34 shall apply to the request.

(6) A party may in the party's notice and in a subpoena name as the deponent a public or private corporation or a partnership or association or governmental agency and describe with reasonable particularity the matters on which examination is requested. In that event, the organization so named shall designate one or more officers, directors, or managing agents, or other persons who consent to testify on its behalf, and may set forth, for each person designated, the matters on which the person will testify. A subpoena shall advise a non-party organization of its duty to make such a designation. The persons so designated shall testify as to matters known or reasonably available to the organization. This subdivision (b)(6) does not preclude taking a deposition by any other procedure authorized in these rules.

(7) The parties may stipulate in writing or the court may upon motion order that a deposition be taken by telephone. For the purposes of this rule and Rules 28(a), 37(a)(1),

37(b)(1), and 45(d), a deposition taken by telephone is taken in the district and at the place where the deponent is to answer questions propounded to the deponent.

(c) EXAMINATION AND CROSS-EXAMINATION; RECORD OF EXAMINATION; OATH; OBJECTIONS. Examination and cross-examination of witnesses may proceed as permitted at the trial under the provisions of the Federal Rules of Evidence. The officer before whom the deposition is to be taken shall put the witness on oath and shall personally, or by someone acting under the officer's direction and in the officer's presence, record the testimony of the witness. The testimony shall be taken stenographically or recorded by any other means ordered in accordance with subdivision (b)(4) of this rule. If requested by one of the parties, the testimony shall be transcribed. All objections made at the time of the examination to the qualifications of the officer taking the deposition, or to the manner of taking it, or to the evidence presented, or to the conduct of any party, and any other objection to the proceedings, shall be noted by the officer upon the deposition. Evidence objected to shall be taken subject to the objections. In lieu of participating in the oral examination, parties may serve written questions in a sealed envelope on the party taking the deposition and the party taking the deposition shall transmit them to the officer, who shall propound them to the witness and record the answers verbatim.

(d) MOTION TO TERMINATE OR LIMIT EXAMINATION. At any time during the taking of the deposition, on motion of a party or of the deponent and upon a showing that the examination is being conducted in bad faith or in such manner as unreasonably to annoy, embarrass, or oppress the deponent or party,.the court in which the action is pending or the court in the district where the deposition is being taken may order the officer conducting the examination to cease forthwith from taking the deposition, or may limit the scope and manner of the taking of the deposition as provided in Rule 26(c). If the order made terminates the examination, it shall be resumed thereafter only upon the order of the court in which the action is pending. Upon demand of the objecting party or deponent, the taking of the deposition shall be suspended for the time necessary to make a motion for an order. The provisions of Rule 37(a)(4) apply to the award of expenses incurred in relation to the motion.

(e) SUBMISSION TO WITNESS; CHANGES; SIGNING. When the testimony is fully transcribed the deposition shall be submitted to the witness for examination and shall be read to or by the witness, unless such examination and reading are waived by the witness and by the parties. Any changes in form or substance which the witness desires to make shall be entered upon the deposition by the officer with a statement of the reasons given by the witness for making them. The deposition shall then be signed by the witness, unless the parties by stipulation waive the signing or the witness is ill or cannot be found or refuses to sign. If the deposition is not signed by the witness within 30 days of its submission to the witness, the officer shall sign it and state on the record the fact of the waiver or of the illness or absence of the witness or the fact of the refusal to sign together with the reason, if any, given therefor; and the deposition may then be used as fully as though signed unless on a motion to suppress under Rule 32(d)(4) the court holds that the reasons given for the refusal to sign require rejection of the deposition in whole or in part.

(f) CERTIFICATION AND FILING BY OFFICER; EXHIBITS; COPIES; NOTICE OF FILING.

(1) The officer shall certify on the deposition that the witness was duly sworn by the officer and that the deposition is a true record of the testimony given by the witness. Unless otherwise ordered by the court, the officer shall then securely seal the deposition in an envelope indorsed with the title of the action and marked "Deposition of [here insert name of witness]" and shall promptly file it with the court in which the action is pending or send it by registered or certified mail to the clerk thereof for filing.

Documents and things produced for inspection during the examination of the witness, shall, upon the request of a party, be marked for identification and annexed to the deposition and may be inspected and copied by any party, except that if the person producing the materials desires to retain them the person may (A) offer copies to be marked for identification and annexed to the deposition and to serve thereafter as originals if the person affords to all parties fair opportunity to verify the copies by comparison with the originals, or (B) offer the originals to be marked for identification, after giving to each party an opportunity to inspect and copy them, in which event the materials may then be used in the same manner as if annexed to the deposition. Any party may move for an order that the original be annexed to and returned with the deposition to the court, pending final disposition of the case.

(2) Upon payment of reasonable charges therefor, the officer shall furnish a copy of the deposition to any party or to the deponent.

(3) The party taking the deposition shall give prompt notice of its filing to all other parties.

(g) FAILURE TO ATTEND OR TO SERVE SUBPOENA; EXPENSES.

(1) If the party giving the notice of the taking of a deposition fails to attend and proceed therewith and another party attends in person or by attorney pursuant to the notice, the court may order the party giving the notice to pay to such

other party the reasonable expenses incurred by that party and that party's attorney in attending, including reasonable attorney's fees.

(2) If the party giving the notice of the taking of a deposition of a witness fails to serve a subpoena upon the witness and the witness because of such failure does not attend, and if another party attends in person or by attorney because that party expects the deposition of that witness to be taken, the court may order the party giving the notice to pay to such other party the reasonable expenses incurred by that party and that party's attorney in attending, including reasonable attorney's fees.

(As amended Jan. 21, 1963, eff. July 1, 1963; Mar. 30, 1970, eff. July 1, 1970; Mar. 1, 1971, eff. July 1, 1971; Nov. 20, 1972, eff. July 1, 1975; Apr. 29, 1980, eff. Aug. 1, 1980; Mar. 2, 1987, eff. Aug. 1, 1987.)

Rule 31. Depositions Upon Written Questions

(a) SERVING QUESTIONS; NOTICE. After commencement of the action, any party may take the testimony of any person, including a party, by deposition upon written questions. The attendance of witnesses may be compelled by the use of subpoena as provided in Rule 45. The deposition of a person confined in prison may be taken only by leave of court on such terms as the court prescribes.

A party desiring to take a deposition upon written questions shall serve them upon every other party with a notice stating (1) the name and address of the person who is to answer them, if known, and if the name is not known, a general description sufficient to identify the person or the particular class or group to which the person belongs, and (2) the name or descriptive title and address of the officer before whom the deposition is to be taken. A deposition upon written questions may be taken of a public or private corporation or a partnership or association or governmental agency in accordance with the provisions of Rule 30(b)(6).

Within 30 days after the notice and written questions are served, a party may serve cross questions upon all other parties. Within 10 days after being served with cross questions, a party may serve redirect questions upon all other parties. Within 10 days after being served with redirect questions, a party may serve recross questions upon all other parties. The court may for cause shown enlarge or shorten the time.

(b) OFFICER TO TAKE RESPONSES AND PREPARE RECORD. A copy of the notice and copies of all questions served shall be delivered by the party taking the deposition to the officer designated in the notice, who shall proceed promptly, in the manner provided by

Rule 30(c), (e), and (f), to take the testimony of the witness in response to the questions and to prepare, certify, and file or mail the deposition, attaching thereto the copy of the notice and the questions received by the officer.

(c) NOTICE OF FILING. When the deposition is filed the party taking it shall promptly give notice thereof to all other parties.

(As amended Mar. 30, 1970, eff. July 1, 1970; Mar. 2, 1987, eff. Aug. 1, 1987.)

Rule 32. Use of Depositions in Court Proceedings

(a) USE OF DEPOSITIONS. At the trial or upon the hearing of a motion or an interlocutory proceeding, any part or all of a deposition, so far as admissible under the rules of evidence applied as though the witness were then present and testifying, may be used against any party who was present or represented at the taking of the deposition or who had reasonable notice thereof, in accordance with any of the following provisions:

(1) Any deposition may be used by any party for the purpose of contradicting or impeaching the testimony of deponent as a witness, or for any other purpose permitted by the Federal Rules of Evidence.

(2) The deposition of a party or of anyone who at the time of taking the deposition was an officer, director, or managing agent, or a person designated under Rule 30(b)(6) or 31(a) to testify on behalf of a public or private corporation, partnership or association or governmental agency which is a party may be used by an adverse party for any purpose.

(3) The deposition of a witness, whether or not a party, may be used by any party for any purpose if the court finds: (A) that the witness is dead; or (B) that the witness is at a greater distance than 100 miles from the place of trial or hearing, or is out of the United States, unless it appears that the absence of the witness was procured by the party offering the deposition; or (C) that the witness is unable to attend or testify because of age, illness, infirmity, or imprisonment; or (D) that the party offering the deposition has been unable to procure the attendance of the witness by subpoena; or (E) upon application and notice, that such exceptional circumstances exist as to make it desirable, in the interest of justice and with due regard to the importance of presenting the testimony of witnesses orally in open court, to allow the deposition to be used.

(4) If only part of a deposition is offered in evidence by a party, an adverse party may require the offeror to introduce any other part which ought in fairness to be considered with the part introduced, and any party may introduce any other parts.

Substitution of parties pursuant to Rule 25 does not affect the right to use depositions previously taken; and, when an action has been brought in any court of the United States or of any State and another action involving the same subject matter is afterward brought between the same parties or their representatives or successors in interest, all depositions lawfully taken and duly filed in the former action may be used in the latter as if originally taken therefor. A deposition previously taken may also be used as permitted by the Federal Rules of Evidence.

(b) OBJECTIONS TO ADMISSIBILITY. Subject to the provisions of Rule 28(b) and subdivision (d)(3) of this rule, objection may be made at the trial or hearing to receiving in evidence any deposition or part thereof for any reason which would require the exclusion of the evidence if the witness were then present and testifying.

[(c) EFFECT OF TAKING OR USING DEPOSITIONS.] (Abrogated Nov. 20, 1972, eff. July 1, 1975)

(d) EFFECT OF ERRORS AND IRREGULARITIES IN DEPOSITIONS.

(1) *As to Notice.* All errors and irregularities in the notice for taking a deposition are waived unless written objection is promptly served upon the party giving the notice.

(2) *As to Disqualification of Officer.* Objection to taking a deposition because of disqualification of the officer before whom it is to be taken is waived unless made before the taking of the deposition begins or as soon thereafter as the disqualification becomes known or could be discovered with reasonable diligence.

(3) *As to Taking of Deposition.*

(A) Objections to the competency of a witness or to the competency, relevancy, or materiality of testimony are not waived by failure to make them before or during the taking of the deposition, unless the ground of the objection is one which might have been obviated or removed if presented at that time.

(B) Errors and irregularities occurring at the oral examination in the manner of taking the deposition, in the form of the questions or answers, in the oath or affirmation, or in the conduct of parties, and errors of any kind which might be obviated, removed, or cured if promptly presented, are waived unless seasonable objection thereto is made at the taking of the deposition.

(C) Objections to the form of written questions submitted under Rule 31 are waived unless served in writing upon the party propounding them within the time allowed for serving the succeeding cross or other questions and within 5 days after service of the last questions authorized.

(4) *As to Completion and Return of Deposition.* Errors and irregularities in the manner in which the testimony is transcribed or the deposition is prepared, signed, certified, sealed, indorsed, transmitted, filed, or otherwise dealt with by the officer under Rules 30 and 31 are waived unless a motion to suppress the deposition or some part thereof is made with reasonable promptness after such defect is, or with due diligence might have been, ascertained.

(As amended Mar. 30, 1970, eff. July 1, 1970; Nov. 20, 1972, eff. July 1, 1975; Apr. 29, 1980, eff. Aug. 1, 1980; Mar. 2, 1987, eff. Aug. 1, 1987.)

Rule 37. Failure To Make or Cooperate in Discovery: Sanctions

(a) MOTION FOR ORDER COMPELLING DISCOVERY. A party, upon reasonable notice to other parties and all persons affected thereby, may apply for an order compelling discovery as follows:

(1) *Appropriate Court.* An application for an order to a party may be made to the court in which the action is pending, or, on matters relating to a deposition, to the court in the district where the deposition is being taken. An application for an order to a deponent who is not a party shall be made to the court in the district where the deposition is being taken.

(2) *Motion.* If a deponent fails to answer a question propounded or submitted under Rules 30 or 31, or a corporation or other entity fails to make a designation under Rule 30(b)(6) or 31(a), or a party fails to answer an interrogatory submitted under Rule 33, or if a party, in response to a request for inspection submitted under Rule 34, fails to respond that inspection will be permitted as requested or fails to permit inspection as requested, the discovering party may move for an order compelling an answer, or a designation, or an order compelling inspection in accordance with the request. When taking a deposition on oral examination, the proponent of the question may complete or adjourn the examination before applying for an order.

If the court denies the motion in whole or in part, it may make such protective order as it would have been empowered to make on a motion made pursuant to Rule 26(c).

(3) *Evasive or Incomplete Answer.* For purposes of this subdivision an evasive or incomplete answer is to be treated as a failure to answer.

(4) *Award of Expenses of Motion.* If the motion is granted, the court shall, after opportunity for hearing, require the party or deponent whose conduct necessitated the motion or the party or attorney advising such conduct or both of them

to pay to the moving party the reasonable expenses incurred in obtaining the order, including attorney's fees, unless the court finds that the opposition to the motion was substantially justified or that other circumstances make an award of expenses unjust.

If the motion is denied, the court shall, after opportunity for hearing, require the moving party or the attorney advising the motion or both of them to pay to the party or deponent who opposed the motion the reasonable expenses incurred in opposing the motion, including attorney's fees, unless the court finds that the making of the motion was substantially justified or that other circumstances make an award of expenses unjust.

If the motion is granted in part and denied in part, the court may apportion the reasonable expenses incurred in relation to the motion among the parties and persons in a just manner.

(b) FAILURE TO COMPLY WITH ORDER.

(1) *Sanctions by Court in District Where Deposition Is Taken.* If a deponent fails to be sworn or to answer a question after being directed to do so by the court in the district in which the deposition is being taken, the failure may be considered a contempt of that court.

(2) *Sanctions by Court in Which Action Is Pending.* If a party or an officer, director, or managing agent of a party or a person designated under Rule 30(b)(6) or 31(a) to testify on behalf of a party fails to obey an order to provide or permit discovery, including an order made under subdivision (a) of this rule or Rule 35, or if a party fails to obey an order entered under Rule 26(f), the court in which the action is pending may make such orders in regard to the failure as are just, and among others the following:

(A) An order that the matters regarding which the order was made or any other designated facts shall be taken to be established for the purposes of the action in accordance with the claim of the party obtaining the order;

(B) An order refusing to allow the disobedient party to support or oppose designated claims or defenses, or prohibiting that party from introducing designated matters in evidence;

(C) An order striking out pleadings or parts thereof, or staying further proceedings until the order is obeyed, or dismissing the action or proceeding or any part thereof, or rendering a judgment by default against the disobedient party;

(D) In lieu of any of the foregoing orders or in addition thereto, an order treating as a contempt of court the failure to obey any orders except an order to submit to a physical or mental examination;

(E) Where a party has failed to comply with an order under Rule 35(a) requiring that party to produce another for examination, such orders as are listed in paragraphs (A), (B), and (C) of this subdivision, unless the party failing to comply shows that that party is unable to produce such person for examination.

In lieu of any of the foregoing orders or in addition thereto, the court shall require the party failing to obey the order or the attorney advising that party or both to pay the reasonable expenses, including attorney's fees, caused by the failure, unless the court finds that the failure was substantially justified or that other circumstances make an award of expenses unjust.

(c) EXPENSES ON FAILURE TO ADMIT. If a party fails to admit the genuineness of any document or the truth of any matter as requested under Rule 36, and if the party requesting the admissions thereafter proves the genuineness of the document or the truth of the matter, the requesting party may apply to the court for an order requiring the other party to pay the reasonable expenses incurred in making that proof, including reasonable attorney's fees. The court shall make the order unless it finds that (1) the request was held objectionable pursuant to Rule 36(a), or (2) the admission sought was of no substantial importance, or (3) the party failing to admit had reasonable ground to believe that the party might prevail on the matter, or (4) there was other good reason for the failure to admit.

(d) FAILURE OF PARTY TO ATTEND AT OWN DEPOSITION OR SERVE ANSWERS TO INTERROGATORIES OR RESPOND TO REQUEST FOR INSPECTION. If a party or an officer, director, or managing agent of a party or a person designated under Rule 30(b)(6) or 31(a) to testify on behalf of a party fails (1) to appear before the officer who is to take the deposition, after being served with a proper notice, or (2) to serve answers or objections to interrogatories submitted under Rule 33, after proper service of the interrogatories, or (3) to serve a written response to a request for inspection submitted under Rule 34, after proper service of the request, the court in which the action is pending on motion may make such orders in regard to the failure as are just, and among others it may take any action authorized under paragraphs (A), (B), and (C) of subdivision (b)(2) of this rule. In lieu of any order or in addition thereto, the court shall require the party failing to act or the attorney advising that party or both to pay the reasonable expenses, including attorney's fees, caused by the failure, unless the court finds that the failure was substantially justified or that other circumstances make an award of expenses unjust.

The failure to act described in this subdivision may not be excused on the ground that the discovery sought is objectionable unless the party failing to act has applied for a protective order as provided by Rule 26(c).

[(e) SUBPOENA OF PERSON IN FOREIGN COUNTRY.] (Abrogated Apr. 29, 1980, eff. Aug. 1, 1980)

[(f) EXPENSES AGAINST UNITED STATES.] (Repealed Oct. 21, 1980, eff. Oct. 1, 1981)

(g) FAILURE TO PARTICIPATE IN THE FRAMING OF A DISCOVERY PLAN. If a party or a party's attorney fails to participate in good faith in the framing of a discovery plan by agreement as is required by Rule 26(f), the court may, after opportunity for hearing, require such party or attorney to pay to any other party the reasonable expenses, including attorney's fees, caused by the failure.

(As amended Dec. 29, 1948, eff. Oct. 20, 1949; Mar. 30, 1970, eff. July 1, 1970; Apr. 29, 1980, eff. Aug. 1, 1980; Oct. 21, 1980, eff. Oct. 1, 1981; Mar. 2, 1987, eff. Aug. 1, 1987.)

Federal Rules of Evidence Applicable to Depositions

Rule 612. Writing Used To Refresh Memory

Except as otherwise provided in criminal proceedings by section 3500 of title 18, United States Code, if a witness uses a writing to refresh memory for the purpose of testifying, either—

(1) while testifying, or

(2) before testifying, if the court in its discretion determines it is necessary in the interests of justice,

an adverse party is entitled to have the writing produced at the hearing, to inspect it, to cross-examine the witness thereon, and to introduce in evidence those portions which relate to the testimony of the witness. If it is claimed that the writing contains matters not related to the subject matter of the testimony the court shall examine the writing in camera, excise any portions not so related, and order delivery of the remainder to the party entitled thereto. Any portion withheld over objections shall be preserved and made available to the appellate court in the event of an appeal. If a writing is not produced or delivered pursuant to order under this rule, the court shall make any order justice requires, except that in criminal cases when the prosecution elects not to comply, the order shall be one striking the testimony or, if the court in its discretion determines that the interests of justice so require, declaring a mistrial.

(As amended Mar. 2, 1987, eff. Oct. 1, 1987.)

Rule 615. Exclusion of Witnesses

At the request of a party the court shall order witnesses excluded so that they cannot hear the testimony of other witnesses, and it may make the order of its own motion. This rule does not authorize exclusion of (1) a party who is a natural person, or (2) an officer or employee of party [1] which is not a natural person designated as its representative by its attorney, or (3) a person whose presence is shown by a party to be essential to the presentation of the party's cause.

(As amended Mar. 2, 1987, eff. Oct. 1, 1987.)

Rule 801. Definitions

The following definitions apply under this article:

(a) Statement.—A "statement" is (1) an oral or written asser-

---

[1] The preposition "a" which originally preceded "party" appears to have been inadvertently eliminated by the 1987 amendment of Rule 615.

tion or (2) nonverbal conduct of a person, if it is intended by the person as an assertion.

(b) Declarant.—A "declarant" is a person who makes a statement.

(c) Hearsay.—"Hearsay" is a statement, other than one made by the declarant while testifying at the trial or hearing, offered in evidence to prove the truth of the matter asserted.

(d) Statements which are not hearsay.—A statement is not hearsay if—

(1) Prior statement by witness.—The declarant testifies at the trial or hearing and is subject to cross-examination concerning the statement, and the statement is (A) inconsistent with the declarant's testimony, and was given under oath subject to the penalty of perjury at a trial, hearing, or other proceeding, or in a deposition, or (B) consistent with the declarant's testimony and is offered to rebut an express or implied charge against the declarant of recent fabrication or improper influence or motive, or (C) one of identification of a person made after perceiving the person; or

(2) Admission by party-opponent.—The statement is offered against a party and is (A) the party's own statement in either an individual or a representative capacity or (B) a statement of which the party has manifested an adoption or belief in its truth, or (C) a statement by a person authorized by the party to make a statement concerning the subject, or (D) a statement by the party's agent or servant concerning a matter within the scope of the agency or employment, made during the existence of the relationship, or (E) a statement by a co-conspirator of a party during the course and in furtherance of the conspiracy.

(As amended Oct. 16, 1975, eff. Oct. 31, 1975; Mar. 2, 1987, eff. Oct. 1, 1987.)

Rule 802. Hearsay Rule

Hearsay is not admissible except as provided by these rules or by other rules prescribed by the Supreme Court pursuant to statutory authority or by Act of Congress.

Rule 803. Hearsay Exceptions; Availability of Declarant Immaterial

The following are not excluded by the hearsay rule, even though the declarant is available as a witness:

(1) Present sense impression.—A statement describing or explaining an event or condition made while the declarant was perceiving the event or condition, or immediately thereafter.

(2) Excited utterance.—A statement relating to a startling event or condition made while the declarant was under the stress of excitement caused by the event or condition.

(3) Then existing mental, emotional, or physical condition.—A statement of the declarant's then existing state of mind, emotion, sensation, or physical condition (such as intent, plan, motive, design, mental feeling, pain, and bodily health), but not including a statement of memory or belief to prove the fact remembered or believed unless it relates to the execution, revocation, identification, or terms of declarant's will.

(4) Statements for purposes of medical diagnosis or treatment.—Statements made for purposes of medical diagnosis or treatment and describing medical history, or past or present symptoms, pain, or sensations, or the inception or general character of the cause or external source thereof insofar as reasonably pertinent to diagnosis or treatment.

(5) Recorded recollection.—A memorandum or record concerning a matter about which a witness once had knowledge but now has insufficient recollection to enable the witness to testify fully and accurately, shown to have been made or adopted by the witness when the matter was fresh in the witness' memory and to reflect that knowledge correctly. If admitted, the memorandum or record may be read into evidence but may not itself be received as an exhibit unless offered by an adverse party.

(6) Records of regularly conducted activity.—A memorandum, report, record, or data compilation, in any form, of acts, events, conditions, opinions, or diagnoses, made at or near the time by, or from information transmitted by, a person with knowledge, if kept in the course of a regularly conducted business activity, and if it was the regular practice of that business activity to make the memorandum, report, record, or data compilation, all as shown by the testimony of the custodian or other qualified witness, unless the source of information or the method or circumstances of preparation indicate lack of trustworthiness. The term "business" as used in this paragraph includes business, institution, association, profession, occupation, and calling of every kind, whether or not conducted for profit.

(7) Absence of entry in records kept in accordance with the provisions of paragraph (6).—Evidence that a matter is not included in the memoranda reports, records, or data compilations, in any form, kept in accordance with the provisions of paragraph (6), to prove the nonoccurrence or nonexistence of the matter, if the matter was of a kind of which a memorandum, report, record, or data compilation was regularly made and preserved, unless the sources of information or other circumstances indicate lack of trustworthiness.

(8) Public records and reports.—Records, reports, statements, or data compilations, in any form, of public offices or agencies, setting forth (A) the activities of the office or agency, or (B) matters observed pursuant to duty imposed by law as to which matters there was a duty to report, excluding, however, in criminal cases matters observed by police officers and other law enforcement personnel, or (C) in civil actions and proceedings and against the Government in criminal cases, factual findings resulting from an investigation made pursuant to authority granted by law, unless the sources of information or other circumstances indicate lack of trustworthiness.

(9) Records of vital statistics.—Records or data compilations, in any form, of births, fetal deaths, deaths, or marriages, if the report thereof was made to a public office pursuant to requirements of law.

(10) Absence of public record or entry.—To prove the absence of a record, report, statement, or data compilation, in any form, or the nonoccurrence or nonexistence of a matter of which a record, report, statement, or data compilation, in any form, was regularly made and preserved by a public office or agency, evidence in the form of a certification in accordance with rule 902, or testimony, that diligent search failed to disclose the record, report, statement, or data compilation, or entry.

(11) Records of religious organizations.—Statements of births, marriages, divorces, deaths, legitimacy, ancestry, relationship by blood or marriage, or other similar facts of personal or family history, contained in a regularly kept record of a religious organization.

(12) Marriage, baptismal, and similar certificates.—Statements of fact contained in a certificate that the maker performed a marriage or other ceremony or administered a sacrament, made by a clergyman, public official, or other person authorized by the rules or practices of a religious organization or by law to perform the act certified, and purporting to have been issued at the time of the act or within a reasonable time thereafter.

(13) Family records.—Statements of fact concerning personal or family history contained in family Bibles, genealogies, charts, engravings on rings, inscriptions on family portraits, engravings on urns, crypts, or tombstones, or the like.

(14) Records of documents affecting an interest in property.—The record of a document purporting to establish or affect an interest in property, as proof of the content of the original recorded document and its execution and delivery by each person by whom it purports to have been executed, if

210

the record is a record of a public office and an applicable statute authorizes the recording of documents of that kind in that office.

(15) Statements in documents affecting an interest in property.—A statement contained in a document purporting to establish or affect an interest in property if the matter stated was relevant to the purpose of the document, unless dealings with the property since the document was made have been inconsistent with the truth of the statement or the purport of the document.

(16) Statements in ancient documents.—Statements in a document in existence twenty years or more the authenticity of which is established.

(17) Market reports, commercial publications.—Market quotations, tabulations, lists, directories, or other published compilations, generally used and relied upon by the public or by persons in particular occupations.

(18) Learned treatises.—To the extent called to the attention of an expert witness upon cross-examination or relied upon by the expert witness in direct examination, statements contained in published treatises, periodicals, or pamphlets on a subject of history, medicine, or other science or art, established as a reliable authority by the testimony or admission of the witness or by other expert testimony or by judicial notice. If admitted, the statements may be read into evidence but may not be received as exhibits.

(19) Reputation concerning personal or family history.—Reputation among members of a person's family by blood, adoption, or marriage, or among a person's associates, or in the community, concerning a person's birth, adoption, marriage, divorce, death, legitimacy, relationship by blood, adoption, or marriage, ancestry, or other similar fact of personal or family history.

(20) Reputation concerning boundaries or general history.—Reputation in a community, arising before the controversy, as to boundaries of or customs affecting lands in the community, and reputation as to events of general history important to the community or State or nation in which located.

(21) Reputation as to character.—Reputation of a person's character among associates or in the community.

(22) Judgment of previous conviction.—Evidence of a final judgment, entered after a trial or upon a plea of guilty (but not upon a plea of nolo contendere), adjudging a person guilty of a crime punishable by death or imprisonment in excess of one year, to prove any fact essential to sustain the

judgment, but not including, when offered by the Government in a criminal prosecution for purposes other than impeachment, judgments against persons other than the accused. The pendency of an appeal may be shown but does not affect admissibility.

(23) Judgment as to personal, family, or general history, or boundaries.—Judgments as proof of matters of personal, family or general history, or boundaries, essential to the judgment, if the same would be provable by evidence of reputation.

(24) Other exceptions.—A statement not specifically covered by any of the foregoing exceptions but having equivalent circumstantial guarantees of trustworthiness, if the court determines that (A) the statement is offered as evidence of a material fact; (B) the statement is more probative on the point for which it is offered than any other evidence which the proponent can procure through reasonable efforts; and (C) the general purposes of these rules and the interests of justice will best be served by admission of the statement into evidence. However, a statement may not be admitted under this exception unless the proponent of it makes known to the adverse party sufficiently in advance of the trial or hearing to provide the adverse party with a fair opportunity to prepare to meet it, the proponent's intention to offer the statement and the particulars of it, including the name and address of the declarant.

(As amended Dec. 12, 1975; Mar. 2, 1987, eff. Oct. 1, 1987.)

Rule 804. Hearsay Exceptions; Declarant Unavailable

(a) Definition of unavailability.—"Unavailability as a witness" includes situations in which the declarant—

(1) is exempted by ruling of the court on the ground of privilege from testifying concerning the subject matter of the declarant's statement; or

(2) persists in refusing to testify concerning the subject matter of the declarant's statement despite an order of the court to do so; or

(3) testifies to a lack of memory of the subject matter of the declarant's statement; or

(4) is unable to be present or to testify at the hearing because of death or then existing physical or mental illness or infirmity; or

(5) is absent from the hearing and the proponent of a statement has been unable to procure the declarant's attendance (or in the case of a hearsay exception under subdivisions

(b)(2), (3), or (4), the declarant's attendance or testimony) by process or other reasonable means.

A declarant is not unavailable as a witness if exemption, refusal, claim of lack of memory, inability, or absence is due to the procurement or wrongdoing of the proponent of a statement for the purpose of preventing the witness from attending or testifying.

(b) Hearsay exceptions.—The following are not excluded by the hearsay rule if the declarant is unavailable as a witness:

(1) Former testimony.—Testimony given as a witness at another hearing of the same or a different proceeding, or in a deposition taken in compliance with law in the course of the same or another proceeding, if the party against whom the testimony is now offered, or, in a civil action or proceeding, a predecessor in interest, had an opportunity and similar motive to develop the testimony by direct, cross, or redirect examination.

(2) Statement under belief of impending death.—In a prosecution for homicide or in a civil action or proceeding, a statement made by a declarant while believing that the declarant's death was imminent, concerning the cause or circumstances of what the declarant believed to be impending death.

(3) Statement against interest.—A statement which was at the time of its making so far contrary to the declarant's pecuniary or proprietary interest, or so far tended to subject the declarant to civil or criminal liability, or to render invalid a claim by the declarant against another, that a reasonable person in the declarant's position would not have made the statement unless believing it to be true. A statement tending to expose the declarant to criminal liability and offered to exculpate the accused is not admissible unless corroborating circumstances clearly indicate the trustworthiness of the statement.

(4) Statement of personal or family history.—(A) A statement concerning the declarant's own birth, adoption, marriage, divorce, legitimacy, relationship by blood, adoption, or marriage, ancestry, or other similar fact of personal or family history, even though declarant had no means of acquiring personal knowledge of the matter stated; or (B) a statement concerning the foregoing matters, and death also, of another person, if the declarant was related to the other by blood, adoption, or marriage or was so intimately associated with the other's family as to be likely to have accurate information concerning the matter declared.

213

(5) Other exceptions.—A statement not specifically covered by any of the foregoing exceptions but having equivalent circumstantial guarantees of trustworthiness, if the court determines that (A) the statement is offered as evidence of a material fact; (B) the statement is more probative on the point for which it is offered than any other evidence which the proponent can procure through reasonable efforts; and (C) the general purposes of these rules and the interests of justice will best be served by admission of the statement into evidence. However, a statement may not be admitted under this exception unless the proponent of it makes known to the adverse party sufficiently in advance of the trial or hearing to provide the adverse party with a fair opportunity to prepare to meet it, the proponent's intention to offer the statement and the particulars of it, including the name and address of the declarant.

(As amended Dec. 12, 1975; Mar. 2, 1987, eff. Oct. 1, 1987.)

Rule 901. Requirement of Authentication or Identification

(a) General provision.—The requirement of authentication or identification as a condition precedent to admissibility is satisfied by evidence sufficient to support a finding that the matter in question is what its proponent claims.

(b) Illustrations.—By way of illustration only, and not by way of limitation, the following are examples of authentication or identification conforming with the requirements of this rule:

(1) Testimony of witness with knowledge.—Testimony that a matter is what it is claimed to be.

(2) Nonexpert opinion on handwriting.—Nonexpert opinion as to the genuineness of handwriting, based upon familiarity not acquired for purposes of the litigation.

(3) Comparison by trier or expert witness.—Comparison by the trier of fact or by expert witnesses with specimens which have been authenticated.

(4) Distinctive characteristics and the like.—Appearance, contents, substance, internal patterns, or other distinctive characteristics, taken in conjunction with circumstances.

(5) Voice identification.—Identification of a voice, whether heard firsthand or through mechanical or electronic transmission or recording, by opinion based upon hearing the voice at any time under circumstances connecting it with the alleged speaker.

(6) Telephone conversations.—Telephone conversations, by evidence that a call was made to the number assigned at the time by the telephone company to a particular person or business, if (A) in the case of a person, circumstances, including self-identification, show the person answering to be the

one called, or (B) in the case of a business, the call was made to a place of business and the conversation related to business reasonably transacted over the telephone.

(7) Public records or reports.—Evidence that a writing authorized by law to be recorded or filed and in fact recorded or filed in a public office, or a purported public record, report, statement, or data compilation, in any form, is from the public office where items of this nature are kept.

(8) Ancient documents or data compilation.—Evidence that a document or data compilation, in any form, (A) is in such condition as to create no suspicion concerning its authenticity, (B) was in a place where it, if authentic, would likely be, and (C) has been in existence 20 years or more at the time it is offered.

(9) Process or system.—Evidence describing a process or system used to produce a result and showing that the process or system produces an accurate result.

(10) Methods provided by statute or rule.—Any method of authentication or identification provided by Act of Congress or by other rules prescribed by the Supreme Court pursuant to statutory authority.

Rule 1007. Testimony or Written Admission of Party

Contents of writings, recordings, or photographs may be proved by the testimony or deposition of the party against whom offered or by that party's written admission, without accounting for the nonproduction of the original.

(As amended Mar. 2, 1987, eff. Oct. 1, 1987.)

UNIFORM AUDIO-VISUAL DEPOSITION
[ACT] [RULE]

Drafted by the

NATIONAL CONFERENCE OF COMMISSIONERS ON UNIFORM STATE LAWS

and by it

APPROVED AND RECOMMENDED FOR ENACTMENT
IN ALL THE STATES

at its

ANNUAL CONFERENCE
MEETING IN ITS EIGHTY-SEVENTH YEAR
IN NEW YORK, NEW YORK
JULY 28 - AUGUST 4, 1978

WITH
PREFATORY NOTE AND COMMENTS

APPROVED BY THE AMERICAN BAR ASSOCIATION AT ITS MEETING IN
ATLANTA, GEORGIA, FEBRUARY 13, 1979

SPECIAL COMMITTEE ON UNIFORM AUDIO-VISUAL DEPOSITION [ACT] [RULE]

RICHARD E. FORD, 203 West Randolph Street, Lewisburg, WV 24901, *Chairman*

CLARKE A. GRAVEL, 109 South Winooski Avenue, Burlington, VT 05401

RICHARD C. HITE, 200 West Douglas Avenue, Wichita, KS 67202

FRANK F. JESTRAB, Room 602, 1730 K Street, N.W., Washington, DC 20006

CARLYLE C. RING, JR., 710 Ring Building, Washington, DC 20036

MICHAEL P. SULLIVAN, 300 Roanoke Building, Minneapolis, MN 55402

PETER F. LANGROCK, P. O. Drawer 351, Middlebury, VT 05753, *Chairman, Division E, Ex Officio*

GEORGE C. KEELY, 1600 Colorado National Building, 950 Seventeenth Street, Denver, CO 80202, *President, Ex Officio*

JOHN C. DEACON, P. O. Box 1245, Jonesboro, AR 72401, *Chairman, Executive Committee, Ex Officio*

WILLIAM J. PIERCE, University of Michigan, School of Law, Ann Arbor, MI 48109, *Executive Director, Ex Officio*

UNIFORM AUDIO-VISUAL DEPOSITION [ACT] [RULE] REVIEW COMMITTEE

LLOYD R. GIBSON, 837 United States Courthouse, Kansas City, MO 64106, *Chairman*

DAVID S. KUNZ, 300 Bank of Utah Building, Ogden, UT 84401

HARRY D. LEINENWEBER, Room 306, 81 North Chicago Street, Joliet, IL 60434

Copies of all Uniform and Model Acts and other printed matter issued by the Conference may be obtained for a minimal fee from

National Conference of Commissioners
on Uniform State Laws
676 North St. Clair Street, Suite 1700
Chicago, Illinois 60611

218

UNIFORM AUDIO-VISUAL DEPOSITION [ACT] [RULE]

PREFATORY NOTE

The use of audio-visual depositions (e.g. videotape) is expanding in both state and federal courts. Thus, uniformity in rules and standards for the taking and use of audio-visual depositions is most desirable to assure commonality of procedure and compatibility of media and equipment.

In 1970, the Federal Rules of Civil Procedure were amended to permit recording of depositions by other than stenographic means (FRCP 30(b) (4)). The Federal Judicial Center has commenced projects in Pittsburgh, Philadelphia, Cleveland, and Detroit in 1970 and in New York City in 1975 that include studios and court installations for the recording and use of videotape depositions.

At the time the drafting committee began its work, 12 states had adopted the substance of the federal rule. Thirteen additional states expressly permitted audio-visual depositions under their own standards. Twenty-five states did not specifically authorize audio-visual depositions. Nonetheless, some courts have ruled that it is within the general power of the trial court to authorize audio-visual depositions. *State of Vermont v. Arthur H. Moffitt*, 133 Vt. 366; 340 A.2d 39 (1975); *Blumberg v. Dornbusch*, 139 N.J. Super. 433; 354 A.2d 351 (1976) and *Bailey v. Sears, Roebuck & Company* (Court of Appeals of the State of California 5th Appellate District, 53124, Superior Court No. 137438).

Three states had adopted definitive provisions to encourage audio-visual depositions. They are Nebraska, Ohio, and Wisconsin.

In addition to the projects of the Federal Judicial Center, bar associations in a number of cities have established studios for taking audio-visual depositions. The equipment for such studios is available at modest cost. A number of law firms have established their own studios. The equipment is portable and can be set up readily in a conference room or library and playback equipment is set up easily in courtrooms. Commercial services are available in most cities at prices comparable to stenographic services. The tapes, discs, or other media are usable over and over again. There is no developing or processing. The deposition can be played back immediately, showing exactly what has been recorded. An audio cassette of the audio portion can be made simultaneously to provide a convenient and exact record of the verbal portion of the deposition. The Federal Judicial Center has prepared and periodically updates a manual setting forth comprehensive guidelines and suggestions for taking videotaped depositions.

The Special Committee was aided substantially in its efforts by the assistance of Judge Joseph F. Weis, Jr., Circuit Judge, United States Court of Appeals, Third Circuit; Judge James L. McCrystal, the Court of Common Pleas, Erie County, Sandusky, Ohio; Joseph C. Richmond, National Bureau of Standards, Department of Commerce; John Shepard and Joseph Ebersole of the Federal Judicial Center; James D. Hawkins, Executive Director, and Harry Foster, Director, National Shorthand Reporters Association; and Eldon L. Boisseau, representing the American Bar Association.

Experience with this new technology was described by Judge Weis in 1973 in a seminar for newly appointed judges:

> "I first became interested in the use of videotape in the courts while a member of the bench of the Court of Common Pleas, the court of general trial jurisdiction of Pennsylvania. At my suggestion, the Allegheny County Bar Association decided to purchase cameras and viewers and offer them at reasonable rental fees to members of the Bar for use in taking depositions. Three years ago, I was appointed to the United States District Court in Western Pennsylvania and soon thereafter was privileged to begin work on the pilot project of the Federal Judicial Center to experiment with the use of videotape in the presentation of depositions during trials.
>
> "During the past 12 months, approximately 25 videotape depositions have been taken by the use of the facilities in our courthouse. About 5 of these have been used in actual trials. Additionally, some depositions have been taken by outside organizations for use at our trials.

"Thus far I have presided over 4 trials in which videotape depositions were used. Three of them were jury trials and the one a non-jury proceeding. In each instance, the deposed witnesses were physicians who were not available for the trial for varying reasons. In addition, I presided over a moot jury trial in a competition between the law school students at the University of Pittsburgh and Duquesne University, sponsored by the Academy of Trial Lawyers of Allegheny County. This trial was held in one of the courtrooms in our Federal Court and parts of the trial were videotaped to test the feasibility of this method of preparing a trial record and to uncover some problems which might be solved.

"The first case in which I presided in which videotape depositions were used provided a dramatic example of the difference between the traditional court reporter question and answer testimony and an audio-visual presentation. The case actually was tried twice. The first trial which used the stenographically recorded deposition of several out-of-town physicians ended in a hung jury. Before the second trial was held, the attorneys arranged to take videotaped depositions of the physicians and these were used at the second trial. It's not possible to say if the first trial might have ended differently had video been used, but the second jury did come to a decision. I had the opportunity of hearing the dry reading of the deposition and comparing it with the video which revealed the idiosyncrasies and personalities of the witnesses, the mannerisms and methods of explaining things which added so much more interest and lasting impressions.

"In the non-jury proceeding, the attorneys had decided to have a court stenographer take down the depositions as well as putting them on videotape. Again, I had the opportunity of contrasting the reading of a deposition with seeing the witness actually testify. I can tell you unequivocally that the difference between reading a cold page of testimony and seeing the witness is startling. The videotape did affect my feelings toward certain points in the testimony of these doctors differently than the simple reading of the depositions had accomplished."

There are a number of advantages to taking a deposition in this manner, rather than by stenographer. The use of an audio-visual deposition will provide:

1. A method of presenting deposition testimony superior to reading a transcript of a deposition into the record.[1]

2. The presentation of visual and oral testimony of witnesses otherwise unavailable by reason of distance, illness, death, etc.[1]

3. Alleviation of problems associated with scheduling witnesses, particularly medical experts, in a visual and oral form.[2]

4. Presentation of visual and oral evidence in logical progression without respect to scheduling requirements.

5. A shorter trial by enabling the judge to delete objectionable testimony before its presentation to the jury.

6. Immediate availability and greater accuracy than that inherent in stenographic transcriptions.

7. Opportunity to take on location thereby visually showing, for example, the surroundings in which an incident occurred.[3]

The time generator, a device that records the date and time in tenths of seconds, guarantees that the recording is a complete and faithful record of the deposition. The instant replay capability affords an opportunity to check the operability of the system at the outset and periodically during the taking of the deposition. Signal lights and decibel meters indicate power and operability. A complete reproduction of the recording can be made immediately and the simultaneous taking of an audio cassette assures the preservation of the verbal portion of the deposition. Just as the reporter's notes may sometimes be lost or misplaced, or the transcription misfiled, it is possible that the parties or the clerk of court may mishandle the audio-visual recording. The risk of loss or

---

[1]See *Malter v. Daniels,* 69 F.R.D. 579 (D. Ga. 1975); see also *Lamb v. Grove Seaways, Inc.,* 516 F.2d 1352, 1357 (Ft. 3) (2d Cir. 1975); *U.S. v. LaFatch,* 382, F. Supp. 360 (D.N.D. Ohio, 1974); *Mayor and Aldermen of City of Savannah v. Palmerio,* 135 Ga. App. 147, 217 S.E.2d 430 (1975).

[2]*State ex. rel. Johnson v. Circuit Court of Milwaukee Cty,* 61 Wis.2d 1, 212 N.W. 2d 1 (1972).

[3]See *Carson v. Burlington Northern Inc.,* 52 F.R.D. 492 (D. Neb. 1971).

damage does not appear any more substantial than that inherent in the stenographic record. The parties may guard against even that unlikely possibility by a duplicate recording.

Many attorneys are accustomed to working with a stenographic transcript for trial preparation. To the extent this may be the case, the [Act] [Rule] permits any party to order, at his expense, the taking of a stenographic record. Also, a typed transcript in whole or part can be prepared by a party from the audio-visual record or the audio cassette recording. Finally, bracketed Section 1(c), if adopted by a state, permits the court to direct the preparation of a typewritten transcription either by a simultaneous stenographic recording or from the videotaped recording. A flat requirement for a duplicate stenographic recording would double the cost, which for preservation of testimony or discovery purposes certainly is not necessary. Indeed, as attorneys become familiar with the new technology, they may find it more efficient to have transcribed only limited relevant portions of the audio track and rely upon the audio cassette and audio-visual recording to obtain an overview of the testimony given.

While there have not been as yet any United States Supreme Court decisions concerning the constitutionality of the use of audio-visual depositions under the Fourth, Fifth, Sixth and Fourteenth Amendments, the rulings of state and lower courts to date have upheld the use of such depositions against constitutional challenges. *Paramore v. State of Florida,* 229 S.2d 855 (1969); *State v. Lusk,* 452 S.W.2d 219 (Mo. 1970); *Illinois v. Ardella,* 49 Ill.2d 517, 296 N.E.2d 302 (1971); *Hendrick v. Swenson,* 456 F.2d 503 (1972); *Vermont v. Moffit,* 133 Vt. 366 (1975); *State of California v. Moran,* 114 Ca. Rptr. 413, 39 Cal. App. 398 (1974) and *Kansas City v. McCoy,* 525 S.W.2d 336 (1975).

BIBLIOGRAPHY

1. "Guidelines for Pre-recording Testimony on Videotape Prior to Trial." Manual prepared by The Federal Judicial Center, Nov. 1974, Pub. No. 74-9.

2. "Recording of Testimony at Deposition by Other Than Stenographic Means Under Rule 30(b) (4) of Federal Rules of Civil Procedure." John A. Glenn, J.D. Annot., 16 A.L.R. Fed. 969 (1973).

3. "Symposium: The Use of Videotape in the Courtroom.

   Introduction by Tom C. Clark.

   'The Effects of Videotape Testimony in Jury Trials' by Gerald R. Miller, David C. Bender, Frank Boster, B. Thomas Florence, Norman Fontes, John Hocking and Henry Nicholson.

   'Juror Perceptions of Trial Testimony as a Function of the Method of Presentation' by Gerald R. Williams, Larry C. Farmer, Rex E. Lee, Bert P. Cundick, Robert J. Howell and C. Keith Rooker.

   'An Assessment of Videotape in the Criminal Courts' by Ernest H. Short, B. Thomas Florence and Mary Alice Marsh.

   'Critique-Data in Search of Theory in Search of Policy: Behavioral Responses to Videotape in the Courtrooms' by Gordon Bermant.

   'Opening Pandora's Box: Asking Judges and Attorneys to React to the Videotape Trial', Comment."

   Brigham Young University Law Review, Vol. 1975, No. 2.

4. "Teletest," Thomas E. Sims; Judicature, Vol. 59, No. 9, April 1976.

5. "Trial by Videotape—Can Justice Be Seen To Be Done?", David M. Doret; 47 Temple L.Q. 228 (1974).

6. "Videotape: Pre-recorded Trials—A Procedure For Judicial Expediency, Comment."; Ohio Northern University Law Review, Vol. III, No. 3, 1976.

7. "Videotape for the Legal Community," Sherwood Allen Salvan; Judicature, Vol. 59, No. 5, Dec. 1975.
8. "Videotape Recording in the California Criminal Justice System," Ernest H. Short and Associates, and McGeorge School of Law, University of the Pacific for the Sacramento County District Attorney, March, 1975.
9. "Videotape Trials: Legal and Practical Implications."; 9 Colum. J. of L. & Soc. Prob. 363 (1973).
10. "Video Technology in the Courts," Genevieve V. Coleman; MITRE Technical Report MTR-7235, Rev. 1.
11. "Use of Videotape in the Preparation and Trial of Lawsuits," Thomas J. Murray, Jr.; The Forum, Vol. XI, No. 4, Summer 1976.
12. "Videotaped Trials: A Primer," Judge James L. McCrystal; "Second Thoughts on Videotaped Trials," Marshall J. Hartman; "Videotaped Depositions: The Ohio Experience," Thomas J. Murray, Jr., Judicature, Vol. 61, No. 6, Dec.-Jan. 1978.

UNIFORM AUDIO-VISUAL DEPOSITION [ACT] [RULE]

1 SECTION 1. [*Authorization of Audio-Visual Deposition.*]
2 (a) Any deposition may be recorded by audio-visual
3 means without a stenographic record. Any party may
4 make at his own expense a simultaneous stenographic or
5 audio record of the deposition. Upon his request and at
6 his own expense, any party is entitled to an audio or
7 audio-visual copy of the audio-visual recording.
8 (b) The audio-visual recording is an official record of
9 the deposition. A transcript prepared by an official court
10 reporter is also an official record of the deposition.
11 [(c) On motion the court, for good cause, may order the
12 party taking, or who took, a deposition by audio-visual
13 recording to furnish, at his expense, a transcript of the
14 deposition.]

COMMENT

Section 1(a) has its roots in Federal Rule 30(b) (4) which reads:

"The court may upon motion order that the testimony at a deposition be recorded by other than stenographic means, in which event the order shall designate the manner of recording, preserving and filing the deposition, and may include other provisions to assure that the recorded testimony will be accurate and trustworthy. If the order is made, a party may nevertheless arrange to have a stenographic transcription made at his expense."

However, this [Act] [Rule] (1) does not require a court order for the taking of an audio-visual deposition; (2) sets out uniform standards for recording, preserving, filing, and using the depositions rather than leaving it to individual orders; and (3) specifically designates the audio-visual recording as an official record of the deposition.

The provisions for audio-visual depositions contained in this [Act] [Rule] supplement, and are in addition to, the general provisions applicable to the taking and use of depositions. Those general provisions remain in effect, except as they may be repealed or modified under Section 9 to eliminate inconsistency.

Subsection (b) provides that the audio-visual recording is an official record of the deposition. If a typewritten transcript is prepared by an official court reporter, it too is an official record of the deposition. Both can be used by the parties for briefing, argument, and appeal. In the event of conflict between the two records, the court would have to resolve the disparity, just as it might now, if the witness contended the stenographic transcription was inaccurate. Because the audio-visual recording is an exact recording, it would normally be relied upon to resolve any disparity; but, in rare circumstances, perhaps the stenographic transcription might be adopted by the court as a better recording.

Bracketed subsection (c) is available in those states where it is felt that the proponent of the deposition in certain circumstances should bear the expense of preparing a typewritten transcript. Because the added cost might well discourage the use of audio-visual depositions, the Special Committee felt that "good cause" should be shown to impose the cost on the proponent. The court can order the transcription to be made either by simultaneous stenographic recording or preparation of the transcript from the audio track of the videotape or from the audio cassette.

In many states, the bracketed provision may be considered unnecessary or counterproductive. Inasmuch as litigation is expensive, many forego judicial resolution of disputes. Omission of bracketed subsection (c) would minimize this problem compelling the party wanting the transcript to weigh the anticipated benefit against the cost to his client.

1   SECTION 2. [*Use.*] An audio-visual deposition may be
2   used for any purpose and under any circumstances in
3   which a stenographic deposition may be used.

COMMENT

This [Act] [Rule] does not expand the use of depositions; however, as is true with other depositions, the parties may wish to stipulate the use of an audio-visual deposition in a situation where its use is not authorized hereby. In such an event, an audio-visual recording is superior to the reading of a stenographic deposition, because it provides an exact visual and audio recording of the testimony. It has many of the attributes of live testimony and will be advantageous for taking of medical and other expert testimony where both delay and cost may be minimized substantially by an audio-visual recording.

1   SECTION 3. [*Notice.*] The notice for taking an audio-
2   visual deposition and the subpoena for attendance at
3   that deposition must state that the deposition will be
4   recorded by audio-visual means.

1   SECTION 4. [*Procedure.*] The following procedure must
2   be observed in recording an audio-visual deposition:
3   (1) (Opening of Deposition.) The deposition must be-
4   gin with an oral or written statement on camera which
5   includes:

6   (i)   the operator's name and business address;
7   (ii)   the name and business address of the oper-
8 ator's employer;
9   (iii) the date, time, and place of the deposition;
10   (iv) the caption of the case;
11   (v)   the name of the witness;
12   (vi) the party on whose behalf the deposition is
13 being taken; and
14   (vii) any stipulations by the parties.

15 (2) (Counsel.) Counsel shall identify themselves on
16 camera.

17 (3) (Oath.) The oath must be administered to the
18 witness on camera.

19 (4) (Multiple Units.) If the length of a deposition re-
20 quires the use of more than one recording unit, the end of
21 each unit and the beginning of each succeeding unit
22 must be announced on camera.

23 (5) (Closing of Deposition.) At the conclusion of a
24 deposition, a statement must be made on camera that
25 the deposition is concluded. A statement may be made
26 on camera setting forth any stipulations made by
27 counsel concerning the custody of the audio-visual re-
28 cording and exhibits or other pertinent matters.

29 (6) (Index.) Depositions must be indexed by a time gen-
30 erator or other method specified pursuant to Section 6.

31 (7) (Objections.) An objection must be made as in the
32 case of stenographic depositions.

33 (8) (Editing.) If the court issues an editing order, the
34 original audio-visual recording must not be altered.

35 (9) (Filing.) Unless otherwise stipulated by the parties,
36 the original audio-visual recording of a deposition, any
37 copy edited pursuant to an order of the court, and ex-
38 hibits must be filed forthwith with the clerk of the court.

COMMENT

A general guide of appropriate procedures is necessary and desirable to assure integrity of the recording and uniformity in procedures facilitating inter- and intra-state use of depositions.

However, provisions have been made for improved technology. For example, "audio-visual" recording is used rather than "videotape" because disc and other methods of recording may soon develop.

In paragraph (6), indexing is by "time generator or other method specified pursuant to Section 6" in anticipation that yet better techniques for indexing may be developed. The rules promulgated under Section 6 would specify the kind of time generator and the information (date, hour, minute, section, etc.) required, depending upon the evolving state of the art.

Paragraph (7) provides that objections will be handled in the same manner as for stenographic depositions. However, the Special Committee anticipates that, for ease of editing of objections and testimony ordered to be struck, the parties may frequently wish to stipulate that objections may be made immediately after the answer.

The [Act] [Rule] does not set out alternative methods of editing because improving technology may develop better techniques than those presently employed. Various techniques are currently used for editing, including (1) preparation of an edited copy omitting testimony that has been struck and (2) suppressing the audio, or audio-visual, display of any portion of the testimony struck. The integrity of the recording, regardless of the editing technique employed, requires that the original recording remain unaltered and thus paragraph (8) so provides.

No provisions are included for retention and storage of the recording by the clerk of court or its return at the conclusion of the proceedings. Local rules can best make provision for those matters. If the clerk of court has display equipment that cannot erase, free accessibility under his supervision would be appropriate. If not, controls should be developed by local rule or court order to preserve the integrity of the recording from inadvertent, or intentional, erasing or destruction of the recording. The videotape itself is reusable and normally should be returned to the party supplying it when the case is concluded.

1   SECTION 5. [*Costs.*] The reasonable expense of recording,
2   editing, and using an audio-visual deposition may be
3   taxed as costs.

COMMENT

It is anticipated that the total cost of employing an audio-visual deposition will be comparable to that of stenographic depositions and thus should be taxed in the same manner.

1   SECTION 6. [*Standards.*] [The [Supreme Court, Court Ad-
2   ministrator, Clerk] may promulgate rules establishing
3   standards for audio-visual equipment and guidelines for
4   taking and using audio-visual depositions.] Incompatible

5 audio-visual recordings must be conformed to the stan-
6 dards at the expense of the proponent. Both recordings
7 are originals.

COMMENT

The purpose of the brackets is to provide flexibility to each state as to the means by which they will standardize the equipment and promulgate guidelines for its use. If state adoption is by court rule, the court should include in its rule standards for equipment and guidelines for its use or delegate that responsibility. If state adoption is by legislative enactment, the [Act] [Rule] should authorize the appropriate agency or official to establish state-wide standards and guidelines.

Many depositions will be taken in other states or other political subdivisions of the state. Uniformity thus is very important. Equipment standardization also needs to be compatible with display equipment used or available to the court. Uniformity in taking and using the recording will avoid problems in its use by various jurisdictions that otherwise might consider nonuniform techniques or procedures improper. The court or appropriate agency should coordinate its standards with other states by adopting in substance the standards and guidelines promulgated by the Federal Judicial Center, or other similar uniform standards.

1 SECTION 7. [*Uniformity of Application and Construc-*
2 *tion.*] This [Act] [Rule] shall be applied and construed to
3 effectuate its general purpose to make uniform the law
4 with respect to the subject of this [Act] [Rule] among
5 states enacting it.

1 SECTION 8. [*Short Title.*] This [Act] [Rule] may be cited
2 as the "Uniform Audio-Visual Deposition [Act] [Rule]".

1 SECTION 9. [*Time of Taking Effect.*] This [Act] [Rule]
2 shall take effect ...

1 [SECTION 10. [*Repeal.*] The following acts and parts of
2 acts are repealed:]

COMMENT

If state adoption is by court rule, this section is not necessary.

Index

Page